LEARN ITALIAN
FAST FOR
ADULT BEGINNERS

3 in 1 Book

CONTENTS

DISCLAIMER NOTICE:

Please note that the information contained within this document is for educational and entertainment purposes only.

All effort has been executed to present accurate, up-to-date, reliable, complete information. No warranties of any kind are declared or implied. Readers acknowledge that the author is not engaged in the rendering of legal, financial, medical or professional advice. The content within this book has been derived from various sources.

Please consult a licensed professional before attempting any techniques outlined in this book.

By reading this document, the reader agrees that under no circumstances is the author responsible for any losses, direct or indirect, that are incurred as a result of the use of the information contained within this document, including, but not limited to, errors, omissions, or inaccuracies.

Speak Abroad
Academy

INTRODUCTION

Let me guess, you're interested in learning Italian, you've tried formal lessons and apps, but you feel stuck and you don't know why. No matter how excited you are at the beginning, you always end up losing your motivation. You start having difficulty finding time to sit down and practice until you finally give up. Will you ever be able to learn Italian?

Of course, you will! While we all know that learning a new language requires effort and commitment, with the right approach you will regain your motivation and look forward to learning.

So, what is the right approach?

Scheduling a time for lessons is a great way to keep your motivation high. But this will only happen if learning is pleasant and easy; that is, if you're not overwhelmed by new information. If you feel you're in control of the process, you will find yourself being excited about new content and tasks.

That is precisely what we have focused on with this book: delivering micro lessons with tiny pieces of key information. By providing simple-to-follow lessons and lots—yes, lots! — of practice, the *Learn Italian Fast for Adult Beginners* will help you learn Italian quickly and thoroughly.

Our easy-to-follow workbook engages readers from the very first page with short, to-the-point grammar explanations and fun exercises. Our program has put you, the learner, at the center of the learning journey, keeping in mind that every day you have a long list of tasks that will be competing for your time and energy.

Learning Italian should not be placed on the overflowing to-do list that fills people with stress and anxiety. Instead, it should be an enjoyable activity you turn to when you want to relax and distract yourself.

Think of learning a language in the same way as doing exercise: if you want it to stick, you need to make it enjoyable. When you're enjoying the learning process, it feels effortless—even though, many times, it isn't! — and you'll end up learning the new language more effectively.

The *Learn Italian Fast for Adult Beginners 3 in 1 Book* helps you build Italian into your life by understanding words in context, as they appear naturally, and presenting grammar explanations in real-life situations. You'll pick up vocabulary from short stories and everyday scenarios. This extensive practice applies the concepts learnt and reviews what you have already mastered. Our bite-sized lessons are based on gradual, cumulative learning: each new class builds on the previous ones to keep your memory fresh. You will constantly review

what you already acquired about the language as you take in new knowledge. This has the two-fold benefit of boosting your self-confidence as you train your brain to recognize new language patterns.

When you start identifying and remembering past lessons, you will feel that you're finally making progress and the learning journey will continue to be more enjoyable. Italian, spoken by about 85 million people worldwide, is not just the official language in Italy, San Marino, Switzerland (Ticino and the Grisons), and the primary language of Vatican City, but it also holds official minority status in Croatia and parts of Slovenian Istria.

Learning Italian can help individuals expand both their personal and professional horizons, unlocking doors to a myriad of different opportunities and fostering a deeper appreciation for the rich tapestry of Italian literature and culture, even with just basic proficiency.

As you begin your lessons with the grammar workbook, you will feel a sense of accomplishment because of the structure of each class. Clear explanations of grammatical rules and exercises that connect directly will help you make quick strides to push you forward.

Moreover, practicing what you learn will give you confidence and make you feel motivated to move on to the next step. Before you know it, you will start to express your thoughts and feelings in Italian and understand a variety of Italian-language resources. We will also provide you excerpts from poems, songs, and social media to keep you engaged and entertained so you never get bored!

Worried about finding the time to study? Don't worry! Our engaging, short and easy lessons will keep you concentrated and won't be overwhelming. Each class highlights one specific grammar point at a time and makes sure you practice it with our exercises which include a wide variety of topics that can always be applied to real-life situations. In addition, each new grammar concept builds on the previous ones, making sure you review the material already learnt before jumping into new content.

So why wait any longer? Start right now! Boost your Italian learning today with our *Learn Italian Fast for Adult Beginners* and step into a lifetime of possibilities: new friends, exciting trips, and a host of career-growth opportunities.

One final thing before you start: **Find your bonus content immediately before Chapter 1 begins. You can go check it out right now. Enjoy!**

Speak Abroad
Academy

We invite you to scan this "QR code"

By using the camera of your phone aiming at the QR code and clicking on the link that appears

to access your bonus content:

SCAN TO CLAIM YOUR BONUSES

OR

ENTER THIS URL IN YOUR WEB BROWSER:

bit.ly/speakithg

(only use lowercase letters)

SECTION I:
GRAMMAR WORKBOOK

Speak Abroad
Academy

LESSON 1 :

SUBJECT PRONOUNS
GOOD MORNING AND GOODBYE

First things first! The initial step to learning any language always begins with subject pronouns. In English, these are words like '*I*,' '*You*,' and '*They*.' They indicate *who* exactly we're talking about and they're essential for everyday conversation! Without them, it would be impossible to describe ourselves, other people, and how things or events have affected us. They are some of the most basic building blocks to any language.

So, let's take a look at what subject pronouns in Italian are!

1.1 Subject Pronouns

English	Italian	Pronunciation
I	io	[ee-oh]
You (informal, singular)	tu	[too]
You (formal, singular)	Lei	[leh-ee]
He	lui* (egli)	[loo-eeh] / [eh-lyh]
She	lei* (ella)	[leh-ee] / [ehl-lah]
They (masculine)	loro* (essi)	[loh-ro] / [ehs-sih]
They (feminine)	loro* (esse)	[loh-ro] / [ehs-seh]
We (masculine) We (feminine)	noi	[noh-ee]
You (formal and informal, plural.)	voi	[voh-ee]

lui (he) and *lei* (she) are predominately and most commonly used when communicating in Italian. The variants *egli* (he) and *ella* (she) are less commonly used but are still important to know in case you come across them in a conversation. The same goes for *loro* (they-for both female and male groups of people) and its variant *esse**

You'll notice that, in Italian , there are a lot more subject pronouns than in English! Aside from *who* they reference, they're also categorized based on:

- ⮐ Formality of the situation.
- ⮐ Genders of the people you're talking about.
- ⮐ Quantity of subjects (i.e., whether you're just talking to or about one person or more.

Unlike English, there are different Italian pronouns for *'you'* and *'they'* depending on how many people you're talking to or talking about. Saying **voi** would be like the equivalent of saying *'you all'* or *'both of you.'*

Let's get familiar with these pronouns, shall we?

Note on Abbreviations: masculine (m.), feminine (f.), informal (inf.), formal (form.), singular (sing.), plural (pl.), archaic (arc.)

1.1 Practice

A. Translate the following pronouns.

1. We (f.): _____
2. I: _____
3. They (f.): _____
4. They (pl.): _____
5. You (inf. pl. in Italy): _____
6. You (inf. sing): _____
7. You (form. and inf. pl. in Italy): _____
8. We (m.): _____
9. You and I: _____
10. He and she: _____

B. Write the correct subject pronoun.

1. _____ vengo a casa tua. (*I'm going to your house*)
2. _____ siamo tuoi amici. (*we—m.—are your friends*)
3. _____ siete i migliori. (*you—m. inf. pl. in Italy—are the best*)
4. _____ siete uomini. (*you— form. and inf. pl. in Italy—are men*)
5. _____ sono amici. (*they—m.—are friends*)

Speak Abroad
Academy

C. Replace the names in parentheses with the correct pronoun.

1. (Paolo) _____ e (Maria) _____ si sposeranno (*will get married*).
2. (They) _____ si sposeranno (*will get married*) in una chiesa (*in a church*).
3. (You – m. pl. inf. in Italy) _____ siete invitati al matrimonio (*are invited to the wedding*).
4. _____ (Luisa and you inf.), volete andare al matrimonio? (*want to go to the wedding*)
5. (Tommaso and I) _____ abbiamo una sorpresa (*have a surprise*) per (they m.) _____.
6. (Pietro) _____ vive in Messico (*lives in México*).
7. (Julia) _____ vive in Ecuador (*lives in Ecuador*).
8. (Olivia and Emma) _____ studiano Italiano (*study Italian*).
9. (Christian) _____ gioca a tennis (*plays tennis*).
10. (Your boss – formal) _____ lavora tanto (*works a lot*).

1.2 The Difference Between Formal (*Lei*) and Informal (*tu*) Pronouns

Earlier, we briefly touched on how different pronouns are used based on the formality of a situation. For example, if you were speaking directly to one person ('*you*'), you'd use the word **tu** in an informal situation and **Lei** in a formal situation. But what exactly constitutes an informal or formal situation?

You'd use the formal word **Lei** in interactions with people like:

- Your boss
- A stranger or new acquaintance (unless you dislike them and want them to know it!)
- A salesperson
- Elderly
- The cashier at the bank
- Someone of high ranking (doctor, lawyer)

You'd use the informal pronoun **tu** with:

- Your friends
- Your family
- Children and animals
- People you intend to insult
- Other young people (if you're young, too)

What if you're not sure whether to use *tu* or *Lei*?

Situations may arise where you're not sure whether to go with the informal or formal pronoun. In this case, be safe and go with the formal *Lei*! It's much better to be overly polite than to risk coming across as rude or insulting.

Tip: The masculine plural form **essi** refers to a group of males or to a group that includes both males and females. The feminine plural form **esse** only refers to a group of females. In other words, the default word for 'They' is **essi**, unless you're referring to a group of people that's entirely female. If you want to address a group of both males and females you can simply say **loro** which does not reflect gender.

Interesting fact: In Italian, there is no subject pronoun, **it**. You use **egli** and **ella** to refer to people, and sometimes animals. You don't use **egli** and **ella** to refer to things. It would be like calling a shoe or a potato *'he'* and *'she.'* Quirky, but not exactly accurate!

1.2 Practice

A. Insert the correct informal or formal pronoun with , *tu* or *Lei*?

1. Your grandmother _____
2. A co-worker _____
3. A flight attendant _____
4. Your boss _____
5. A little boy _____

6. A professor _____
7. A repair person _____
8. Your cousin _____
9. Your best friend _____
10. Your father-in-law _____

B. Write the correct pronoun according to the situation: *tu or voi ?*

1. You ask the waiter at a restaurant in Italian when your table will be ready. He answers: "_____ siete i prossimi." (*You're up next.*)
2. You ask your friends in Italian if they want to come with you to the park: "_____ volete venire con me?" (*Do you want to come with me?*)
3. You tell your friends in Italian that they're your best friends: "_____ siete i miei migliori amici." (*You are my best friends.*)
4. You tell your friends in Italian that they are the best Instagram followers you could have: "_____ siete i migliori follower su Instagram che possa avere." (*You are the best Instagram followers I could have.*)
5. You tell your friend in Italian that they know how to cook very well: "_____ sai cucinare molto bene." (*You know how to cook very well.*)

1.3 Greetings and Expressions of Politeness

As we mentioned earlier, your choice of words will vary depending on the formality of the situation. This applies to pronouns, and it also applies to longer exchanges, like greetings. In English, formality and informality matter too! For example, you probably wouldn't enter a formal meeting with your boss and say, "Hey, what's up?"

In Italian, it's no different. You'll have different greetings for different types of situations. The words might essentially mean the same thing, but the choice of words helps to convey whether you're familiar or unfamiliar with the person or people you're addressing.

Informal Greeting

Consider the following informal greeting between Maria and Pedro, two young housemates that go to the same college. Since they're both peers, they'll use informal language with each other, even if they're not that close.

Maria:	Ciao, Pietro.
	(Hi, Pietro.)
Pietro:	Ciao, Maria. Come va?
	(Hi, Maria. How's it going?)
Maria:	Bene. E tu?
	(Good. And you?)
Pietro:	Molto bene! A dopo.
	(Very good! See you later.)
Maria:	Ciao! Ci vediamo dopo.
	(Bye! See you later.)

Formal Greeting

Now, let's look at a formal greeting between il signor Pérez and la signorina Sofia. Il signor Pérez is a security guard at signorina Sofia's apartment building. Even though they're both middle-aged, they would use formal language with each other since they don't know each other well and they aren't exactly peers. Il signor Pérez is providing a service for la signorina Sofia, therefore he should address her in a formal manner.

Signor Pérez:	Buon pomeriggio, signorina Sofia.
	(Good afternoon, Ms. Sofia.)
Signorina Sofia:	Buon pomeriggio, signor Pérez. Come sta?
	(Good afternoon, Mr. Pérez. How are you?)
Signor Pérez:	Molto bene, grazie. E Lei?
	(Very good, thank you. And you?)
Signorina Sofia:	Molto bene, grazie. Arrivederci.
	(Very good, thanks. Goodbye.)
Signor Pérez:	A presto.
	(See you soon.)

Both the informal and formal greetings are essentially saying the same thing, but the formal phrases and subject pronouns specifically express politeness. With that said, some words and phrases may also remain the same. You can still say **bene** or **molto bene** to say you're doing well or very well, and in either situation, you can still say **arrivederci** to say goodbye.

Vocabulary: Greetings

English	Italian	Pronunciation
Hi	**Ciao**	*[chee-ah-oh]*
How's it going?	**Come va?**	*[coh-meh vah]*
Good	**Bene**	*[beh-neh]*
And you?	**E tu?**	*[he too]*
Very good	**Molto bene**	*[mohl-toh beh-neh]*
See you later	**A dopo**	*[ah doh-poh]*
Goodbye	**Arrivederci**	*[ahr-ree-veh-dehr-chee]*
Bye	**Ciao**	*[chee-ah-oh]*

Come va?, Come stai?, and **E tu?** are greeting expressions used in informal situations, with people you know well, on a first-name basis.

Speak Abroad
Academy

Vocabulary: More Greetings

English	Italian	Pronunciation
Good morning	**Buongiorno**	[bwon-johr-noh]
Good afternoon	**Buon pomeriggio**	[bwon poh-meh-ree-joh]
Good evening	**Buonasera**	[bwon-ah-seh-rah]
Good night	**Buonanotte**	[bwoh-nah-noht-teh]
Mr.	**Signor (Sig.)**	[see-nyohr]
Mrs.	**Signora (Sig.ra)**	[see-nyoh-rah]
Miss	**Signorina (Sig.na)**	[see-nyoh-ree-nah]
How are you?	**Lei come sta?**	[leh-ee koh-meh stah]
And you?	**E Lei?**	[eh leh-ee]
See you later	**A dopo**	[ah doh-poh]
See you tomorrow	**A domani**	[ah doh-mah-nee]
See you soon	**A presto**	[ah preh-sto]

Come stai? and **E Lei?** are used to address someone with whom you have a more formal relationship, like your boss or a salesperson.

Language Etiquette

Next are the "magic" words and phrases that will help you address others politely in everyday life. Say your please and thank you in Italian, just like you do in English.

English	Italian	Pronunciation
Thanks. / Thank you	**Grazie**	[grah-tsee-eh]
Thanks a lot. / Thank you very much	**Molte grazie/ Grazie mille**	[mohl-the grah-tsee-eh] / [grah-tsee-eh mih-leh]
You're welcome	**Prego**	[preh-go]
You're welcome	**Di nulla/ Di niente**	[dee nuhl-lah] / [dee nyen-teh]
Please	**Per favore**	[pehr fah-voh-reh]
Excuse me / Pardon me (to get someone's attention or to apologize to someone or for something you did)*	**Scusa**	[skoo-zah]

English	Italian	Pronunciation
Excuse me / Pardon me (to ask for permission to go through a group of people)	**Con permesso/ Permesso**	[kohn pehr-mehs-soh]/ [pehr-mehs-soh
It's nothing - don't worry	**Non è niente/ Non fa niente**	[nohn eh nah-dah] / [nohn fah nyen-teh]
Don't worry	**Non preoccuparti**	[nohn preh-oh-coo-pahr-tee]
Excuse me (to get someone's attention or to apologize to someone for something you did)	**Scusate/ Mi scusi**	[skoo-zah-teh] / [mee skoo-zee]

Now let's dive into some hands-on practice!

1.3 Practice

A. Choose the most appropriate response from the list on the right for the following greetings or expressions.

1. Molte grazie/ Grazie mille _____   a. Ciao, buon pomeriggio!
2. Buongiorno _____   b. Bene, grazie. E Lei?
3. Scusa _____   c. Di niente
4. Come va? _____   d. Buongiorno, come sta?
5. Arrivederci _____   e. Non fa niente
6. Buon pomeriggio _____   f. A dopo
7. Come sta? _____   g. Bene E tu?
8. Buonanotte _____   h. A domani!
9. Ci vediamo domani _____   i. Benissimo, grazie!
10. Tutto bene? _____   k. Buonanotte!

B. What might these people say to each other if they met at the time given?

1. Laura and Mathew at 2:00 p.m. _____
2. Mary and her boss at 7:00 a.m. _____
3. You and your friend at 12:00 a.m. _____
4. Joe and Ann at 10:00 p.m. _____
5. You and your Math teacher at 11 a.m. _____

C.   Match the situation with the correct response.

Permesso – Non fa niente – Scusate/ Mi scusi – Scusa – Di niente/ Di nulla

1.   _____ You accidentally bump into a person on the street.
2.   _____ You're trying to squeeze your way out of a packed subway.
3.   _____ A waiter apologizes for spilling water on your shirt.
4.   _____ You're trying to exit the aisle at the movie theater to use the restroom.
5.   _____ You're trying to draw the cashier's attention at the supermarket, who's sitting with his back to you.

D.   Choose the most appropriate response for the following statements and questions

1.   Molte grazie/Grazie mille. _____   a. A dopo
2.   Come va? _____   b. Non fa niente
3.   Come stai? _____   c. Bene. E tu?
4.   Arrivederci. _____   d. Molto bene, grazie
5.   Scusate/ Mi scusi. _____   e. Di niente

E.   Complete the following dialogue with the correct greeting or phrase.

YOU: Ciao, Martino, _____ [1] ?

MARTINO: Bene, grazie, _____ [2] ?

YOU: Molto _____ [3] .

MARTINO: Arrivederci. _____ [4] mattina.

YOU: _____ [5] .

Common Mistake: Remember it's "Buongiorno," but "Buon pomeriggio" and "Buonanotte." *

Ciao, vuoi sapere qualcosa? *(Do you want to know something?)*

Italian became an official language in 1861 and it has only 21 letters! That's right, 5 letters less than English. With 16 consonants and 5 vowels, Italian stands strong even without the letters k, j, w, x and y. *

LESSON 2 :

NOUNS AND ARTICLES
THE DOG AND A CAT

2.1 The Gender of Nouns and the Singular Definite Article

We covered pronouns, but now let's focus on what qualifies as a noun? Nouns are objects, places, and things.

In Italian, nouns are called **sustantivos**, but don't worry you don't need to remember this just yet. Unlike English, all nouns in Italian are either masculine or feminine. This doesn't mean that objects are perceived as having literal gender differences, of course, but rather, they are just classified into different groups depending on the final vowel at the end of each word *(o-i-a-e)*

Some of these are straightforward, such as *l'uomo* and *la donna,* which mean *the man* and *the woman* respectively. As you'd expect, **l'uomo** is a masculine noun and **la donna** is a feminine noun. Although they're represented using different articles , *il* and *la* both mean 'the' – they simply apply to different genders *(il-masculine / la-feminine)*. You would never ever say 'la uomo' or 'il donna' as it would be grammatically incorrect.

It's easy with people, but can be confusing when we speak about objects and places as they don't have any obvious gender. To speak fluent Italian, you'll need to get used to the genders of different nouns. For example, you'll need to remember that a book is masculine *(il libro)* while a door *(la porta)* is feminine.

The definite article (the) should always agree with the gender of the noun. This is a hard one for English speakers, because we only have one definite article—*the*—and don't have to worry about the rest. Let's break it down for you!

Masculine: il + nouns ending in 'o'

Feminine: la + nouns ending in 'a'

Singular Masculine Nouns

So, is there a way to distinguish masculine from feminine nouns? Well, most masculine nouns end in **-o** while most feminine nouns end in **-a**.

As we mentioned earlier, the masculine singular noun uses the definite article **il**. This shows we are referring to just **one** of the things, places, or objects. Don't worry about plural nouns for now, we'll get to those later.

The following table contains singular masculine nouns:

English	Italian	Pronunciation
The man	**l'uomo**	*[lwoh-moh]*
The friend (male)	**l'amico**	*[lah-mee-koh]*
The boy	**il ragazzo**	*[eel rah-gaht-tsoh]*
The son	**il figlio**	*[eel fee-lyoh]*
The brother	**il fratello**	*[eel frha-tehl-loh]*
The grandfather	**il nonno**	*[eel nohn-noh]*
The uncle	**lo zio**	*[loh tsee-oh]*
The cat	**il gatto**	*[eel gaht-toh]*
The tomato	**il pomodoro**	*[eel poh-moh-doh-roh]*
The book	**il libro**	*[eel lee-broh]*
The telephone	**il telefono**	*[eel teh-leh-foh-noh]*

Some masculine nouns end in -e:

English	Italian	Pronunciation
the coffee	**il caffè**	*[eel kahf-feh]*
the student	**lo studente**	*[loh stuh-dehn-teh]*
the dog	**il cane**	*[eel kah-neh]*
the youngster	**il giovane**	*[eel-joh-vah-neh]*

Alright, so not *all* masculine nouns end in -o. Most of them do, but there are some exceptions. Here are some masculine nouns that end in *-a* or *-ma*. Regardless of how the word ends, you'll still need to use *il* if it's masculine. Let's take a look at some examples below.

English	Italian	Pronunciation
the climate	il clima	[eehl klee-mah]
the program	il programma	[eehl proh-grahm-mah]
the system	il sistema*	[eehl see-steh-mah]
the map	la mappa	[lah mahp-pah]
the language	la lingua	[lah leen-gwah]
the planet	il pianeta	[eehl pee-ah-neh-tah]
the problem	il problema	[eehl proh-bleh-mah]
the tourist	il turista	[eehl too-ree-stah]
the sofa	il sofá	[eehl soh-fah]

> **Tip: Be careful!** Many English speakers say "la sistema," thinking this word is feminine. Remember, it's "*il sistema*."

> **Tip**: Since there is no clear rule about what ending a noun should have in order to be qualified as masculine, you'll need to simply memorize which noun is what gender. Don't worry, this gets easier with practice!

Singular Feminine Nouns

On the other hand, feminine nouns usually end in *-a*. The feminine singular noun uses the definite article *la*.

Pay attention! When a noun begins with a vowel (*a, e, i, o, u*) you must drop the vowel and replace it with an apostrophe, essentially joining the article with the noun to create a unified word. This is seen in words like, **l'amica, l'elefante, l'acqua.**

Please take a look at the following table containing singular feminine nouns:

English	Italian	Pronunciation
the person	la persona	[lah pehr-soh-nah]
the woman	la donna	[lah dohn-nah]
the mother	la madre	[lah mah-dreh]
the friend (female)	l'amica	[lah ah-mee-kah]

Nouns and articles

Speak Abroad
Academy

English	Italian	Pronunciation
the girl	**la bambina**	[lah bahm-bee-nah]
the girl	**la ragazza**	[lah rah-gaht-tsah]
the daughter	**la figlia**	[lah fee-lyah]
the sister	**la sorella**	[lah soh-rehl-lah]
the grandmother	**la nonna**	[lah nohn-nah]
the aunt	**la zia**	[lah tsee-ah]
the cat (female)	**la gatta**	[lah gaht-tah]
the house	**la casa**	[lah kah-sah]
the chair	**la sedia**	[lah seh-deeah]

Some feminine nouns end in, **-zione, -sione, -tà, -cia, or -zia**.

English	Italian	Pronunciation
the conversation	**la conversazione**	[lah kohn-vehr-sah-tsyoh-neh]
the television	**la televisione**	[lah teh-leh-vee-syoh-neh]
the truth	**la verità**	[lah veh-ree-tah]
the city	**la città**	[lah cheet-tah]
The drugstore	**la farmacia**	[lah fahr-mah-chee-ah]
the friendship	**l'amicizia**	[lah-mee-chee-tsyah]

And even some feminine nouns end in **-o!**

English	Italian	Pronunciation
the photograph	**la foto**	[lah foh-toh]
the hand	**la mano**	[lah mah-noh]
the radio	**la radio**	[lah rah-dyoh]
the motorcycle	**la moto**	[lah moh-toh]

Again, since many feminine nouns don't follow a regular pattern, you need to learn each noun with its article, so you don't make mistakes like saying, "*il mano*," when it should be "***la mano***." Slowly but surely, practice makes perfect!

2.1 Practice

Write the appropriate masculine or feminine form of the definite article (the) for each noun. And while you're at it, try translating the word to see if you remember the meaning!

1. _____ foto
2. _____ ospedale
3. _____ televisore
4. _____ casa
5. _____ acqua
6. _____ città
7. _____ conversazione
8. _____ figlio
9. _____ pianeta
10. _____ amico

11. _____ mappa
12. _____ amica
13. _____ sistema
14. _____ problema
15. _____ hotel
16. _____ persona
17. _____ animale
18. _____ cibo
19. _____ mano
20. _____ telefono

> **Common Mistake:** The noun *delta* (*estuary of a river*) ends in **-a** but is masculine: *il delta* (*the delta*). So don't say, *la delta*!

2.2 Plural Nouns and the Plural Definite Article

Plural Nouns

So far, we've only covered singular nouns. That is, just one object, place, or thing. But what if you wanted to refer to multiple friends, not just one friend? Or many books, not just a single book? This is where plural nouns come in.

In English, we usually indicate that there is *more* than one thing by simply adding "s" to the end of the word, like 'friends' or 'books.' In Italian, plurality is also indicated by modifying the ending of the word but as we learned earlier with singular nouns, the final letter of plural nouns also depends on gender

For Italian male nouns ending in **-o** (*amico – friend*) or **-e** (*studente – student*), the plural form would use the letter **-i** (*amici, studenti*). If you're referring to more than one friend, you would say **amic**i, and for more than one student, you would say **studenti**.

For Italian female nouns ending in **-a** (*porta-door*), the plural form would use the letter **-e**. If you are referring to more than one door, you would say **port**e.

Hopefully, you're getting the hang of this by now! If you're referring to multiple pencils, you'd use the word **matit**e. And for multiple noses, you would use the word **nasi**.

You might notice that something is missing – the definite article. Are you wondering if they also change if the noun is plural? Well you are correct, they do!

Just like the nouns, the definite articles are also modified to indicate plurality. We must also continue to keep in mind the gender of the noun!

The masculine definite article **il/lo** becomes **i/gli.**

The feminine definite article **la** becomes **le.**

In Italian, for nouns starting with a vowel, the article "loses" the vowel, due to the encounter of two vowels. If you think about it, we have a similar rule in English. Before a noun starting with a vowel, we always use the article **"an"** not **"a".** In Italian, the vowel is replaced with an apostrophe connecting the article and the noun making it look like one word.

Examples:

l'arte (*the art*) instead of la arte; **l'amico** (*the friend),* instead of "lo amico"; **l'incontro** (*the encounter*) instead of "lo incontro"; **l'uomo** (*the man*) instead of "lo uomo".

If you are talking about plural nouns beginning with a vowel, this rule does not apply. Instead, you will go back to using the regular plural forms of the articles:

For example...

L'amico → gli amici

L'acqua → le acque

In some cases, the plural form is indicated by the article, whereas the noun does not change. For example:

la città (*singular – the city*) **le** città (*plural – the cities*)

> **Tip**: Remember that in Italian, if we're referring to multiple people that consist of both females and males, we use the masculine plurality by default. So, you would use the term **gli amici** when referring to your friends if your friends include both males and females.
>
> To clarify...
>
> **Gli amici =** male friends OR male friends + female friends

> **Tip:** Keep in mind that, just like in English, we don't always need to use the definite article. In English, the definite article is the word 'the,' and in Italian, this is **il/ lo, la, i/ gli,** and **le.** So, when do you need to use the definite article?
>
> First, let's just quickly go over the purpose of the definite article. Let's use an English example.

If you have a salad in your fridge that you really need to eat before it goes bad, you would say 'I need to eat *the* salad.' Using the definite article indicates that you have a specific salad in mind. It's already there and it's just waiting to be eaten!

However, if you feel like you've been eating too much fast food lately, you might say 'I need to eat *a* salad.' In this case, you don't have a specific salad in mind, you just need to eat any salad. That's why we call it the *definite* article because there is more certainty and specificity implied.

These rules about when to use the definite article also apply to Italian – but with a couple of additions. Let's summarize!

In Italian, the definite article (**il/lo, la, gli, le**) is used...

➲ Like English, to refer to a specific person or thing.
La donna di Adamo è Eva (*Eve is Adam's woman*).

➲ Unlike English, to refer to something in a general, broad sense.
Mi piace la carne (*I like meat*) or **Mi piace la musica** (*I like music*)

➲ Unlike English, to refer to parts of your own body.
Mi hai rotto il braccio (*You broke my arm*)

Now, let's roll up our sleeves and get some practice in!

2.2 Practice

A. Write the plural version of each singular noun. When you finish, read each pair out loud.

1. L'uomo _____
2. L'amica _____
3. La conversazione _____
4. L'animale _____
5. Il sistema _____
6. Il bambino _____
7. La casa _____
8. Il treno _____
9. La città _____
10. Il dottore _____

B. Write the singular version of each plural noun. When you finish, read each pair out loud.

1. Le verità _____
2. Le televisioni _____
3. Le mani _____
4. Le forchette _____
5. Le matite _____
6. Le bambine _____
7. Le radio _____
8. Le cene _____
9. Le sedie _____
10. Le gambe _____

Speak Abroad
Academy

2.3 The Indefinite Article

So, we've already talked about the definite article. But what about the indefinite article? Remember when we talked about the difference between 'I need to eat *the* salad' and 'I need to eat *a* salad'? As you can probably guess, we can find the indefinite article in, '*a* salad'. We use the indefinite article to refer to a thing that is non-specific.

In English, the indefinite article is *a* or *an*. In Italian, the indefinite articles are…

Masculine/Neutral, singular: **un/uno** (*an/a*)

> *use **un** for all masculine nouns beginning with a vowel or consonant
> **(un ombrello – un libro)**

> *use **uno** for all masculine nouns that begin with **z, s,** or **x** **(uno zaino, uno studio)**

Masculine, plural: **dei/ degli** (*some*)

> *use **dei** for all masculine plural nouns beginning with a consonant
> **(dei figli)**

> *use **degli** for all masculine plural nouns beginning with a vowel
> **(degli animali)**

Feminine, singular: **una/un'** (*a/an*)

> *use **una** for all feminine singular nouns beginning with a consonant
> **(una mappa)**

> *use **un'** for all feminine singular nouns beginning with a vowel
> **(un'oliva)**

Feminine, plural: **delle** (*some*)

> For example:

> **Un'amica** (*a female friend*) → **delle amiche** (*some female friends*)

Remember: Just like the definite article, you must use an apostrophe to connect the indefinite article with a noun that begins with a vowel **(un'amica)***

When pronouncing the article directly with the noun, imagine it to be one word – the apostrophe joins the two to create a fluent sound. Don't pause between **un** and **amica**. Say them together.

Try it! **un'amica**… 'unamica'

Un figlio *(a son)* → **dei figli** *(some sons)*

Tip* When a word has '..gl..' it sounds like the English letter 'y' as in 'yellow'.

Try saying it out loud, figli → fi-yee

Try saying it out loud, coniglio → coh-nih-yoo

> To summarize, you only use the indefinite article (**un/uno, una/un', dei/delle**) when:
> ⮑ You want to identify someone or something as part of a class or group: **è un animale** *(it's an animal).*
> ⮑ You want to refer to something in a non-specific way: **una barca è per navigare** *(a boat is for sailing)* or **una donna giovane** *(a young woman).*

Quick Recap

	MASCULINE SINGULAR NOUNS	MASCULINE PLURAL NOUNS	FEMININE SINGULAR NOUNS	FEMININE PLURAL NOUNS
DEFINITE ARTICLES	l'amico (the male friend)	**gli** amici (the male friends **or** the female and male friends)	l'amica (the female friend)	**le** amiche (the female friends)
INDEFINITE ARTICLES	**un** amico (a male friend)	**degli** amici (some male friends or some female and male friends)	**una** casa (a house)	**delle** amiche (some female friends)
	uno studente	**degli studenti**	**un'**amica (a female friend)	**delle** amiche (some female friends)

> **Tip: Un** and **una** *(a and an)* can also mean *one* in addition to *a* or *an*. You will understand the difference based on the context of the sentence. For example, Gioco con **un** bambino *(I play with a boy)* vs. Compro **un** pomodoro *(I buy one tomato).*

Ready to flex those newfound skills? It's practice time!

2.3 Practice

A. Turn these singular nouns with indefinite articles into plural nouns with the correct responding indefinite article.

1. un nonno: _____
2. una conversazione: _____
3. un cane: _____
4. una donna: _____
5. uno studente: _____

6. un dottore: _____
7. un hotel: _____
8. un treno: _____
9. una matita: _____
10. una città: _____

B. Translate the following phrases:
1. The (male and female) students: _____
2. The planets: _____
3. A (female) doctor: _____
4. Some photographs: _____
5. The language: _____
6. The tourists: _____
7. Some (male and female) friends: _____
8. A tomato: _____
9. The conversation: _____
10. Some truths: _____

C. Complete the sentences with the correct article: **il/lo, la/l', i/gli, le** or **un/uno, una/un', dei/degli, delle**

1. _____ casa di Giovanni.
2. Ho trovato (*I found*) _____ moneta (*coin*).
3. È _____ testa (*head*) di _____ leone.
4. Quella è _____ impronta (*footprint*).
5. Sono _____ amiche di mia sorella (*they are some friends of my sisters*).
6. Mi piace_____ pollo (I like chicken).
7. Sto portando _____ torta a casa tua (*I'm bringing a cake to your house*).
8. Pietro sta comprando _____ bevande per la festa (*Pedro is buying the drinks for the party*).
9. Olivia sta guardando _____ televisione con sua mamma.
10. Adriano sta leggendo _____ libro molto interessante.

D. Do you remember what these nouns are in English? Remember to translate them with the definite or indefinite article that precedes them.

1. Il libro _____
2. La casa _____
3. I fiori _____
4. Il ragazzo _____
5. I fratelli _____
6. Il caffè _____
7. Il treno _____
8. I pianeti _____
9. Un gatto _____
10. Alcuni cani _____
11. Il telefono _____
12. Le mani _____
13. Un programma _____
14. Alcuni sistemi _____
15. I libri _____

E. Circle the correct article:

1. { La / Una } madre di Tommaso è simpatica.
2. Vorrei { i / alcuni } libri da leggere.
3. Vorrei { il / un } televisore nuovo.
4. { Il / Un } gatto è un animale independente.
5. Ha rotto (*he broke*) { la / una } finestra della casa.
6. Mi piacciono { i / degli } fiori.
7. Ho parlato (*I spoke*) con { il / un } direttore del collegio.
8. Teresa ha trovato { il / un } gatto.
9. Ho messo (*I put*) { le / delle } chiavi (*keys*) nella borsetta (*purse*).
10. Emma ha cucinato (*Emma cooked*) { la / una } pizza per cena.

F. Complete these sentences with the correct definite or indefinite article:

il/lo – la/l' – i/gli – le – un/uno – una/un'- dei/degli – delle

1. Washington è _____ città degli Stati Uniti.
2. Hudson è _____ via di casa tua.
3. Bogotá è _____ capitale della Colombia.
4. _____ casa di Elena è grande.
5. _____ Papa vive a Roma.
6. Ho bisogno (*I need*) _____ giacca (*jacket*) rossa.
7. Hai _____ chiavi (*keys*) di casa?
8. Ho visto (*I saw*) _____ leone (*lion*) grande allo zoo (*zoo*).
9. Hai cucinato _____ piatto di pasta *(a plate of pasta)* per pranzo.
10. _____ uccelli (*birds*) mangiano i semi (seeds).

Ciao! Lo sapevi...? *(Did you know...?)*

Italians always greet people with a kiss on both cheeks, even if you are just meeting them for the first time. Always go to the right cheek first for a proper *'saluto italiano'!* However, the exact number of kisses and the practice itself can vary depending on the region and the relationship between the people meeting. In some regions or among close friends and family, a third kiss might be added, but two kisses are the most common and widely accepted practice.

LESSON 3 :

DESCRIBING PEOPLE AND THINGS
BROWN DOG AND BLACK CAT

3.1 Descriptive Adjectives

Remember what a noun is? It's a person, place, or thing, like 'doctor' 'house' or 'table.'

Sometimes more detail is necessary when talking about objects or subjects– sometimes, we need to describe objects or subjects to give a better understanding. This is where adjectives come in. We use adjectives to describe the nouns we're talking about. For example, we could say that a person is tall or short – or that a table is big or small.

In Italian, we usually put the adjective *after* the noun that we're describing.

So, to say 'big table,' in Italian you would say, '**tavolo grande**'. As you can guess, the word **grande** means big and yes, it is an adjective.

Adjectives are also used to describe other qualities, like the nationality of something or someone. For example, to say 'Italian food,' you would say, '**cibo italiano**'.

Although we usually put the adjective after the noun, there is one exception when we put the descriptor *before* the noun. This happens when we're describing the *quantity* of something. For example, when we say, 'a few pencils,' this would be **qualche matita.**

Just like nouns, adjectives will also change their endings depending on:

- ⟳ The singularity or plurality of the noun
- ⟳ The gender of the noun

So, if you have a feminine singular noun like **la foto** (the photo), you will need to use a feminine singular adjective like **bella** (beautiful) to describe it. In this case, you would say **la foto bella** to say, 'the beautiful photo.'

Singular Form of Adjectives

Adjectives that end in **-o** are masculine and agree with a masculine noun. For example: L'amico **buono** (*the good friend*). Keep in mind that Italian adjectives are the last words in the sentence, since they *usually* go after the noun.

English	Italian	Pronunciation
The tall student	**Lo studente alto**	*[loh stoo-dehn-teh ahl-toh]*
The short boy	**Il bambino basso**	*[eel bahm-bee-noh bahs-soh]*
The good brother	**Il fratello buono**	*[eel frah-tehl-loh bwoh-noh]*
The bad dog	**Il cane cattivo**	*[eel kah-neh kaht-tee-voh]*
The fat cat	**Il gatto grasso**	*[eel gaht-toh grahs-soh]*
The thin uncle	**Lo zio magro**	*[loh tsee-oh mah-groh]*
The friendly boy	**Il bambino simpatico**	*[eel bahm-bee-noh seem-pah-tee-koh]*
The unfriendly youngster	**Il ragazzo antipatico**	*[eel rah-gaht-tsoh ahn-tee-pah-tee-koh]*
The small book	**Il libro piccolo**	*[eel lee-broh peek-koh-loh]*
The hardworking grandfather	**Il nonno lavoratore**	*[eel nohn-noh lah-voh-rah-toh-reh]*
The beautiful sofa	**Il sofa bello**	*[eel soh-fah behl-loh]*
The old man	**L'uomo vecchio**	*[lwoh-moh vehk-kyo]*
The mischievous boy	**Il bambino dispettoso**	*[eel bahm-bee-no dee-speht-toh-soh]*

But what if you're not referring to a masculine noun? Sometimes, you need to describe a female student as tall, not just a male student!

In this case, adjectives change the **-o** to **-a** when they describe a feminine noun. For example: La bambina **buona** (*the good girl*).

English	Italian	Pronunciation
The tall (female) student	**La studentessa alta**	*[lah stoo-dehn-tehs-sah ahl-tah]*
The short girl	**La bambina bassa**	*[lah bahm-bee-nah bahs-sah]*
The good sister	**La sorella buona**	*[lah soh-rehl-lah bwoh-nah]*
The bad (female) teacher	**La maestra cattiva**	*[lah mah-eh-strah]]*
The fat (female) cat	**La gatta grassa**	*[lah gaht-tah grahs-sa]*
The thin aunt	**La zia magra**	*[lah tsee-ah mah-grah]*

English	Italian	Pronunciation
The friendly girl	**La bambina simpatica**	*[lah bahm-bee-na seem-pah-tee-kah]*
The unfriendly (female) youngster	**La ragazza antipatica**	*[lah rah-gaht-tsa ahn-tee-pah-tee-kah]*
The small house	**La casa piccola**	*[lah kah-sah peek-koh-lah]*
The hardworking grandmother	**La nonna lavoratrice**	*[lah nohn-nah lah-voh-rah-tree-cheh]*
The beautiful city	**La città bella**	*[lah ceeht-ta behl-lah]*
The old woman	**La donna vecchia**	*[lah dohn-nah vehk-kya]*

Sometimes, you don't need to change the ending of an adjective. This makes it a little easier!

If the adjective ends in **-e** (*intelligente-intelligent*), it will have the same form whether describing a feminine or masculine noun: uomo **fedele** (*loyal man*) and donna **fedele** (*loyal woman*).

English	Italian	Pronunciation
The excellent book	**Il libro eccellente**	*[eel leeh-broh ehch-chehl-lehn-teh]*
The big planet	**Il pianeta grande**	*[eel pee-ah-neh-tah grahn-deh]*
The loyal friend	**L'amico fedele**	*[lah-mee-koh feh-deh-leh]*
The weak boy	**Il bambino debole**	*[eel bahm-bee-noh deh-boh-leh]*
The difficult conversation	**La conversazione difficile**	*[lah kohn-vehr-sah-tyoh-neh]*
The easy issue	**Il tema facile**	*[eel the-mah fah-cheeh-leh]*
The strong woman	**La donna forte**	*[lah dohn-nah fohr-teh]*
The excellent food	**Il cibo eccellente**	*[eel chee-boh ehch-chehl-ehn-teh]*
The kind lady	**La signora gentile**	*[lah see-nyoh-rah jehn-tee-leh]*
The (male) young student	**Lo studente giovane**	*[loh stoo-dehn-teh joh-vah-neh]*
The intelligent (female) doctor	**La dottoressa intelligente**	*[lah doht-toh-rehs-sah een-tehl-lee-jehn-teh]*

Describing people and things

Now, let's introduce another rule.

Remember when I said that the Italian adjective *usually* goes after the noun? If you want to emphasize the quality of something or add an emotional charge to a description, you can sometimes place the adjective before the noun. In this case, the adjective will be shortened.

For example, **buono** and **grande** may all appear before the noun. When **buono** and **grande** precede a masculine singular noun, **buono** will become **buon** and **grande** will become **gran.**

Un libro buono and **un buon libro** both mean *'a good book,'* but you may choose to say **un buon libro** to *emphasize* just how much you enjoyed this excellent book.

On the other hand, if you thought a program was particularly bad, you might choose to say **un brutto programma** instead of **un programma brutto.** They both mean *'a bad program,'* but the former places more of an emotional charge on the word *'bad.'*

Sometimes, this can slightly change the meaning of the adjectives in question.

When **grande** is placed after a noun, it simply means large or big, like in the sentence **una casa grande** (*a large house*). Instead, when it is placed before a singular noun, it is shortened to **gran** and means impressive or great. You could even say **un gran dottore** to say, *'a great doctor.'*

Plural Form of Adjectives

I'm sure you guessed that this was coming! When the noun is plural and refers to multiple things, the adjectives must be modified to agree with the plurality. We do the same exact thing when we modify nouns depending on gender and quantity! Let's take a look at some examples:

If you want to say *'the good girls'*, In Italian you would say **'le bambine buone'**

The ending vowel e represents that the noun is plural-feminine, therefore we use the same vowel e at the end of the adjective

If you want to say *'the fat cats'*, In Italian you would say **'i gatti grassi'**

The ending vowel i represents that the nouns is plural-masculine, therefore we use the same vowel i at the end of the adjective

Keep this in mind for when we dive into this topic in more detail in Lesson 4!

Time to get your learning hat on – it's time for some hands-on practice!

3.1 Practice

A. Translate the English adjective into its Italian equivalent. Make sure it matches the noun.

Example: Il gatto _____ (fat) <u>il gatto grasso</u>

1. La bambina _____ (tall)
2. L'uomo _____ (poor)
3. Il cane _____ (loyal)
4. La ragazza _____ (beautiful)
5. Il problema _____ (difficult)
6. Il bambino _____ (good)
7. I nonno _____ (happy)
8. Il libro _____ (interesting)
9. L'amicizia _____ (strong)
10. La mano _____ (weak)

B. Translate the English adjective into its Italian equivalent. Make sure it matches the noun.

1. La zia _____ (short)
2. Il cibo _____ (excellent)
3. La città _____ (small)
4. Lo zio _____ (friendly)
5. L'hotel _____ (old)
6. Il gatto _____ (bad)
7. L'amica _____ (intelligent)
8. Il cane _____ (loyal)
9. Il ragazzo _____ (hardworking)
10. Il turista _____ (fat)

C. Write the opposite adjectives to the one in the phrases below.

1. La tema facile _____
2. Il bambino basso _____
3. Il ristorante pieno _____
4. La bambina antipatica _____
5. Il cane piccolo _____

D. Write the plural form of each of the following nouns and adjectives.
1. Il pomodoro grande _____
2. L'uomo alto _____
3. Il cane intelligente _____
4. La bambina forte _____
5. La persona laboriosa _____
6. La città piccola _____
7. Il gatto magro _____
8. La donna allegra _____
9. Il libro difficile _____
10. Il cibo eccellente _____

E. Complete the sentence with the correct form of the adjectives:
1. I libri _____ (eccellente)
2. La nonna _____ (laborioso)
3. La città _____ (bello)
4. I libri _____ (piccolo)
5. I sofà _____ (bello)
6. Le sorelle _____ (buono)
7. I gatti _____ (grasso)
8. I bambini _____ (simpatico)
9. La casa _____ (nuovo)
10. Le scarpe _____ (comodo-comfortable)

3.2 Adjectives of Nationality

As we mentioned earlier, nationalities are also adjectives. They describe the origin of a thing or person. In Italian, the word for a country's language is sometimes the same as the word for the singular form of their nationality.

For example: **l'inglese** (English), **l'italiano** (Italian), and **il francese** (French).

This is similar to English, where the language 'English' uses the same word as the nationality 'English.' The same goes for 'Italian' and 'French.'

In the Italian examples above, you'll notice that all three languages/nationalities are masculine. This means that the words for language and nationality are only interchangeable when the noun is masculine. When the noun is feminine, however, the adjective (in this case, the nationality) must be modified to a feminine form.

This means that you would say **lei è <u>italiana</u>** (she is Italian) when you're talking about a female Italian person.

But if you were talking about a male Italian person, you would say **lui è** <u>italiano,</u> using the same word that we use for the language itself (*italiano*)

English	Italian	Pronunciation
Spanish	**spagnolo**	*[spah-nyoh-loh]*
English	**inglese**	*[een-gleh-seh]*
French	**francese**	*[frahn-cheh-seh]*
German	**tedesco**	*[teh-deh-skoh]*
Italian	**italiano**	*[ee-tah-lyah-noh]*
Portuguese	**portoghese**	*[pohr-toh-geh-seh]*
Northamerican/ American	**nordamericano/americano**	*[nohrd-ah-meh-ree-kah-noh]/ [ah-meh-ree-kah-noh]*

> **Tip:** In Italian, you do not capitalize the names of languages and adjectives of nationality, though you do capitalize the names of countries and cities.

Let's make it real! Time for some practical exercises to solidify your skills.

3.2 Practice

Write the correct nationality next to each noun, making it match in gender and quantity.

1. La Statua della Libertà è _____ .
2. La Torre Eiffel è _____ .
3. Il Big Ben è _____ .
4. La Torre di Pisa è _____ .
5. Il Museo El Prado è _____ .
6. Angela Merkel è _____ .
7. Il Duomo di Milano è _____ .
8. Simone Biles è _____ .
9. Chanel è _____ .
10. Cristiano Ronaldo è _____ .

3.3 Describing a Person

In Italian, there's more than one way to write a descriptive sentence – just like in English. You can say 'the intelligent woman' or you can say 'the woman is intelligent.'

To say someone or something *is* something, you use the Italian word **è**. This means that 'the woman is intelligent' – in Italian, '**la donna** è **intelligente**.'

Of course, you don't always have to specify '*the* woman,' you can also use pronouns to indicate who you're talking about, just like in English. In this case, just replace the noun with the pronoun. To simply say 'she is intelligent,' you would say, '**lei è intelligente**.'

Fortunately, the words '*is*' and è are only different by one letter, so this should be somewhat easy to remember! You'll also be glad to hear that you use the word è for both masculine and feminine nouns. For example, '*he is friendly*' would be, '**lui** è simpatico.'

Got the concept down? Now, let's apply it with some good old practice!

3.3 Practice

A. Which adjectives are the most appropriate for each sentence?
1. La zia Maria è { bassi / intelligente / bella / forti }
2. Il signor García è { lavoratrice / allegro / interessante / poveri }
3. La città è { grande / interessante / vecchio / bello }
4. Il bambino è { cattivi / buono / magra / simpatico }
5. I gatti sono { buono / cattivi / bianchi / nero }

B. Using the word è, choose two adjectives to describe the following people/ things:

grande – pulito/a – simpatico/a – grasso/a
laborioso/a – buono/a – interessante – bello/a

1. Mio padre è _____
2. Mia madre è _____
3. Mio fratello è _____
4. Il mio gatto è _____
5. Il mio cane è _____

C. Translate the following:
1. Monique is French: Monique è _____
2. Carlo is Italian: Carlo è _____
3. Helmut is German: Helmut è _____
4. Sofía is Spanish: Sofia è _____
5. María is Portuguese: Maria è _____

D. Do you remember where these famous people are from? Write the correct nationality.
1. Pablo Picasso è _____
2. Emmanuel Macron è _____
3. Daniel Craig è _____
4. Marco Polo è _____
5. Antonio Banderas è _____

Common Error: Remember not to make the mistake of placing the adjectives before the subject when you speak Italian.

X Don't say : Un **difficile** esame (*a difficult exam*)

✓ Say : Un esame **difficile**!

Ciao! Vuoi sapere qualcosa?

The word 'boh' in Italian is an actual term that expresses a confused feeling. It is often used when you are perplexed or do not know the answer to something. Try shrugging your shoulders up, lifting your hands as if you are confused and say 'boh..?'

"Dov'è il cane?"

"Boh, non lo so."

LESSON 4 :

DESCRIBING THINGS
THE YELLOW BRICK ROAD

4.1 Adjectives Continued

Shake off the rulebook for a while! Let's embark on a journey of discovery; it's time to sprinkle some magic into your vocabulary. Unveil the richness of the Italian language, where each adjective is like a brushstroke painting vivid portraits of the world, people, and experiences around you. Did you know that Italian is the language of art, and it brought us masterpieces like Michelangelo's David and Leonardo da Vinci's Mona Lisa? Therefore, it's important that you dive into the linguistic canvas and let the colors of Italian enrich your expression! I mean, how else can we describe the world around and within us in greater detail?

Here are some useful everyday adjectives that you'll need to know!

Descriptive Adjectives

English	Italian	Pronunciation
fast	**veloce**	[veh-loh-cheh]
slow	**lento**	[lehn-toh]
cheap	**economico**	[eh-koh-noh-mee-koh]
expensive	**caro**	[kah-roh]
famous	**famoso**	[fah-moh-soh]
long	**lungo**	[loohn-goh]
short	**corto**	[kohr-toh]
young	**giovane**	[joh-vah-neh]
elderly	**anziano**	[ahn-tsyag-noh]
pretty	**carino**	[kah-ree-noh]
ugly	**brutto**	[bruht-toh]
happy	**felice**	[feh-lee-cheh]
sad	**triste**	[trees-teh]

English	Italian	Pronunciation
rich	**ricco**	*[reek-koh]*
new	**nuovo**	*[nwoh-voh]*
blonde	**biondo**	*[byohn-doh]*
dark-haired / dark-skinned	**moro**	*[moh-roh]*
delicious	**delizioso**	*[deh-leet-tsyoh-soh]*

I'm sure you're now wondering what these adjectives look like in a sentence. Let's use them together to compliment some nouns we learned in prior chapters.

Il problema facile (*the easy problem*)

La moto veloce (*the fast motorcycle*)

La sedia economica (*the cheap chair*)

La bambina famosa (*the famous girl*)

La donna felice (*the happy woman*)

L'uomo triste (*the sad man*)

Il bambino moro (*the dark-skinned boy*)

Il cibo delizioso (*the delicious food*)

La lezione breve (*the short lesson*)

Il treno lungo (*the long train*)

Colors

Of course, just like in English, colors are adjectives too – and they're extremely important ones since we tend to use them very often. But, don't worry – all the rules you've already learned about adjectives so far also apply to colors. Treat them just like you would all the other adjectives you've learned and place them after the noun.

English	Italian	Pronunciation
white	**bianco**	*[byahn-koh]*
black	**nero**	*[neh-roh]*
red	**rosso**	*[rohs-soh]*
blue	**blu**	*[bluh]*
yellow	**giallo**	*[jahl-loh]*
green	**verde**	*[vehr-deh]*
grey	**grigio**	*[gree-joh]*
pink	**rosa/ rosato**	*[roh-sah roh-sah-to]*
brown	**marrone**	*[mahr-roh-neh]*
orange	**arancione**	*[ah-rahn-chee-oh-neh]*

Here are some examples on how to use colors with a noun:

Il pianeta rosso (*the red planet*)   **La sedia verde** (*the green chair*)

La matita nera (*the black pencil*)   **La moto blu** (*the blue motorcycle*)

Il gatto bianco (*the white cat*)   **La casa rosa** (*the pink house*)

Il divano giallo (*the yellow sofa*)   **Il cane marrone** (*the brown dog*)

To modify these colours for plurality or multiple nouns, use the plural form (example: il cavallo nero – i cavalli neri) to the end of each adjective, except blue and pink that remain unchanged (example: la parete rosa – le pareti rosa). For example:

I pianeti rossi (*the red planets*)   **Le sedie verdi** (*the green chairs*)

Le matite nere (*the black pencils*)   **Le moto blu** (*the blue motorcycles*)

I gatti bianchi (*the white cats*)   **Le case rosa** (*the pink houses*)

I sofà gialli (*the yellow sofa*)   **I cani marroni** (*the brown dogs*)

Remember that, in Italian, adjectives change their endings based on the gender (masculine or feminine) and number (singular or plural) of the nouns they accompany.

No time to waste; let's jump straight into some practical exercises!

4.1 Practice

A. It's a good idea to practice what you already know so far: nouns (Second Lesson) and adjectives (Third Lesson and Fourth Lesson).

Find the right adjective for the following nouns according to the noun being masculine or feminine.

> lavoratrice – cara – interessante – moro – difficile – veloce – felice
> intelligente – vecchia – nuovo – fedele – alto – ricco – nuova – facil
> economica – anziana – delizioso – marrone – buono – grasso

1. Il cane è _____ .
2. Il divano è _____ .
3. La ragazza è _____ .
4. Il treno è _____ .
5. Il bambino è _____ .
6. Il televisore è _____ .
7. Il caffè è _____ .
8. La persona è _____ .
9. La casa è _____ .
10. La nonna è _____ .

11. Il problema è _____.
12. La bambina è _____.
13. Il programma è _____.
14. L'uomo è _____.
15. La moto è _____.
16. La sedia è _____.
17. L'idioma è _____.
18. Il pomodoro è _____.
19. Il ragazzo è _____.
20. Il gatto è _____.

B. And now let's practice using colors! Complete the following phrases translating the color adjectives from English to Italian.

1. Il fiore _____ (yellow)
2. La casa _____ (blue)
3. La sedia _____ (orange)
4. La mano _____ (white)
5. La gatta _____ (black)
6. La matita _____ (grey)
7. Il sofá _____ (green)
8. Il telefono _____ (pink)
9. Il cane _____ (brown)
10. Il pomodoro _____ (red)

C. Answer these questions according to the example, by matching the adjectives to the noun.

Example: Il cane è intelligente. E i gatti? <u>Anche loro sono intelligenti.</u>

1. La madre è gentile. E il padre? _____.
2. L'esame di matematica è facile. E l'esame di letteratura? _____.
3. Le zie sono laboriose. E gli zii? _____.
4. Il cane è grasso. E i gatti? _____.
5. I nonni sono buoni. E la nonna? _____.

D. Describe the person or object in the question. Keep in mind that you must write the exact opposite of each of the adjectives that are used in the affirmative sentences.

Example: Olivia and Emma are quite opposite. What is Olivia like?
Emma è alta, bionda, felice e forte, invece Olivia è <u>bassa, mora, triste e pigra.</u>

1. Elena and Sofía are quite opposite. What is Sofía like?
   Elena è bassa, pigra, mora, triste e povera, invece Sofia è
   _____.

2. Tomás and Martín's house are the opposite. What is Martín's house like?
   La casa di Tommaso è piccola, bella, nuova e economica, invece la casa di
   Martino è _____.

3. Germán and Pablo are quite opposite. What is Pablo like?
   Germano è ricco, intelligente, biondo, alto, lavoratore e vecchio, invece Paolo è
   _____.

4. Christian and Adriano are quite the opposite. What is Adriano like?
   Christian è basso, giovane, moro e grasso, invece Adriano è
   _____.

5. Matilda and Anna's cats are quite the opposite. What is Anna's cat like?
   Il gatto di Matilda è lento, lungo e triste. Invece il gatto di Anna è
   _____.

4.2 Demonstrative Adjectives

We've talked primarily about common adjectives so far. Now, let's talk about demonstrative adjectives. You've probably noticed that we're tossing around some very official linguistic terminology here. Let me just say that although it's important for you to be introduced to official terms like 'demonstrative adjectives,' you don't have to remember them *if you remember the rule itself.*

So, let's talk about demonstrative adjectives.

These are words like '*this*' or '*that*,' which draw attention to specific nouns (singular or plural). You already know what purpose they serve in English, and it's essentially the same in Italian.

When we use these words, they go ***before*** the noun, just like in English, and they also change if we're talking about multiple nouns. This is like the difference between 'this' and 'these.' For example, you would say **questo cane** for '*this dog*' and **questi cani** for '*these dogs*.'

And of course, they also need to be modified if you're talking about a feminine noun. For example, **questa casa** (*this house*) and **queste case** (*these houses*).

As you can see from the examples above and the table below, demonstrative adjectives also change the final vowel depending on gender and quantity, following the same rules for singular and plural nouns.

this	**questo** (masculine, singular)	*[kweh-stoh]*	**questa** (feminine, singular)	*[kweh-stah]*
these	**questi** (masculine, plural)	*[kweh-stee]*	**queste** (feminine, plural)	*[kweh-steh]*
that	**quello** (masculine, singular)	*[kwehl-loh]*	**quella** (feminine, singular)	*[kwehl-lah]*
those	**quelli** (masculine, plural)	*[kwehl-lee]*	**quelle** (feminine, plural)	*[kwehl-leh]*

The forms of **quello** change depending on the gender and number of the noun, as well as the initial letter or sound of the noun. Let's take a look!

Masculine Singular

quel → before a masculine singular noun that begins with a consonant
quel ragazzo (that boy)

quell' → before a masculine singular noun that begins with a vowel
quell'uomo (that man)
quello → before a masculine singular noun that begins with consonants:

z, pn, ps, gn, x, y
quello studente (that student)

Describing things

Masculine Plural

quei → before a masculine plural noun that begins with a consonant
quei ragazzi (those boys)

quegli → before a masculine plural noun that begins with a vowel and consonants:

z, pn, ps, gn, x, y
quegli uomini (those men)
quegli studenti (those students)

Feminine Singular

quella → before a feminine singular noun that begins with a consonant
quella ragazza (that girl)

quell' → before a feminine singular noun that begins with a vowel
quell'amica (that friend – female)

Feminine Plural

quelle → before a feminine plural noun that begins with a consonant or a vowel

quelle ragazze (those girls)
quelle amiche (those friends – females)

Time to transition from theory to action! Let's practice and perfect these skills.

4.2 Practice

A. Beatriz and her friend go shopping. Check out what they say about the clothes, using the demonstrative adjective **questo** in the correct form. Use è (*is*) or **sono** (*are*) depending on whether the subject is singular or plural.

Example: vestito (dress) / rosso (red) → Questo vestito è rosso.

1. camicia (shirt) / bella → _____
2. scarpe (shoes) / care → _____
3. maglione (sweater) / lana (wool) → _____
4. vestiti (dresses) / seta (silk) → _____
5. pantaloni (pants) / economici → _____

B. Now use the demonstrative adjective **quello** in the correct form.

        Example: calze (socks) / lunghe → Queste calze sono lunghe.

1. camicia (*blouse*) / bianca → _____
2. maglietta (*t-shirt*) / rossa → _____
3. gonne (*skirt*) / corte → _____
4. giacca (*jacket*) / **molto*** economica → _____
5. scarpe sportive (*sneakers*) / belle → _____

*Molto: Is an adverb that means **very**. Adverbs go before adjectives and verbs. Check out some more adverbs here:

Adverb	How it is used	Example
molto *(very)*	**molto** + adjective/ adverb	Quei fiori sono **molto** belli. *(Those flowers are very beautiful.)*
tanto *(a lot)*	verb + **tanto**	Carlo viaggia **tanto**. *(Carlos travels a lot.)*
abbastanza *(quite)*	**abbastanza** + adjective/ adverb/ verb	Lei cammina **abbastanza** veloce. *(She walks quite fast.)*
poco *(not a lot)*	adjective/ adverb/ verb + **poco**	Martino mangia **poco**. *(Martín doesn't eat a lot.)*
troppo *(too much)*	adjective/ adverb/ verb + **troppo**	Elena parla **troppo**. *(Elena talks too much.)*

C. Complete these sentences with **questo** or **quello**.

1. Chi (*Who*) è _____ (that) dottore? (This) _____ dottore è un cardiologo (*cardiologist*).
2. _____ (This) pianeta è molto grande.
3. _____ (that over there) casa è bella.
4. _____ (that over there) treno è grande.
5. _____ (that) moto è nuova.

D. Complete each sentence with the correct form of **questo, questa, questi, queste**. Next answer in the reverse, using the adjective that means the opposite.

Example: È buono _____ **professore?** _____ **: È buono questo professore? No, è cattivo.**

1. È felice _____ bambina? _____ .
2. Sono ricchi _____ ragazzi? _____ .
3. È brutto _____ cane? _____ .
4. Sono vecchi _____ edifici? _____ .
5. È anziana _____ donna? _____ .
6. Sono forti _____ ragazze? _____ .
7. È grande _____ casa? _____ .
8. È alto _____ bambino? _____ .
9. Sono debole _____ ragazze? _____ .
10. È felice _____ bambina? _____ .

4.3 Describing People and Adjectives in the Plural Form

Remember when we talked about using è to describe a singular noun? For example, **la donna è intelligente** to say, 'the woman is intelligent'?

It also becomes necessary to describe plural nouns in the same way. In English, 'is' becomes 'are' when we're talking about plural nouns, like in the sentence 'the books are boring.'

In Italian, è becomes **sono**.

Instead of...

> **lui è**: he (masculine) is
> **lei è**: she (feminine) is

You would say...

> **quelli sono**: they (masculine) are
> **quelle sono**: they (feminine) are

Just like è, you use the word **sono** regardless of whether the noun is feminine or masculine. The demonstrative verb tells us whether the noun is feminine, masculine, or both!

For example:

They (a group of men) are thin. → Quell**i** **sono** magri.

They (a group of women) are intelligent. → Quell**e** **sono** intelligenti.

They (a group of men **and** women) are happy. → Quell**i** **sono** felici.

Now, you know how to say 'he/she is' and 'they are'! Try and practice this with different adjectives.

Vocabulary: The Neighborhood

Time to expand your vocabulary! Let's look at some nouns that you'll encounter in your typical neighborhood, town, and city.

English	Italian	Pronunciation
tree	albero	[ahl-beh-roh]
flower	fiore	[fyoh-reh]
street	strada	[strah-dah]
post office	ufficio postale	[oof-fee-chee-oh poh-stah-leh]
fish store	pescheria	[peh-skeh-ree-ah]
supermarket	supermercato	[soo-pehr-mehr-kah-toh]
office	ufficio	[oof-fee-chee-oh]
car	automobile	[aw-toh-moh-bee-leh]
theatre	teatro	[teh-ah-troh]
salesperson	commesso	[kohm-mehs-soh]
fruit and vegetable store	fruttivendolo	[froot-teeh-vehn-doh-loh]
park	parco	[pahr-koh]
garden/yard	giardino	[jahr-dee-noh]
school	scuola	[skwoh-lah]
college/university	università	[oo-nee-vehr-see-tah]
movie theatre	cinema	[chee-neh-mah]
church	chiesa	[kyeh-sah]
airport	aeroporto	[ah-eh-roh-pohr-toh]
museum	museo	[moo-seh-oh]
bar	bar	[bahr]
restaurant	ristorante	[reeh-stoh-rahn-teh]
avenue	viale	[vee-ah-leh]
building	edificio	[eh-dee-fee-chyoh]

Eager to see your knowledge in action? Let's practice and make it happen!

Speak Abroad
Academy

4.3 Practice

A. Imagine you're showing your friend around your neighborhood from your car. Point out some places of interest, completing the sentences with the right form of: **quello, quella, quelli, quelle**.

1. _____ casa è molto grande. 2. _____ edificio (*building*) è l'ufficio postale (*post office*) e _____ albero è molto vecchio. 3. _____ strada (*street*) è nuova e _____ cani sono cattivi. 4. _____ viale è ampio. 5. _____ aeroporto è grande.

B. Rewrite these sentences using the correct demonstrative adjective and corresponding verb *to be* (è or **sono**, depending on whether the subject is singular or plural), and the right form of the adjective (singular or plural).

Example: Questa / strada / è / lunga: Queste strade sono lunghe.

1. Questo / sistema / è / eccellente _____
2. Questa / pescheria / è / cara _____
3. Questa / città / è / bella _____
4. Questo / teatro / è / piccolo _____
5. Quello / ufficio / è / nuovo _____

Common Error: When using the word **persona**, it's not necessary to use a masculine adjective, even if the sex of the person you are referring to is male. **Persona** always agrees with a **feminine adjective**:

X	✓
Giuseppe è una persona buono.	Giuseppe è una **persona** buon**a**.
Martino è una persona lavoratore.	Martino è una **persona** lavo>tr**ice**.
Luigi è una persona simpatico.	Luigi è una **persona** simpatic**a**.

Ciao, senti questo! (*Listen to this!*)

Don't be confused, although **buono/a** and **bene** both mean 'good' they cannot be used interchangeably! Say **buono/a** when you want to say that **food** is good or if you are describing **good behavior** in a person or animal. Say **bene** to describe a **good feeling** or to describe **situations** – it can also be used as an adverb to describe **verbs**.

LESSON 5 :

THE VERB ESSERE (TO BE)

TO BE OR NOT TO BE

Present Tense of Essere

Remember the words è and **sono**? They mean *'is'* and *'are,'* which essentially mean the same thing, but one is singular and the other is plural. The Italian words è and **sono** are all rooted in the same Italian verb **essere**, which means *'to be'*- one of the most used and important verbs in almost any language!

In English, we use the word è *(is)* for basically everything. You use it to say both *'the car is red'* (*description*) and *'the car is here'* (*location*), even though you're describing different types of attributes about the car.

In Italian, you wouldn't use the same word for different types of descriptions.

Let's look at the two verbs in these sentences, è and **sta**. While è is rooted in the verb **essere**, which means *'to be,'* **sta** is rooted in the verb **stare**. And guess what? It also means *'to be'*! That's right, in English, **essere** and **stare** both mean the same thing, but in Italian, they describe different types of indications.

For example, you can say:

La ragazza **sta** bene. *(The girl is well./ The girl is fine.)*

La ragazza **è** una studentessa. *(The girl is a student.)*

But don't worry, we will get into the difference between **essere** and **stare** later on!

Before we learn more about **stare**, let's make sure you're familiar with all the forms of **essere**. You already know è and **sono** (*'is' and 'are'*), which can be used to say **lui/lei è** (*he/she is*) and **essi/esse sono** (*they are*). But what if you wanted to say, *'we are'* or *'I am'*? To refer to different pronouns, you'll need to make modifications.

Let's take a look at these modifications and let's roll up our sleeves to get some practice in. Read the following dialogue and use the table below (modifications for **'essere'**) to identify exactly what they're saying.

La città

TOMMASO: Scusi, questo è l'ufficio postale?

LUIGI: Mi dispiace, non **sono** di qui.

TOMMASO: Ah, di dov'è Lei?

LUIGI: **Sono** di un'altra città. Non **sono** di Roma.

TOMMASO: Ah, **è** un turista, come me.

LUIGI: Sí, **sono** un turista. **Sono** degli Stati Uniti. E Lei?

TOMMASO: **Sono** francese.

LUIGI: Ah. **Siamo** due turisti. Quella signora là è italiana. Lei è di qui.

Glossary:

Di qui: *from here*

Di dove...?: *Where... from?*

Un'altra: *another*

Come: *like*

Qui: *here*

***Note on abbreviations:** form. (formal), inf. (informal), sing. (singular), pl. (plural), arc. (archaic)*

essere *(to be)*			
io *(I)*	**sono**	noi *(we)*	**siamo**
tu *(you)*	**sei**	voi *(you - inf. pl.)*	**siete**
lui *(he)* lei *(she)* esso,essa *(it - arc.)* ella,egli *(s/he - arc.)* Lei *(You - form.)*	**es**	loro *(they)* essi,esse *(it - arc. pl.)*	**sono**

***Tip:** Back in the day and in some traditional households, Italians may use the pronoun 'Voi' when referring to (You-formal) instead of 'Lei' as seen on the table above. Nowadays, 'Lei' (You-formal) predominates the Italian language as the pronoun for You-Singular-Formal. But, keep 'Voi' in mind as an option!
Lei (You-formal)   è
Voi (You-formal)   siete*

We mentioned that verbs meaning '*to be*' are used to describe things in different ways. So, when exactly is **essere** (io **sono, sei, è, sono,** etc) used? Generally, **essere** is used to describe:

⊃ The nature of something or someone

⊃ The identity of something or someone

⊃ The qualities or characteristics of something or someone

⊃ Time

⊃ Events

This means you would use **essere** in these ten situations:

1. To *describe*

Io **sono** bionda.	=	*I am blonde.*
Tu **sei** alto.	=	*You're tall.*
Lui **è** giovane.	=	*He is young.*
Lei **è** intelligente.	=	*She is intelligent.*
Siamo simpatici.	=	*We are nice.*
Voi **siete** celibi.	=	*You (formal) are single.*
Voi **siete** romantici.	=	*You all are romantic.*
Loro sono mori.	=	*They are dark-haired.*

> **Tip:** Note that in Italian you do not need to add the pronoun to a sentence—unless you want to stress it—because it is already included in the verb: **siamo** simpatici (*we are nice*).

2. To *indicate a profession*

Marco **è** avvocato.	=	*Marcos is a lawyer.*
Io **sono** studente.	=	*I am a student.*
Lei **è** architetta.	=	*She is an architect.*
Siamo dottori.	=	*We are doctors.*
Siete professori.	=	*You (formal) are professors.*
Voi **siete** dirigenti.	=	*You all are managers.*
Loro sono ingegneri.	=	*They are engineers.*

> **Tip**: Unlike English, Italian omits the indefinite article **un/una** before an unmodified profession. For example: **Loro sono dottoresse**. But if you modify the profession with detail, you need to add the indefinite article: **Loro sono <u>delle</u> dottoresse <u>eccellenti</u>**.

3. To *indicate where someone comes from*

Io **sono** del Perú.	=	*I am from Peru.*
Tu **sei** della Colombia.	=	*You are from Colombia.*
Lui **è** di New York.	=	*He is from New York.*
Lei **è** spagnola.	=	*You are Spanish.*
Noi **siamo** italiani.	=	*We are Italians.*
Voi **siete** francesi.	=	*You are all French.*
Essi **sono** irlandesi.	=	*They are Irish.*

4. To *identify specific attributes about a person, such as relationship, nationality, race, or religion*

Io **sono** cattolica.	=	*I am Catholic.*
Tu **sei** argentino.	=	*You are Argentinian.*
Lui **è** asiatico.	=	*He is Asian.*
Siamo celibi.	=	*We are single.*
Voi **siete** compagne di scuola.	=	*You are friends from school.*
Marco e Luisa **sono** amici.	=	*Marcos and Luisa are friends.*

5. To say *what material something is made of*

Il tavolo **è** di legno.	=	*The table is of wood.* (The table is made of wood)
La casa **è** di mattoni.	=	*The house is of bricks.* (The house is made of bricks)
La sedia è di plastica.	=	*The chair is of plastic.* (The chair is made of plastic)
Le scarpe **sono** di pelle.	=	*The shoes are of leather.* (The shoes are made of leather)
Le finestre **sono** di vetro.	=	*The windows are of glass.* (The windows are made of glass)

6. To say *who something belongs to*

Il cane **è** di Maria.	=	*The dog is María's.* (The dog belongs to Maria)
Gli amici **sono** di Pietro.	=	*The friends are Pedro's.* (The friends belong to Pedro)

Il libro **è** del ragazzo.	=	*The book is the boy's.*
		(The book belongs to the boy)
La foto **è** di lei.	=	*The photograph is hers.*
		(The photograph belongs to her)
La moto **è** loro.	=	*The motorcycle is theirs.*
		(The motorcycle belongs to them)

Tip: di + il = del. When **di** (*of*) is followed by **il** (*the*), the words contract to **del** (*of the*)

*di in this case is referring to possession → **il cane è <u>di</u> Sofia** (*The dog is Sofia's/ The dog belongs to Sofia*)

7. To say for *whom or for what something is intended*

Il televisore **è** per lei.	=	*The television is for her.*
La matita **è** per loro.	=	*The pencil is for them.*
La gatta **è** per mio fratello.	=	*The female cat is for my brother.*

8. To describe *where an event takes place*

| La festa **è** a casa di Maria. | = | *The party is at Maria's house.* |
| La cerimonia **è** all'università. | = | *The ceremony is at the university.* |

9. To *indicate a generalization*

| **È** importante studiare. | = | *It's important to study.* |

10. To express time, dates, and days of the week.

Sono le 3:00 del pomeriggio.	=	*It's 3:00 p.m.*
È il 14 di agosto.	=	*It's August 14th.*
È lunedì.	=	*It's Monday.*

Tip: Note that in Italian, the days of the week and the months of the year are NOT capitalized like in English.

Speak Abroad
Academy

Vocabulary: Types of Materials

English	Italian	Pronunciation
Paper	**carta**	[kahr-tah]
Wood	**legno**	[leh-nyoh]
Glass	**vetro**	[ve-troh]
Plastic	**plastica**	[plahs-tee-kah]
Metal	**metallo**	[meh-tahl-loh]
Fabric	**tessuto**	[tehs-soo-toh]

The moment of truth has arrived—let's practice what we've learned!

Practice 5

A. Answer these questions about the dialogue "La città" (*The City*) from the beginning of the lesson.

1. Di dov'è Luigi? _____

2. Di dov'è Tommaso? _____

3. In quale città stanno? _____

4. Cosa sono Luigi e Tommaso? _____

5. Di dov'è la signora? _____

B. Where are these famous people from? Use the 3rd person singular of **essere – È** *(to be)* to say where they are from and what nationality they are.

Example: David Beckham: È dell'Inghilterra. È inglese.

Inghilterra (*England*)   **Francia** (*France*)
Italia (*Italy*)   **Portogallo** (*Portugal*)
Germania (*Germany*)   **Stati Uniti** (*the United States*)
Spagna (*Spain*)   **Messico** (*Mexico*)

1. Luciano Pavarotti _____

2. Frida Kahlo _____

3. Johnny Depp _____

4. Albert Einstein _____

5. Coco Chanel _____

6. Rafael Nadal _____

7. Cristiano Ronaldo _____

8. Paul McCartney _____

9. Madonna _____

10. Carlos Santana _____

C. Complete the following sentences with the appropriate form of **essere** and include in parentheses *why* you're using this verb:

- Description
- Profession
- Origin
- Identification
- Material something is made of

- Possession
- For whom something is intended
- Generalizations
- Where an event takes place
- Time, date, or day of the week

Example: Il ragazzo è simpatico. (description)

1. Mick Jagger _____ inglese.   (_____)
2. Le sedie _____ di plastica.   (_____)
3. Noi _____ della Colombia.   (_____)
4. I tavoli _____ di legno.   (_____)
5. Il cibo _____ per la bambina.   (_____)
6. _____ lunedì.   (_____)
7. Marco e Luigi _____ avvocati.   (_____)
8. La festa _____ nel club.   (_____)
9. Il cane _____ di Maria.   (_____)
10. Il libro _____ giallo.   (_____)

D. What are these objects made of?

Example: Di cosa è fatta la tavola? La tavola è fatta di legno.

1. Di cosa è fatta la bottiglia (*bottle*)? _____
2. Di cosa è fatta la sedia? _____
3. Di cosa è fatta la casa? _____
4. Di cosa sono fatte le scarpe? _____
5. Di cosa sono fatte le finestre? _____
6. DI cosa è fatto il pavimento (*floor*)? _____
7. Di cosa è fatta l'automobile? _____
8. Di cosa è fatta la pagina (*page*)? _____
9. Di cosa è fatta la matita (*pencil*)? _____
10. Di cosa è fatta la pallina (*little ball*)? _____

E. Fill in the blank with the right form of the verb essere: è or **sono**, depending on the subject.

1. Il cane _____ di Maria.
2. Gli amici _____ di Marco.
3. La casa _____ di Teresa.
4. Le foto _____ dei nonni.
5. Le automobili _____ degli zii.

F. Now let's try to use all the forms of the verb *"to be"*. Complete the sentences with the right form of the verb **essere** ("to be") and the country suggested in each case.

Example: Io (Perú) <u>Io sono del Perú</u>

1. Loro (Germania) _____

2. Tu e Alessandra (Argentina) _____

3. Voi (Colombia) _____

4. Noi (Messico) _____

5. Io (Francia) _____

G. Use the correct form of the verb **essere**.

1. Voi _____ musulmani.

2. Io _____ sposata.

3. Noi _____ celibi.

4. Martino _____ cinese.

5. Elena e Sofia _____ brasiliane.

6. Tu _____ bianco.

7. Voi _____ cristiani.

8. Maria _____ messicana.

9. Tu e Martino _____ amici.

10. Emma e Matilda _____ compagni di scuola.

H. Translate the following sentences. Remember that you use è or **sono** to express time, dates, and days of the week.

1. It's three o'clock in the afternoon (tre del pomeriggio):

    _____

2. It's first of May (primo di maggio):

    _____

3. It's November 3rd (novembre):

    _____

4. It's Wednesday (mercoledì):

    _____

5. It's ten o'clock in the morning (dieci del mattino):

    _____

I. Answer these questions with the appropriate form of **essere**:

1. Lei è simpatica? _____

2. Siete studenti? _____

3. È piccola la casa di Marianna? _____

4. Di dov'è Elena? (Inghilterra) _____

5. Che cos'è importante? (studiare) _____

J. Rewrite these sentences contracting di + il.

Example: L'automobile è <u>di il</u> signor Pérez: <u>L'automobile è del signor Pérez.</u>

1. I cani sono di il bambino: _____

2. Il libro è di il collegio: _____

3. Quella casa è di il signore ricco: _____

4. La moto è di il giovane: _____

5. Il cibo è di il ristorante: _____

Ciao! Lo sapevi che ... (Did you know?)

Spaghetti and meatballs is an American invention. Separately, they are original Italian dishes, but you'll never come across 'Spaghetti and Meatballs' on a menu in Italy! In Italy, spaghetti, or any type of pasta is typically never served together with meat – unless of course if it is accompanied with a meat sauce, like ragù. Pasta is a 'primo piatto' (first dish) and meat or fish is a "secondo piatto" – essentially, two separate categories.

The verb essere (to be)

LESSON 6 :

STARE (*TO BE*) AND AVERE (*TO HAVE*)
I HAVE YOUR LOVE

6.1 Present Tense of Stare (*To Be*)

As we said in the previous chapter, **stare** also means 'to be.' However, it's used in different types of contexts and situations.

In Italian, **stare** is used to express:

- ➲ location: lei **sta** nella casa (*she is in the house*)
- ➲ health: lui **sta** male (*he is sick*)
- ➲ changing mood or condition: **stai** tranquillo (*be quiet*)
- ➲ personal opinion: Questo vestito ti **sta** bene (*You are fine with this dress*)

Notice that what most of these examples have in common is that they are interchangeable situations. For example, he is sick **(lui sta male)**, but he might not be sick soon. It's a temporary state, not a permanent one. 'Sick' is his condition, but it's not his nature. Just like the example, she is at home **(lei sta acasa)**, she is home now but she may leave soon.

Tip: When using **stare** for location, use the preposition **in + the article (il/lo/l', la/l' i/gli, le)**. For example: **Sara sta in dentro la macchina.**

---

stare (to be)			
io *(I)*	sto	noi *(we)*	stiamo
tu *(you)*	stai	voi *(you - inf. pl.)*	state
lui *(he)* lei *(she)* esso,essa *(it - arc.)* ella,egli *(s/he - arc.)* Lei *(You - form.)*	sta	loro *(they)* essi,esse *(it - arc. pl.)*	stanno

Now let's learn some more adjectives to practice with the verb **stare**.

Vocabulary: More Adjectives

English	Italian	Pronunciation
Handsome	**bello**	[behl-loh]
Thin	**magro**	[mah-groh]
Stressed	**stressato**	[strehs-sah-toh]
Tired	**stanco**	[stahn-koh]
Happy	**contento**	[kohn-tehn-toh]
Delicious	**delizioso**	[deh-lee-tsyoh-soh]
Sick	**malato**	[mah-lah-toh]
Angry	**arrabbiato**	[ahr-rahb-byah-toh]
Clean	**pulito**	[puh-lee-toh]
Dirty	**sporco**	[spohr-koh]
Furious	**furioso**	[foo-ryoh-soh]
Nervous	**nervoso**	[nehr-voh-soh]
Busy	**occupato**	[oh-koo-pah-toh]
Bored	**annoiato**	[ahn-noh-yah-toh]
Worried	**preoccupato**	[preh-ohk-koo-pah-toh]
Open	**aperto**	[ah-pehr-toh]
Closed	**chiuso**	[kyoo-soh]

Got the concepts down? Now, let's apply them with some good old practice!

6.1 Practice

A.   Write the appropriate form of **stare**. Say why you chose that option:

- ⟳   location
- ⟳   health
- ⟳   changing mood or condition
- ⟳   personal opinion.

1.   Parigi e Lione _____ in Francia.   (_____)
2.   La bambina _____ male.   (_____)
3.   _____ giù di morale.   (_____)
4.   Gianmarco _____ a pezzi.   (_____)
5.   Noi _____ qui.   (_____)
6.   Il cibo _____ in frigorifero.   (_____)
7.   Voi _____ calmi.   (_____)
8.   Tu _____ dormendo.   (_____)
9.   Mia mamma _____ lavorando.   (_____)
10. Adriano e Lorenzo _____ alla partita.   (_____)

B. And now, see if you can tell which verb to use, **essere** or **stare**, according to the meaning of each sentence, and match the verb to the subject depending on gender and quantity.

Example: Maria e Giovanni <u>stanno</u> giù di morale.

1. Il tavolo e le sedie_____ in cucina.
2. Lui _____ avvocato.
3. Noi _____ stanchi.
4. _____ importante studiare.
5. Voi _____ all'università.
6. Martino e Luigi _____ intelligenti.
7. Il caffè _____ per la donna.
8. La città _____ bella.
9. Tu _____ una turista.
10, In _____ di Milano.
11. La lezione _____ facile.
12. Il bambino _____ al collegio.
13. Voi _____ contenti.
14. Noi _____ italiani.
15. Sara _____ triste.

C. Make complete sentences using the appropriate form of **essere** or **stare** + the words in parentheses.

Example: La nonna? (male) <u>La nonna sta male</u>

1. Tim? (spagnolo) _____
2. Il ristorante? (chiuso) _____
3. Le figlie di Pietro? (bionde e intelligenti) _____
4. Il problema? (molto facile) _____
5. Il libro? (interessante) _____
6. Tu? (furioso) _____
7. La banana? (gialla) _____
8. Noi? (felici) _____
9. La foto? (sedia) _____
10. La macchina? (rosso) _____

> **Common Mistake:** Of course, since English speakers only have one verb (*to be*) to express all these situations, it's completely normal to be confused about when to use each verb when speaking or writing in Italian. You'll get the hang of it with more practice!
>
> **X** Don't say: **Io sono bene**.
>
> **✓** Right way to say: **Io sto bene**. (changing mood)

D. Write **essere** or **stare** according to whether the adjective refers to an inherent feature or a changing condition.

Example: Lui _____ **giù di morale → Lui <u>sta</u> giù di morale. (changing condition)**

1. Lei _____ intelligente.
2. Lui _____ studioso.
3. Paola _____ furiosa.
4. Gli avvocati _____ occupati.
5. Il tavolo _____ sporco.
6. L'anziano _____ stanco.
7. L'anziano _____ simpatico.
8. La bambina _____ nervosa.
9. Il nonno _____ male
10. Le bambine _____ amiche.

Summary of the Uses of Ser	
⮑ To describe	**Il fiore è bello**
⮑ To indicate a profession	**Sono avvocatessa**
⮑ To indicate someone's origin/nationality	**Loro sono del Messico**
⮑ To identify inherent qualities about a person	**Lui è intelligente**
⮑ To say what material something is made of	**La sedia è di plastica**
⮑ To say who something belongs to	**Il libro è della bambina**
⮑ To say for whom something is intended	**Il cane è per lui**
⮑ To describe where an event takes place	**La festa è nella casa**
⮑ To use a generalization	**È importante studiare**
⮑ To express time, dates, and days of the week	**È martedì** (*It's Tuesday*)

Summary of the Uses of Estar	
⮑ To express location	**Sto nel ristorante**
⮑ To describe health	**Maria sta male**
⮑ To express a changing mood or condition	**Luigi sta giù di morale**
⮑ To express a personal opinion	**Il vestito ti sta bene**

Speak Abroad
Academy

Common Mistake:

Keep in mind that **essere** is used to express **inherent** qualities of a person, such as...

Luisa è affettuosa. Luisa has a sweet-loving character. That's her nature. She is nice because that's who she is.

Stare is used to express a **transitory** condition, such as...

Luisa sta a pezzi. Luisa is tired now, but she won't be after she rests.

X Don't say	✓ Say
Luisa sta affettuosa.	Luisa è affettuosa.
Luisa è a pezzi.	Luisa sta a pezzi.
Io sono dormendo.	Io sto dormendo.
Mio padre è alsupermercato	Mio padre sta alsupermercato.
Lui sta medico.	Lui è medico.

Then again, many adjectives can be used with either **essere** or **stare**, depending on the exact message that you're trying to convey. But as a rule, **essere** is used for unalterable qualities (**sono bionda** – *I am blonde*) and **stare** is used for variable qualities (**sto male** – *I'm not well*).

E. Say if these sentences are right (✓) or wrong (X) according to their use of essere or stare. **Example: (X) Lui sta moro.**

1. _____ Teresa e Michele sono nel cinema.
2. _____ Voi state male.
3. _____ Questo vestito ti sta bene.
4. _____ Tu sei un bravo studente.
5. _____ Tu stai una brava avvocatessa.
6. _____ Tu stai del Perú.
7. _____ I fiori sono gialli.
8. _____ Le sedie stanno di plastica.
9. _____ Susanna sta intelligente.
10. _____ Miguel e Juan sono professori.

F. Now rewrite the incorrect sentences using the correct verb form on the lines below:

Example: (X) Lui sta moro. → (✓) Lui è moro.

_____

_____

_____

_____

_____

6.2 Present Tense of Avere (*to have*)

Now that we're getting the hang of different verbs, let's introduce another one! **Avere** is an extremely useful verb to know as it indicates possession and is used quite often in all languages. In English this would mean '*to have*.'

avere (to have)			
io *(I)*	**ho**	noi *(we)*	**abbiamo**
tu *(you)*	**hai**	voi *(you - inf. pl.)*	**avete**
lui *(he)* lei *(she)* esso,essa *(it - arc.)* ella,egli *(s/he - arc.)* Lei *(You - form.)*	**ha**	loro *(they)* essi,esse *(it - arc. pl.)*	**hanno**

Read the Story

How do you feel about reading a short story so we can practice getting to know the verb, **avere**? This is a story about a family going on vacation. Let's make sure they have everything they need before they leave!

Oggi si parte per una vacanza al mare!
(*Today we leave for a vacation at the beach!*)

Abbiamo due biglietti per il treno alle 7:00 che ci porta a Cinque Terre.
(*We have two tickets for the train at 7:00 that brings us to Cinque Terre.*)

Io porto mia sorella con me. Lei ha vent'anni.
(*I bring my sister with me. She is 20 years old.*)

Lei ha due borse, un capello, la crema solare e tante merende, se abbiamo fame.
(*She has two bags, a hat and sunscreen and a lot of snacks if we are hungry.*)

Io ho gli asciugamani. Sono sicura che ci divertiamo tanto!
(*I have the towels. I am sure that we will have a lot of fun!*)

Tanto and Poco

You can also describe nouns through quantifiers. In English these are words like *'many, much, a lot, a few, a little)* saying something about their quantity. For example, we might say something like *'many dogs'* or *'a few dogs.'* There are words for these descriptors in Italian, too.

*Unlike regular adjectives, they go **before** the noun instead of after.*

Tanto/a/i/e *(a lot, many)*

This word must agree in gender and plurality with the noun that follows it.

E.g. **Ho tanti cani** (*I have many dogs*).

Tanto can also be an adverb, and remains invariable. Adverbs are words that describe verbs: **legge tanto** (*he reads a lot*). In this case, **tanto** will go after the verb.

Poco/a/chi/che *(little, few, not many)*

This word also must agree in gender and plurality with the noun, too!

E.g. **Ho pochi vestiti** (*I have few dresses*).

Poco can also be an adverb, which means that it describes a verb, not just a noun. E.g. **Martino mangia poco** (*Martín doesn't eat much*). Just like **tanto**, when poco is used as an adverb, it will go after the verb.

Let's make it real! Time for some practical exercises to solidify your skills.

6.2 Practice

Complete the sentences with the correct form of **avere**.

Example: Voi _____ **tanti ospiti → Voi** <u>avete</u> **tanti ospiti.**

1. Noi _____ una casa molto bella.
2. Sofia e Paolo _____ sei televisioni.
3. Tu e Sara _____ tanti libri.
4. La nonna _____ pochi problemi.
5. Io _____ due mani.
6. Il cinema _____ tanti posti a sedere.
7. Quel giardino _____ tanti alberi.
8. Roberto e io _____ un ristorante.
9. Tu _____ un giardino molto bello.
10. Quel museo _____ tanti quadri interessanti.

6.3 Avere to Express Age

In Italian, we use the verb **avere** (*to have*) to say how old we are. Instead of saying you *are* of a certain age, you say that you *have* a certain number of years.

I am [number] years old. = **Ho** [number] **anni**.

In Italian, you cannot omit the word **anni** in this expression. Therefore it is necessary to say the word **anni** when talking about how old you are or someone else is!

As for numbers, we'll dive into them more extensively in the next chapter! But for now, here are some translations of sentences expressing age.

Ho trent'anni.	*I am thirty years old.*
Hai ventitré anni.	*You are twenty-three years old.*
Lui/lei ha quarant'anni.	*He/she is forty years old.*
Abbiamo quindici anni.	*We are fifteen years old.*
Avete tutti due anni.	*You all are two years old.*
Hanno diciotto anni.	*They are eighteen years old.*

> **Common Mistake:** Of course, English speakers tend to translate the structure they use in English directly into Italian; word for word, but this doesn't always work! In Italian, you never use the verbs **essere** (*to be*) or **stare** (*to be*) to talk about age. Even if its direct translation makes sense, always use the verb **avere!**
>
> **X Don't say** | **✓ Say**
> ---|---
> Io sono vent'anni. | Io <u>ho</u> vent'anni.
> Io sto vent'anni. |

6.3 Practice

A. Write the correct form of **avere** to convey these people's ages:

1. Manuel e Giuseppe _____ ventuno anni.
2. Io _____ cinquant'anni.
3. Tu _____ diciotto anni.
4. Marina e io _____ trent'anni.
5. Voi _____ venticinque anni.
6. Mio nonno _____ settant'anni.
7. Mia nonna _____ sessantacinque anni.
8. Lei _____ quarantadue anni.
9. Il gatto _____ sette anni.
10. Lucia e io _____ ventidue anni.

B. Indicate if these sentences are right (✓) or wrong (X). Remember, to express age in Italian you use the verb **avere**, not **essere** or **stare** like in English.

Example: Lui sta vent'anni. X

1. _____ Noi siamo sessant'anni.
2. _____ Voi state quarant'anni.
3. _____ Io ho cinquantadue anni.
4. _____ Giuseppe e Daniele hanno trentacinque anni.
5. _____ Tu sei quindici anni.
6. _____ Maria sta sei anni.
7. _____ Tu e Michele siete settanta anni.
8. _____ Josefina sta ventitré anni.
9. _____ Lui ha cinque anni.
10. _____ La bambina sta a casa.

C. Now rewrite the incorrect sentences using the correct verb form on the lines below:

Example: X Lui sta vent'anni. >>> ✓ Lui ha vent'anni.

_____

_____

_____

_____

_____

D. Fill in the blank with the correct verb form of **avere**.

1. Io _____ tante scarpe.
2. Noi _____ tanti amici.
3. Marco _____ un libro.
4. Tu _____ tanti gatti.
5. Voi _____ una nonna buona.
6. Lei _____ una matita rossa.
7. Carlo e Maria _____ una figlia.
8. Voi _____ un sistema eccellente.
9. Laura _____ 32 anni.
10. La bambina _____ capelli biondi.

> **Ciao! Lo sapevi che ...** (*Did You Know...?*)
>
> In Italian you can NEVER use the verb <u>essere-to be</u> to say your age or that you are hungry or sleepy like we do in English. Instead, use the verb <u>avere-to have</u>! This is a common misconception from English and Italian. Make sure you sound like a 'vero italiano' try it yourself!
>
> **ho fame, ho sonno, ho ventitre anni.**

Speak Abroad
Academy

LESSON 7:

NUMBERS

ONE, TWO, BUCKLE MY SHOE

If we're going to express the quantity of something, we obviously need to know our numbers. Numbers are also essential for telling the date and time, just like in English. Here's how to say your numbers in Italian:

7.1 Numbers

#	English	Italian	Pronunciation
0	zero	**zero**	*[tseh-roh]*
1	one	**uno**	*[oo-noh]*
2	two	**due**	*[doo-eh]*
3	three	**tre**	*[treh]*
4	four	**quattro**	*[kwaht-troh]*
5	five	**cinque**	*[cheen-kweh]*
6	six	**sei**	*[say]*
7	seven	**sette**	*[seht-teh]*
8	eight	**otto**	*[oht-toh]*
9	nine	**nove**	*[noh-veh]*
10	ten	**dieci**	*[dee-eh-chee]*
11	eleven	**undici**	*[oon-dee-chee]*
12	twelve	**dodici**	*[doh-dee-chee]*
13	thirteen	**tredici**	*[treh-dee-chee]*
14	fourteen	**quattordici**	*[kwaht-tohr-dee-chee]*
15	fifteen	**quindici**	*[kween-dee-chee]*
16	sixteen	**sedici**	*[seh-dee-chee]*
17	seventeen	**diciassette**	*[dee-chee-ahs-seht-teh]*
18	eighteen	**diciotto**	*[dee-chee-oht-toh]*
19	nineteen	**diciannove**	*[dee-chee-ahn-noh-veh]*
20	twenty	**venti**	*[vehn-teeh]*

> **Tip: The number one in Italian:**
>
> **Uno** is the form you use when counting (the number): **Uno, due, tre...**
>
> **Un** is the form you use before masculine singular nouns (the article): **un cane**
>
> **Una/Un'** is the form you use before feminine singular nouns (the article): **una casa/Un'amica**

Ready to play with words? Let's practice!

7.1 Practice

Complete with **uno, una,** or **un** according to each sentence.

Example: ____ cane → <u>un</u> cane.

1. Ha _____ anno.
2. Ha _____ matita.
3. Abbiamo _____ gatta.
4. _____ , due, tre, quattro.
5. _____ uomo sta camminando (*a man is walking*).
6. _____ fiore giallo
7. _____ bambina felice.
8. Hai _____ gatto molto grande (*a big cat*).
9. _____ signore sta lavorando.
10. _____ pizza per te!

7.2 There Is and There Are: *C'è and Ci sono*

Statements with c'è/ ci sono

The words **c'è/ ci sono** (pronounced like the English *cheh/ tʃi sono*) means 'there is' and 'there are.' As you know, it's a useful way of describing the contents or arrangement of something. You can also use **c'è** to ask simple questions by simply saying **c'e...?** – *'is there...?'* or **ci sono** *'are there...?'*

C'è un gatto in casa (singular)
Ci sono gatti in casa (plural)

> **Common Mistake:** Don't use the Italian definite articles **il/lo/l', la/l', i/gli,** and **le** (*the*) after **c'è**. Instead, use the definite articles after **c'è: un, dei, una, delle,** etc.
>
> X   Don't say: <u>C'è la matita</u> sul tavolo.
>
> ✓   Say: <u>C'è una matita</u> sul tavolo. (*There is a pencil on the table.*)

> **Tip:** When **c'è** is followed by a plural noun, you don't need the article. Instead you must say **ci sono** and remove the article:
>
> X   Don't say: **C'e i fiori nel giardino**.
>
> ✓   Say: **Ci sono fiori nel giardino**.

Ci sono quindici cani per strada	*There are fifteen dogs in the street*
C'è una persona nell'ufficio	*There is one person in the office*
C'è un albero nel cortile	*There is a tree in the yard*
C'è tanto cibo nel supermercato	*There is a lot of food in the supermarket*
Ci sono due turiste tedesche sul treno	*There are two German tourists on the train*

The Negative with C'è

To make a sentence negative, just add **'non'** before **c'è/ci sono**:

Non c'è acqua nel bicchiere.	*There isn't water in the glass.*
Non ci sono quindici cani per strada.	*There are not fifteen dogs in the street.*

The Interrogative With C'è

To ask a question with **c'è** or **ci sono**, follow the same order as you do with regular sentences but just add a question mark at the end.. If you're saying this sentence out loud, you can change the tone of your voice to indicate that you're asking a question, just like you do in English. With a simple rising intonation in your voice, you can convey that you're asking a question, not making a statement.

Ci sono due cani per strada?	*Are there two dogs in the street?*
C'è una persona in ufficio?	*Is there one person in the office?*
C'è un albero nel giardino?	*Is there a tree in the yard?*
C'è tanto cibo nel supermercato?	*Is there a lot of food in the supermarket?*
Ci sono due turiste tedesche sul treno?	*Are there two German tourists on the train?*

> **Difference between c'è and stare**
>
> Use **c'è/ci sono** (there is/there are) when you're talking about the existence of something/someone. For example, **c'è un museo nella mia città** (*There is a museum in my city*).
>
> Use **stare**, which means 'to be,' when you're talking about where something or someone *is*. For example, **il collegio sta dietro l'angolo** (*The school is behind the corner*).

Ready to apply what you've learned? Let's practice!

7.2 Practice

A. Look at these sentences and decide if they are correct or incorrect. Write a ☰ if they are correct and an **X** if it's incorrect. Rewrite the incorrect sentences on the lines provided.

Examples: C'è un gatto nel giardino. ✓
         C'e i libri sul tavolo. <u>X Ci sono libri sul tavolo.</u>

1. C'è il tappeto nella casa. _____
2. Ci sono le tigri allo zoo. _____
3. Ci sono mele dal fruttivendolo. _____
4. C'è un quadro nel museo. _____
5. Ci sono gli uffici nell'edificio. _____
6. Ci sono tanti bambini nel collegio _____
7. Ci sono i turista in città. _____
8. Ci sono le persone nel cinema. _____
9. Ci sono una pizza sul tavolo. _____
10. C'è l'acqua nel frigo. _____

B. Translate the following to English:

Example: Ci sono matite in casa tua? <u>Are there pencils in your house?</u>

1. Ci sono fiori nel giardino? _____
2. Ci sono sedie nell'ufficio? _____
3. Ci sono gatti per strada? _____
4. Ci sono hotel in città? _____
5. C'è un televisore in casa? _____
6. Ci sono dottori all'ospedale? _____
7. C'è un cane nel cortile? _____
8. C'è una radio nell'automobile? _____
9. Ci sono due donne nella pescheria? _____
10. Ci sono tavoli nel ristorante? _____

C. Turn these affirmative sentences into negative sentences. Place **non** before **c'è** or **ci sono**.

1. Ci sono animali allo zoo: _____
2. Ci sono tanti bambini al parco: _____
3. C'è tanta gente al ristorante: _____
4. C'è un buon hotel in città: _____
5. Ci sono tanti pianeti nel cielo: _____

D. Fill in the blanks with **c'è, ci sono** or **sta**:
1. Dove _____ l'ufficio postale?
2. Nel collegio _____ un grande parco.
3. La chiesa _____ dietro l'angolo.
4. L'università _____ accanto al parco.
5. _____ ristoranti molto buoni nella mia città.
6. Sulla piazza centrale _____ due bar.
7. _____ un parco lì?
8. Sí, il parco _____ lì.
9. Dove _____ il parco?
10. _____ un parco vicino.

7.3 Fare: *To do / To make*

Let's learn some more verbs. **Fare** is a useful verb that allows you to say, 'to do' or 'to make.' It's helpful when we're talking about activities and daily habits!

Fare is an irregular verb like some of the others we've covered, which means that the spelling looks different depending on the pronouns that are next to it.

fare *(to do/ to make)*			
io *(I)*	**faccio**	noi *(we)*	**facciamo**
tu *(you)*	**fai**	voi *(you - inf. pl.)*	**fate**
lui *(he)* lei *(she)* esso,essa *(it - arc.)* ella,egli *(s/he - arc.)* Lei *(You - form.)*	**fa**	loro *(they)* essi,esse *(it - arc. pl.)*	**fanno**

Fare is an irregular verb of the 1st conjugation (suffix *-are*) – this means that when conjugated, the ending letters (*-are*) change, as seen in the table above. It can be used to talk about the weather in an impersonal way, to say whether it is hot or cold. You can also use fare to say something is funny or sad. In this case, we use it as a third-person verb, just like we would use it for the pronouns for 'he' or 'she.' It looks like this...

It's cold: **fa freddo**

It's hot: **fa caldo**

It's funny: **fa ridere**

It's sad: **fa piangere**

Vocabulary: the weather

Nuvole: clouds → ci sono nuvole/ si sta annuvolando/nuvoloso

Pioggia: rain → c'è pioggia/ sta piovendo/piove

Neve: snow → c'è neve/ sta nevicando/nevica

Vento: wind → c'è vento/ sta soffiando il vento/ventosa

Let's spice things up with a practical exercise!

7.3 Practice

A. What is the weather like according to what the people are wearing/doing?
1. Maria is wearing shorts and a T-shirt: _____
2. Tommaso is wearing a scarf, gloves, and a jacket: _____
3. Luigi is wearing a windbreaker: _____
4. Teresa is wearing sunblock: _____
5. Paola is wearing a raincoat: _____
6. Giulio is looking at the snow through the window: _____
7. Carlo is looking at the clouds in the sky: _____
8. Sofia is wearing rain boots: _____
9. Giulia is wearing a hat and gloves at work today: _____
10. Federico is walking to the beach to go for a swim: _____

Vocabulary: Everyday Objects

English	Italian	Pronunciation
The suitcase	la valigia	[lah vah-lee-jah]
The exercise	l'esercizio	[leh-sehr-chee-tsyoh]
The homework	il compito	[eel kohm-pee-toh]
The yoga	lo yoga	[loh yoh-gah]
The sports	lo sport	[loh spohrt]
The swimming	il nuoto	[eel nwoh-toh]
The breakfast	la colazione	[lah koh-lah-tsyoh-neh]
The lunch	il pranzo	[eel prahn-tsoh]
The tea	il tè	[eel teh]
The dinner	la cena	[lah cheh-nah]

B. Fill in the blank with the appropriate form of **fare** (*to do/ to make*):
1. Noi _____ le valigie (*suitcases*).
2. Juan e Isabella _____ un dolce.
3. Io _____ esercizio (*exercise*)
4. I bambini _____ il compito (*homework*)
5. _____ caldo.
6. Mia sorella _____ yoga.
7. Tu _____ sport.
8. Voi _____ nuoto.
9. _____ tanto freddo.
10. Il cuoco _____ la pasta.

7.4 The Interrogative Quanto/a? Quanti/e?

Questions are important! How else can we discover information from other people? Let's start off with some of the most important interrogative words for everyday life.

Quanto/a? *How much?*

Quanti/e? *How many?*

In English, '*much*' is used for nouns that are uncountable, whereas '*many*' is used for nouns that *are* countable. It's the same in Italian! The only difference is that the ending vowel will change as we already know depending on gender and quantity.

When you're asking someone how much coffee they want, you're expecting a reply like '*a lot*' or '*not that much*,' which is essentially uncountable. However, if you were to phrase it as how *many* coffees they want, you're expecting a countable response like '*two cups*' or '*just one*.'

Keep this concept in mind when determining whether to use **quanto/a** (not countable) or **quanti/e** (countable).

Put on your linguistic explorer hat—it's expedition time, we're venturing into the realm of practice!

7.4 Practice

A. Fill in the blanks with the right form of **quanto/a** or **quanti/e**.
1. _____ cani avete?
2. _____ cibo c'è al supermercato?
3. _____ gatti ci sono nel parco?
4. _____ lingue parli (*speak*)?
5. _____ caffè c'è?

B. Now we're going to tie in **quanti/e?** with **c'è** and **ci sono**. Answer the following questions using the written number.

Example: Quanti sofà **ci sono** in casa tua? <u>**Ci sono** due sofà in casa mia.</u>

1. Quanti giorni ci sono in una settimana (*week*)?
   _____

2. Quante settimane (*weeks*) ci sono in un mese (*month*)?
   _____

3. Quanti mesi ci sono in un anno (*year*)?
   _____

4. Quanti giorni ci sono in un fine settimana (*weekend*)?
   _____

5. Quanti giorni ci sono nel mese di febbraio (February)?
   _____

6. Quante dita (*fingers*) ci sono nella tua (*your*) mano?
   _____

7. Quanti ospedali ci sono nella tua (*your*) città?
   _____

8. Quanti televisori hai nella tua (*your*) casa?
   _____

9. Quanti alberi ci sono nel tuo (*your*) giardino?
   _____

10. Quante sedie ci sono in casa tua?
    _____

C. Write sentences using the words that are suggested. Modify the words as needed to match the nouns and numbers – add articles when necessary.

Example: Ci sono | tre | elefante | allo | zoo: <u>Ci sono tre elefanti allo zoo.</u>

1. ci sono | due | università | in | città _____
2. ci sono | venti | mele | nel | cestino (*basket*) _____
3. ci sono | dodici | mese | in | anno _____
4. c'è | una | Statua della Libertà | a | New York _____
5. ci sono | due | occhi | sul | viso _____

Ciao! Vuoi sapere qualcosa? (*Did you know?*)

Some Italian words are misused in English. Like the word 'panini': in English is used to describe a specific type of Italian sandwich – one singular sandwich. But the real Italian meaning of 'panini' is two or more sandwiches. And not a specific type of sandwich, just any ol' single sandwich!

LESSON 8 :

SAPERE E CONOSCERE
TO KNOW IS KNOWING YOU KNOW NOTHING

8.1 To Know – Sapere

The verb **sapere** means *'to know'* in English. However, just like some of the verbs we've discussed in prior chapters, it's not the only Italian verb that has this meaning! **Sapere** refers to a very specific type of knowledge. It's only used when we're talking about knowing **facts**, **information**, and **skills**. It *can't* be used when talking about knowing people, places, or things. Those things will be used with the verb **conoscere** which we'll take a closer look at below.

When *know* refers to *knowing facts* and *learned skills*, use **sapere**.

For example, **so la matematica** (*I know mathematics*) or **so nuotare** (*I know how to swim*).

sapere *(to know facts)*			
io *(I)*	**so**	noi *(we)*	**sappiamo**
tu *(you)*	**sai**	voi *(you - inf. pl.)*	**sapete**
lui *(he)* lei *(she)* esso,essa *(it - arc.)* ella,egli *(s/he - arc.)* Lei *(You - form.)*	**sa**	loro *(they)* essi,esse *(it - arc. pl.)*	**sanno**

Sapere is an irregular verb and belongs to the 2nd conjugation (suffix *-ere*). But the irregularity is in its conjugation. For example, io **so** (*I know*), which is used when talking about yourself in singular form. Normally, with regular verbs that end in *-ere*, you would knock off the *ere*, and add an *o* (**sapo** X). But with **sapere**, it's just **so** if you're talking only about yourself.

For example: **Io so.** (*I know*)
          Non so. (*I don't know*)

The journey continues! Time to dive into the sea of practice!

Speak Abroad
Academy

8.1 Practice

Write the appropriate form of the verb **sapere** in each sentence.

1. Noi _____ l'italiano.
2. Tu _____ il telefono di Luigi.
3. Voi _____ la verità.
4. Elena _____ quel poema?
5. Io _____ il francese.
6. Maria _____ la lezione.
7. Pietro e José _____ il tedesco.
8. Lui _____ ballare il valzer. *(waltz)*
9. Loro _____ come aiutare *(how to help)*
10. La maestra _____ parlare bene.

8.2 To Know – *Conoscere*

The other word for 'to know' is **conoscere.** We use **conoscere** when talking about knowing
certain **people** or **things**.

When *know* refers to *being familiar or being acquainted with something or someone,* use
conoscere. For example, **Io conosco Luigi** (*I know Luigi*).

conoscere *(to be familiar with or to meet)*			
io *(I)*	**conosco**	noi *(we)*	**conosciamo**
tu *(you)*	**conosci**	voi *(you - inf. pl.)*	**conoscete**
lui *(he)* lei *(she)* esso,essa *(it - arc.)* ella,egli *(s/he - arc.)* Lei *(You - form.)*	**conosce**	loro *(they)* essi,esse *(it - arc. pl.)*	**conoscono**

Conoscere is also an irregular verb of the 2ⁿᵈ conjugation (suffix *-ere*).

For example: **Io conosco.** (*I know*)
    Non conosco. (*I don't know*)

It's showtime for practice! Get ready to shine in the language spotlight.

8.2 Practice

A. Fill in the blanks with the appropriate form of the verb **conoscere** in each sentence.

1. Elena e Pietro _____ la professoressa.
2. Juan _____ il dottor Pérez.
3. Voi _____ il sistema.
4. Noi _____ il cibo francese.
5. Io _____ la casa.
6. Maria _____ la città.
7. Tu _____ il Louvre.
8. Lui _____ il turista.
9. Io _____ il giocatore.
10. I ragazzi _____ te.

B. Complete the sentences with the correct form of **sapere** or **conoscere:**

Example: Maria _____ **(conoscere/sapere) l'inglese → Maria sa l'inglese.**

1. Tommaso _____ (conoscere/sapere) il sud della Spagna.
2. Voi _____ (conoscere/sapere) contare fino a dieci in tedesco.
3. Elena e Paolo _____ (conoscere/sapere) giocare a golf.
4. Non _____ (lui – conoscere/sapere) se fa freddo.
5. Maria _____ (conoscere/sapere) quel viale.
6. Tu _____ (conoscere/sapere) quella storia.
7. Io _____ (conoscere/sapere) dove vive Jorge (*where Jorge lives*).
8. Tu e Sara _____ (conoscere/sapere) le regole del Monopoli.
9. Noi _____ (conoscere/sapere) come insegnare la matematica.
10. La professoressa _____ (conoscere/sapere) una famosa autrice.

C. Choose the right verb and conjugate it. You do not need to use the pronoun; it's just a cue to tell you how to conjugate the verb.

1. _____ (io- conoscere/sapere) Mattia.
2. Non _____ (noi- conoscere/sapere) dove sta il gatto.
3. _____ (voi – conoscere/sapere) molto bene le opere di Albéniz.
4. Mia sorella non _____ (conoscere/sapere) quel gruppo musicale (*band*).
5. _____ (tu – sapere/conoscere) a che ora inizia (*starts*) il film?
6. I miei cugini _____ (sapere/conoscere) cinque lingue.
7. _____ (io – conoscere/sapere) il Brasile molto bene.
8. _____ (lui – conoscere/sapere) il tuo fidanzato (*boyfriend*)?
9. Isabella e Luisa _____ (conoscere/sapere) la lezione molto bene.
10. Olivia _____ (conoscere/sapere) la ballerina, Matilda.

Speak Abroad
Academy

8.3 Sapere + Infinitive: To know how to do something

We've mentioned a lot of infinitive verbs so far. In fact, **sapere** itself is an infinitive verb. When you use **sapere** before an infinitive verb, you're saying that you *know* how to do something. Therefore the verb that goes after **sapere** must be in the infinitive form, while **sapere** must be conjugated.

For example: **So parlare francese.** (*I know how to speak French*)

Here are some verbs and specific activities in the infinitive form that you can combine with **sapere** to express your knowledge of a certain ability. Like, for example, **sa nuotare** (*he/she knows how to swim*), **sa parlare spagnolo** (*he/she knows how to speak Spanish*).

Which of the following do you know how to do?

English	Italian	Pronunciation
To swim	nuotare	[nwoh-tah-reh]
To dance	ballare	[bahl-lah-reh]
To sing	cantare	[kahn-tah-reh]
To do artistic gymnastics	fare ginnastica artistica	[fah-reh jeen-nah-stee-kah ahr-tee-stee-kah]
To play tennis	giocare a tennis	[joh-kah-reh ah then-nees]
To play the piano	suonare il pianoforte	[swoh-nah-reh eel pyah-noh-fohr-teh]
To play basketball	giocare a pallacanestro	[joh-kah-reh ah pahl-lah-kah-neh-stroh]
To play golf	giocare a golf	[joh-kah-reh ah golf]
To play football	giocare a calcio	[joh-kah-reh a kahl-chee-oh]
To write novels	scrivere romanzi	[skree-veh-reh roh-mahn-tsee]
To speak	parlare	[pahr-lah-reh]
To act	recitare	[reh-chee-tah-reh]

The spotlight is on you in the grand theater of language practice – 3,2,1... action!

8.3 Practice

A. What do these people know how to do? Use the verb **sapere** + the infinitive form and direct object to complete the sentences.

Example: Serena Williams sa giocare a tennis. → <u>Serena Williams knows how to play tennis</u>.

1. Novak Djokovic _____
2. LeBron James _____
3. Tiger Woods _____
4. J. K. Rowling _____
5. Lionel Messi e Cristiano Ronaldo _____
6. Taylor Swift _____
7. Michael Phelps _____
8. Shakira _____
9. Meryl Streep _____
10. Simone Biles _____

B. Who do these famous people know? Write the appropriate sentence on the lines provided, picking a person from the right row and finding the correct match on the left. Remember that we use **conoscere** for people!

Sherlock Holmes	Dakota Johnson
Ashton Kutcher	Eva
Rhett Butler	Watson
Chris Martin	Mila Kunis
Adamo	Scarlett O'Hara

1. _____
2. _____
3. _____
4. _____
5. _____

C. Write a sentence with the verb "conoscere" following the cues given:

Example: (Laura | la zia Julia) → <u>Laura conosce la zia Julia</u>

1. (io | il professore De Luca)
2. (mia sorella e io | la madre di Gianmarco)
3. (Maria e Luigi | Sergio)
4. (voi | direttore dell'area commerciale)
5. (tu | zia Teresa)

Speak Abroad
Academy

D. Translate the sentences using **sapere** or **conoscere** depending on the context. Remember:

Conoscere = to be familiar with something or someone.

Sapere = to know facts and learned skills.
1. I know the truth. _____
2. She knows Maria. _____
3. They know how to swim. _____
4. Pedro and Elena know New York. _____
5. We know the answer. _____
6. We know the student. _____
7. You know my name. _____
8. He knows the truth. _____
9. The dog knows Lorenzo. _____
10. I know how to play the piano. _____

E. Sapere or Conoscere? Choose the right verb to complete the sentence.
1. Maria non { sa | conosce } ancora nuotare (*yet*).
2. No { so | conosco } questo computer.
3. { Sai | Conosci } l'Australia?
4. { Conoscono | Sanno } il numero di telefono di Luigi?
5. Carlo non { conosce | sa } il dottore.

Ciao, hai sentito? *(Did you know?)*

Pizza originated from the city of Naples, Italy. It didn't take long for immigration to run its course, making America the second country in the world to sponsor pizza as an Italian delicacy!

You may not know that when you order a pizza in Italy, you get your own personal pie – no slices, only a beautiful full pizza always garnished with fresh basil just for you and it is never cut into slices! Yes, that's right, you will be eating your pizza with a fork and knife, or like most families who use scissors at home to cut each slice.

However, in casual settings like pizzerias that serve pizza al taglio (pizza by the slice), the pizza is pre-cut into squares or rectangles for easy takeaway and consumption. Buon appetito!

LESSON 9 :

THE INDICATIVE MOOD – PRESENT TENSE OF REGULAR VERBS
SPEAKING OF WHICH

Verbs in Italian ending in **-are, -ere,** and **-ire** are called *regular verbs* because they all follow a regular pattern. As we've discussed, Italian verbs change according to the person and the quantity of the subject. They're much easier to modify when we're dealing with regular verbs!

9.1 Verbs Ending in -are

The -are verbs follow the pattern of **parlare.** Below are some of them:

English	Italian	Pronunciation
To work	lavorare	[lah-voh-rah-reh]
To study	studiare	[stoo-dyah-reh]
To look	guardare	[gwahr-dah-reh]
To arrive	arrivare	[ahr-ree-vah-reh]
To look for/ to search	cercare	[chehr-kah-reh]
To teach	insegnare	[een-seh-nyah-reh]
To buy	comprare	[kohm-prah-reh]
To need	necessitare	[neh-chehs-see-tah-reh]
To pay	pagare	[pah-gah-reh]
To return (to a place)	ritornare	[reeh-tohr-nah-reh]
To eat	mangiare	[mahn-gyah-reh]
To prepare	preparare	[preh-pah-rah-reh]
To fix/ to repair	riparare/sistemare	[ree-pah-rah-reh] / [sihs-teh-ma-reh]
To travel	viaggiare	[vee-ahj-jah-reh]
To explain	spiegare	[spee-eh-gah-reh]

Speak Abroad
Academy

The present tense form of verbs ending in **-are** is conjugated by removing the infinitive **-are** ending and replacing it with an ending corresponding to the person that is performing the action of the verb. See below:

parlare *(to speak)*			
io *(I)*	**parlo**	noi *(we)*	**parl-iamo**
tu *(you)*	**parli**	voi *(you - inf. pl.)*	**parlate**
lui *(he)* lei *(she)* esso,essa *(it - arc.)* ella,egli *(s/he - arc.)* Lei *(You - form.)*	**parl-a**	loro *(they)* essi,esse *(it - arc. pl.)*	**parlano**

Ready to apply what you learned? Let's practice!

9.1 Practice

A.   Check this dialogue. Can you translate what Luisa, and the grocer are saying?

Dal fruttivendolo

LUISA: Buenos días, ¿tiene bananas?

FRUTTIVENDOLO: Buenos días. Sí, tengo bananas.

LUISA: Ah, quanto costano?

FRUTTIVENDOLO: Costano 20 euro al chilo.

LUISA: Ottimo. Ne compro due chili.

FRUTTIVENDOLO: D'accordo. Ecco a Lei.

LUISA: Tante grazie. Arrivederci.

Glossary:

Avere: *to have*

Quanto costa…?: *how much are…?*

Chilo: *kilogram*

Ecco a Lei: *Here you are*

Vocabulary: The House

Here are some helpful vocabulary words that you'll need to know. They all refer to various parts of the house and some common household items.

English	Italian	Pronunciation
The living room	il salotto	[eel sah-loht-toh]
The dining room	la sala da pranzo	[lah sah-lah dah prahn-tsoh]
The kitchen	la cucina	[lah kooh-chee-nah]
The cup (for coffee or tea)	la tazza	[lah taht-tsah]
The glass	il bicchiere	[eel beek-kyeh-reh]
The refrigerator	Il frigorifero	[eel free-goh-ree-feh-roh]
The oven	Il forno	[eel fohr-noh]
The bedroom	la camera da letto	[lah kah-meh-rah dah leht-toh]
The garage	il garage	[eel gah-rah-djeh]
The stairs	le scale	[leh skah-leh]
The bathroom	il bagno	[eel bah-nyoh]
The mirror	lo specchio	[loh spehk-kyoh]
The roof	il tetto	[eel teht-toh]

B.   Write the corresponding subject pronouns depending on the verb ending.

Example: <u>tornate voi</u>

1.   insegno _____
2.   cantiamo _____
3.   studiano _____
4.   paga _____
5.   desidero _____

6.   cerca _____
7.   compra _____
8.   parlate _____
9.   lavorano _____
10. ritorni _____

C. Confirm whether these statements are true (**vero**) or false (**falso**), based on the information in the paragraph below.

In biblioteca

Marco sta in biblioteca. Studia per un esame di matematica. L'esame è domani (*tomorrow*). Ha tanti libri da leggere. Marco sta in ansia. Ha bisogno di studiare tanto. L'esame è molto difficile.

---

1. Marco è un professore _____
2. Marco studia a (*his*) casa _____
3. Marco ha un esame domani _____
4. L'esame è molto facile _____
5. Marco studia per un esame di inglese _____

D. Answer these questions by conjugating the verbs ending in **-are** to match the person performing the action.

1. Mio padre _____ (lavorare) dal lunedì al venerdì.
2. I tuoi figli _____ (guardare) troppa televisione.
3. Voi _____ (cercare) scarpe buone.
4. La professoressa Oliva _____ (insegnare) in tre classi.
5. _____ (io/comprare) frutta e verdura tutte le settimane.
6. Teresa e Pietro _____ (viaggiare) in treno al lavoro.
7. Noi _____ (spiegare) ai nostri figli come comportarsi (*how to behave*).
8. Il signor Romanelli _____ (riparare) borse.
9. Il cuoco _____ (cucinare) la pasta molto bene.
10. Emma _____ (giocare) con la pallina.

E. Fill in the blanks with the correct verb form:

Infinitive	parlare	insegnare	lavorare	guardare
io		insegno		
tu	parli			guardi
egli, ella, esso, essa, lui, lei, Lei			lavora	
noi	parliamo			guardiamo
voi			lavorate	
loro, essi, esse		insegnano		

9.2 Verbs Ending in -ere

The **-ere** verbs follow the pattern of **prendere**, simply ending in **-ere**. Below are some of other examples:

English	Italian	Pronunciation
To learn	**apprendere**	*[ahp-prehn-deh-re]*
To take	**prendere**	*[prehn-deh-reh]*
To drink	**bere**	*[beh-reh]*
To understand	**comprendere**	*[kohm-prehn-deh-reh]*
To think/ to believe in	**credere**	*[kreh-deh-reh]*
Should, must, ought to (do something)	**dovere (+ infinito)**	*[doh-veh-reh]*
To read	**leggere**	*[lehj-jeh-reh]*
To sell	**vendere**	*[vehn-deh-reh]*
To put	**mettere**	*[meht-teh-reh]*
To run	**correre**	*[kohr-reh-ehr]*
To break	**rompere**	*[rohm-peh-reh]*

You'll notice that all these verbs end in **-ere**! When we're speaking in the present tense, we remove the **-ere** and we add a new ending depending on the pronoun that goes before it. In other words, the ending of the word changes depending on who and how many people are being referred to. This follows the same rule as **-are** verbs.

Refer to the diagram box below for the rules on how to modify the endings of these verbs for each pronoun.

prendere *(to take)*			
io *(I)*	**prend-o**	noi *(we)*	**prend-iamo**
tu *(you)*	**prend-i**	voi *(you - inf. pl.)*	**prend-ete**
lui *(he)* lei *(she)* esso,essa *(it - arc.)* ella,egli *(s/he - arc.)* Lei *(You - form.)*	**prend-e**	loro *(they)* essi,esse *(it - arc. pl.)*	**prend-ono**

> **Tip: Anche** is an adverb. It means *'as well,' 'too,'* or *'also.'*

Speak Abroad
Academy

9.2 Practice

A. Answer the following questions regarding the text below.

Al ristorante

Stiamo al ristorante "Carlitos". Siamo quindici persone. Lavoriamo tutte insieme nello stesso ufficio. Abbiamo un tavolo grande. La carne di questo ristorante è molto deliziosa. Ci sono anche del pollo e del pesce. È tutto squisito. Il cameriere prende l'ordinazione e torna con il cibo. Mangiamo e beviamo molto bene.

Glossary:

in: in	**carne**: meat	**pesce**. fish
tutte: all	**di**: of	**tutto**: everything
insieme: together	**questo**: this	**cameriere**: waiter
lo stesso: the same	**anche**: also	**ordinazione**: order
colleghi: coworkers	**pollo**: chicken	**con**: with
molto bene: very well		

Example: La carne di questo ristorante è cattiva? <u>No, la carne di questo ristorante è deliziosa.</u>

1. Siete venti persone a tavola?

   _____

2. Lavorate tutti allo stesso ufficio?

   _____

3. Avete del pollo e del pesce?

   _____

4. Avete un tavolo piccolo?

   _____

5. Hai una bambina bionda?

   _____

B. Complete the sentences with the appropriate form of the correct verb. Use each verb once.

**comprendere – prendere – leggere – correre – apprendere – vedere
vendere – lavorare – mangiare – scrivere**

1. Il bambino non _____ la lezione.
2. Luigi e Maria _____ la televisione.
3. La ragazza _____ al collegio per (*to*) non arrivare tardi (*late*).
4. Noi _____ la casa e compriamo un appartamento.
5. Voi _____ in quel (*that*) ristorante eccellente.
6. Tu e io _____ molte lettere.
7. Tutte le domeniche _____ (io) il giornale.
8. Tutti i giorni _____ (tu) qualcosa.
9. Loro _____ il cielo (*the sky*).
10. La maestra _____ a scuola.

C. Fill in the blanks with the correct verb form:

Infinito	mangiare	vendere	credere	apprendere
io	mangio			apprendo
tu		vendi		
egli, ella, lui, lei			credi	
noi	mangiamo			apprendiamo
voi		vendete		
esse, essi, loro			credono	

9.3 Verbs Ending in -ire

The **-ire** verbs follow the pattern of **aprire**, simple ending in **-ire**. Below are some more examples:

English	Italian	Pronunciation
To open	**aprire**	[ah-pree-reh]
To write	**dormire**	[dohr-mee-reh]
To offer	**offrire**	[of-ree-reh]
To have fun	**divertire**	[dee-verh-tee-reh]
To leave/ to depart	**partire**	[pahr-tee-reh]
To heal/To feel	**sentire**	[sehn-tee-reh]
To go up	**salire**	[sah-lee-reh]
To suffer	**soffrire**	[sohf-free-reh]

We talked about how to modify verbs ending in **-ere**, but what about verbs that end in **-ire**? To use these verbs in the present tense, we remove the **-ire** ending and change it according to the subject, just like the other verbs. See below for how to modify these verbs.

partire *(to live)*			
io *(I)*	**parto**	noi *(we)*	**partiamo**
tu *(you)*	**parti**	voi *(you - inf. pl.)*	**partite**
lui *(he)* lei *(she)* esso,essa *(it - arc.)* ella,egli *(s/he - arc.)* Lei *(You - form.)*	**parte**	loro *(they)* essi,esse *(it - arc. pl.)*	**partono**

> **Tip:** In English, a verb must have an expressed subject (**he** eats spaghetti). In Italian, 'he' or 'she' is not always necessary. Why? Because it's obvious from the ending of the verb you are referring to. People tend to omit using subject pronouns unless you want to clarify who's doing the action or place emphasis on it.
>
> **Example: mangio** *(I eat)*

Ready to play with words? Let's practice!

9.3 Practice

A. Complete these sentences with the appropriate form of the correct verbs listed. Use each verb once.

finire – salire – divertire – salire – sentire – ricevere
condividere – decidere – vivere- aprire

1. I bambini _____ le caramelle (*candy*).
2. Tutti gli studenti _____ le scale per (*for*) la lezione di matematica.
3. Marco _____ per la città; Maria _____ per la campagna (*country*)
4. Io _____ la porta (*door*).
5. Tu _____ i tuoi amici in casa tua
6. Voi _____ alla festa.
7. Noi _____ il notiziario (*the news*) con nostri colleghi. (*our colleagues*)
8. Tu _____ di studiare lo spagnolo.
9. Lei _____ la partita (*the game*).
10. Io _____ la musica al concerto.

B. Fill in the blanks with the correct verb form:

Infinito	partire	spedire	aprire	offrire
io	parto			offro
tu		spedisci		
lui, lei, esso, essa, egli, ella			apre	
noi	spartiamo			offriamo
voi		spedite		
esse, essi, loro			aprono	

Ciao, vorresti sapere qualcosa di interessante?

(Would you like to know something interesting?)

Children who live in Italy begin studying English at school as early as preschool and continue throughout highschool. Although Italy is a very traditional country, in recent years, schools and companies have focused on implementing more opportunities to study English.

LESSON 10 :

WHAT TIME IS IT?

Navigating everyday life would be pretty hard without the ability to ask for and to express the time. In this lesson, we'll go over everything you need to know to understand this crucial component of language.

10.1 What Time Is It?

To ask, 'what time is it?' in Italian, you say **Che ora è?** or you can say, **Che ore sono?**

If it's one o'clock, the response will be È l'una.

And if it's a number higher than one, you'll phrase it as **sono le due** or **sono le tre**, and so on. As you can see, we're using è again, which is the singular third-person form of the verb **essere**.

È l'una	*It's one o'clock*
Sono le due	*It's two o'clock*
Sono le quattro	*It's four o'clock*
Sono le dieci	*It's ten o'clock*

> **Tip:**
> If you want to say it is 12:00pm (noon) you can say, È mezzogiorno.
> If you want to say it is 12:00am (midnight) you can say, È mezzanotte.
> If you want to say "sharp" or "exactly", Italian uses **esattamente** or **in punto**.

Sono le undici in punto	*It's eleven o'clock sharp*
Sono le sei in punto	*It's six o'clock sharp*
Sono le otto in punto	*It's sharp eight o'clock*

If, instead, you're hesitant about the time, you can say **più o meno** or **circa** (*about*).

Sono più o meno le nove	*It's about nine o'clock*
È l'una, circa	*It's about one o'clock*

If you want to say it's half past the hour, use **...e mezza** or **...e trenta**. For example, **sono le otto e mezza** or **sono le otto e trenta** (*it's eight thirty*).

Sono le dodici e mezza	*It's twelve thirty*
Sono le dieci e trenta	*It's ten thirty*
Sono le quattro e mezza	*It's four thirty*

To indicate that it's a precise number past the hour, use **e + number of minutes**.

For example: **sono le sette e venti** (it's 7:20)

Sono le due e cinque	*It's 2:05*
Sono le sei e dieci	*It's 6:10*
Sono le otto e venti	*It's 8:20*
È l'una e venticinque	*It's 1:25*

And to say it's a number to the hour, say **meno + number of minutes**.

For example: **sono le tre meno venti** (it's twenty to three)

Sono le nove meno dieci	*It's 8:50*
È l'una meno venti	*It's 12:40*
Sono le quattro meno cinque	*It's 3:55*
Sono le dodici meno venticinque	*It's 11:35*

What about fifteen minutes past the hour?

In Italian, when it's a quarter after the hour, you say **e un quarto** (*and a quarter*) or **e quindici** (*fifteen*).

Sono le sette e un quarto = It's 7:15	Sono le quattro e un quarto = It's 4:15	Sono le sei e quarto = It's 6:15

And when it's fifteen minutes before the hour, in Italiano you say **meno un quarto** or, less frequently, **meno quindici**.

Sono le otto meno un quarto.	*It's 7:45.*
Sono le tre meno un quarto.	*It's 2:45.*
È l'una meno un quarto.	*It's 12:45.*

Another way of expressing the time before the hour is saying the **number of minutes + alle + l'ora** (the hour).

Examples:

Sono dieci <u>alle</u> due.	*It's ten minutes to two o'clock.*
Sono venti alle quattro.	*It's twenty minutes to four o'clock.*
Sono dieci all'una.	*It's ten minutes to one o'clock.*
Sono venticinque alle dodici.	*It's twenty-five minutes to twelve o'clock.*

Here are more examples:

È l'una

Sono le undici

Sono le sei

È l'una meno dieci

Sono le otto e mezza

Sono le sette e venti

Tik-tok, it's practice o'clock. Let's go!

10.1 Practice

A.   Che ora è? State in words what time it is on each clock.

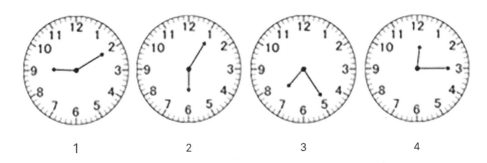

1   2   3   4

1. _____

2. _____

3. _____

4. _____

B.   Che ora è? – Che ore sono?

1.   3:45 = _____   6.   9:20 = _____

2.   11:00 = _____   7.   7:45 = _____

3.   1:30 = _____   8.   12:00 pm = _____

4.   6:45 = _____   9.   12:00 am = _____

5.   8:15 = _____   10. 5:30 = _____

C.   State what time it is and what it's time for.

Example: Mezzogiorno. → Sono le dodici. È ora di pranzo.

Some activities you might use are:
cenare (*have dinner*) – **camminare – lavorare – guardare la televisione – correre –
tornare a casa – andare a prendere i miei figli** (*pick my kids up*) – **mangiare**

1.   8:00 = _____

2.   10:00 = _____

3.   1:15 = _____

4.   4:30 = _____

5.   6:00 = _____

Speak Abroad
Academy

D. At what time do we travel to... Form sentences according to the cues.

Example: Londra / 8:15 → <u>A che ora partiamo per Londra? Alle otto e un quarto.</u>

1. Parigi / 12.00 _____
2. Milan / 1:00 _____
3. Praga / 5:30 _____
4. Lima / 9:15 _____
5. Washington / 5:45 _____

10.2 At what time is...?

To indicate at what time something is happening, in Italian you ask, "**A che ora è...?**" (*At what time is...?*). And the answer is, "**Al/alle...**" (*At...*) or "È al/alle..." (*It's at...*)

A che ora è la cena?	*At what time is dinner?*
È all'una.	*It's at one.*
A che ora è il programma?	*At what time is the program?*
Alle tre.	*It's at three.*

> **Tip**: Note that **colazione/pranzo/cena** can mean *food* in a general sense, but it can also indicate the name of the meal (*breakfast, lunch, dinner*)

What about references to the time of day? Italian also specifies whether something happens in the morning, at noon, in the afternoon, or at night.

del mattino	*in the morning: a.m.*
di/a mezzogiorno	*at noon: p.m.*
del pomeriggio	*in the afternoon: p.m.*
della sera	*at night: p.m.*
di mezzanotte	*at midnight: a.m.*

Sono le tre del mattino	*It's three in the morning (3:00 a.m.)*
Sono le otto di sera	*It's eight in the evening (8:00 p.m.)*
È mezzogiorno	*It's twelve noon (12:00 p.m.)*
È mezzanotte	*It's midnight (12:00 a.m.)*

Vocabulary: Social Events

English	Italian	Pronunciation
The party	**la festa**	*[lah feh-stah]*
The class	**la lezione**	*[lah leh-tsyoh-neh]*
The meeting	**la riunione**	*[lah ryoo-nyoh-neh]*
The lunch	**il pranzo**	*[eel prahn-tsoh]*
The appointment	**l'appuntamento**	*[lahp-poohn-tah-mehn-toh]*
The event	**l'evento**	*[leh-vehn-toh]*

Enough talk; let's do some practice!

10.2 Practice

In everyday language, you can omit the verb è when you're **answering** a time that something happens; for example, **A che ora è la cena?** The answer would be **Alle otto di sera.**

A. Respond to some more questions by spelling out the numbers and including the time indicated. You can add "del mattino", "del pomeriggio" to make it more complete! **Example: A che ora è la cena?** <u>Alle tre del pomeriggio.</u>

1. A che ora è il pranzo? (12:00 p.m.) _____

2. A che ora è l'appuntamento? (4:00 p.m.) _____

3. A che ora è la tua lezione? (8:00 a.m.) _____

4. A che ora è la riunione? (11:00 a.m.) _____

5. A che ora è la festa? (12:00 a.m.) _____

B. Translate these expressions:

1. It's eleven o'clock sharp: _____

2. It's eight thirty: _____

3. It's eight in the morning: _____

4. It's about three o'clock in the afternoon: _____

5. It's ten thirty: _____

6. It's five thirty: _____

7. It's seven twenty: _____

8. It's twenty to one: _____

9. It's five to two: _____

10. It's twenty-five to two: _____

10.3 The Days of the Week

English	Italian	Pronunciation
Monday	**lunedì**	[loo-neh-dee]
Tuesday	**martedì**	[mahr-teh-dee]
Wednesday	**mercoledì**	[mehr-koh-leh-dee]
Thursday	**giovedì**	[joh-veh-dee]
Friday	**venerdì**	[veh-nehr-dee]
Saturday	**sabato**	[sah-bah-toh]
Sunday	**domenica**	[doh-meh-nee-kah]

If you want to say you do something on a certain day every week, you say: **Lavoro il lunedì** *(I work on Mondays)*. This means that in Italian, you must include the article before the day of the week.

If you want to say you do something from one day to another, you say: **Lavoro dal lunedì al venerdì** *(I work from Monday to Friday)*

If you want to say you do something on the weekends, you say: **Gioco a tennis nei fine settimana** *(I play tennis on the weekends)*.

Reading Comprehension

Let's read a short story about an Italian family as they enjoy a traditional Sunday together. Do you do similar things with your family on the weekends? Let's see how much Italian culture you share with them!

È domenica! Domenica è il giorno che stiamo in famiglia.
(It's Sunday! Sunday is the day we stay with family.)

Qualche famiglia va alla messa durante la mattina,
(Some families go to church in the morning;)

altre famiglie vanno al bar per colazione.
(other families go to the bar for breakfast.)

Non dimenticare, c'è la partita a mezzogiorno! Si guarda a casa, o si va allo stadio?
(Don't forget there's the game at noon! Do we watch it at home or go to the stadium?)

Oggi si guarda a casa dopo si mangia pranzo cucinato dalla nonna.
(Today we watch it at home after we eat lunch cooked by grandma.)

Dopo si celebra la vittoria della nostra squadra, si scende in piazza per aperitivo–
(After we celebrate our team's victory, we go to the veranda for appetizers.)

Un aperol spritz e patatine prima di cena.
(An Aperol Spritz and chips before dinner.)

I bambini preparano lo zaino per la scuola domani. Va via il sole, e tutti a dormire!
(Children get their backpacks ready for school tomorrow. The sun sets and everyone goes to sleep!)

Time to roll up your sleeves and practice!

10.3 Practice

A. Answer these questions about the reading comprehension:
1. Cosa fanno le famiglie domenica mattina?

_____

2. Chi cucina il pranzo?

_____

3. Dove si guarda la partita?

_____

4. Cosa si fa dopo che hanno guardato la partita?

_____

5. Cosa fanno i bambini?

_____

B. Look at Monica's schedule and answer the questions below:

	LUNEDÌ	MARTEDÌ	MERCOLEDÌ	GIOVEDÌ
9:15	pagare bollette			prendere il caffé con Elena
10:30	studiare	studiare	studiare	studiare
11:45				
4:15	prendere i bambini a scuola	prendere i bambini a scuola	prendere i bambini a scuola	prendere i bambini a scuola
6:45	cucinare	cucinare	cucinare	cucinare
8:15	cenare	cenare	cenare	cenare

	VENERDÌ	SABATO	DOMENICA
9:15			
10:30	studiare	giocare a tennis	giocare a golf
11:45			
4:15	prendere i bambini a scuola		
6:45	cucinare	ristorante	ordinare pizza (order pizza)
8:15	cenare		

1. A che ora Monica prende i figli a scuola? _____
2. A che ora paga le bollette? _____
3. A che ora studia? _____
4. Quando studia? _____
5. Quando gioca a tennis? _____

10.4 The Months of the Year

English	Italian	Pronunciation
January	**gennaio**	[jehn-nah-yoh]
February	**febbraio**	[fehb-hrah-yoh]
March	**marzo**	[mahr-tsoh]
April	**aprile**	[ah-pree-leh]
May	**maggio**	[mahj-joh]
June	**giugno**	[joo-nyoh]
July	**luglio**	[looh-lyoh]
August	**agosto**	[ah-goh-stoh]
September	**settembre**	[seht-tehm-breh]
October	**ottobre**	[oht-toh-breh]
November	**novembre**	[noh-vehm-breh]
December	**dicembre**	[dee-chehm-breh]

> **Tip:** When you're learning about time in a language, understanding and using adverbs related to time can significantly enhance your ability to communicate effectively. The adverb "quando?" which translates to "when?" in English, Is particularly useful. It helps in asking about the timing of events, which is fundamental for organizing activities, making plans, and understanding historical or future contexts.

Other period expressions:

Che giorno è oggi?	*What day is it today?*
Oggi è il 18 agosto.	*Today is August 18th.*
Oggi è il primo di maggio.	*Today is May 1st.*
Il mio compleanno è il 2 giugno.	*My birthday is June 2nd.*
La festa è l'8 ottobre.	*The party is on October 8th.*

When it's the first day of the month, you should use the ordinal number **primo** *(first)*. After that, cardinal numbers (**due, tre, quattro**, and so on) should be used.

Tip: Remember to use the article il before the date when you're stating when an event takes place: **La riunione è il 7 novembre** *(the meeting is on November 7)*.

Tip: The months of the year and the days of the week are not capitalized in Italian: **Oggi è lunedì, 2 marzo.** *(Today is Monday, March 2nd.)*

Common Error:

When you want to say, "*Today is Thursday,*"

X Don't say: **Oggi è il giovedì**

✓ Instead say: **Oggi è giovedì** (omit the **il**)

Tip: On the other hand, if you want to state when a specific event takes place, always use **il**. For example:

Natale è **il** 25 dicembre.

Capodanno è **il** primo gennaio.

Il mio compleanno è **il** 4 agosto.

L'indipendenza degli Stati Uniti è **il** 4 luglio.

The year is divided into seasons: summer (**estate**), fall or autumn (**autunno**), winter (**inverno**), and spring (**primavera**). In Italian, you often put the article il or la before speaking about a season. See below.

l'estate	**giugno**	**l'autunno**	**settembre**
	luglio		**ottobre**
	agosto		**novembre**
la primavera	**marzo**	**l'inverno**	**dicembre**
	aprile		**gennaio**
	maggio		**febbraio**

Ready to play with words? Let's practice!

10.4 Practice

A.   State when these events take place:

1.   Quando è il tuo compleanno (*birthday*)?

_____

2.   Quando si celebra l'indipendenza degli Stati Uniti?

_____

3.   Quando inizia (*starts*) l'estate in Europa?

_____

4.   Quando è Natale (*Christmas*)?

_____

5.   Quando è Capodanno (*New Year's*)?

_____

B.   Link the words with the appropriate season and write a sentence accordingly

Example: neve → <u>inverno. In inverno c'è neve.</u>

Seasons: primavera – estate – autunno – inverno

1.   Fiori → _____

2.   Sole → _____

3.   Foglie secche (*dry leaves*) → _____

4.   Caldo → _____

5.   Vento → _____

Ciao, lo sapevi che... *(Did you know?)*

As a fashion capital of the world, Italy does not lack in style! Here's a hint for when you travel to Italy...never wear flip flops anywhere but the beach! Italians love looking good wherever they are but there is a time and place for everything. Keep this mind and keep up with Italian fashion!

LESSON 11 :

AFFIRMATIVE AND NEGATIVE SENTENCES
YES, SIR; NO, SIR

Affirmative and negative sentences are an important part of everyday conversations. When we use an affirmative sentence, we're saying that something *is...* or that something *did* happen. It's a positive statement. On the other hand, negative sentences express that something *is not...* or that something *didn't* happen. It's the opposite of an affirmative sentence.

An affirmative sentence would be something like, '*the cat is blue.* On the contrary, a negative sentence would look like, '*the cat is not blue.*'

So, how do we express these positive and negative sentences in Italian? Let's take a look.

Affirmative and Negative Sentences

We've covered a lot of affirmative sentences already, but let's give you a refresher on the construction of these types of sentences.

When constructing an affirmative sentence in Italian, the subject (the noun) usually goes at the beginning of the sentence. After the noun, we add the verb, similar to English. We end up with a sentence such as:

Il cane salta *(The dog jumps)*

noun + verb

There are also words that, by default, are affirmative words.

In Italian, they are:

qualcosa	*something*
qualcuno	*someone*
alcun, alcuno, alcuna	*one, a, an, any*
alcuni, alcune	*some, any*
a volte, alcune volte	*sometimes*
sempre	*always*
anche	*also / too / as well*

Let's go back to the sentence about the dog jumping. What if we wanted to turn this sentence into a negative one and state that the dog is *not* jumping?

To do so, we'd add the word **non** right after the noun and before the verb.

Il cane non salta *(The dog does not jump)*

noun + **non** + verb

Just as there are affirmative words, there are also inherently negative words.

Negative words are:

no	*no*
né	*neither / nor*
niente	*nothing*
nessuno	*no one / nobody*
mai	*never/ever*

Do you know what a double negative is? We use them in English all the time. They're technically not grammatically correct to use in any language, but they're extremely common in everyday, informal speech.

A double negative sentence occurs when we combine two negative words in the same sentence. For example, *'She didn't do nothing'* or *'I didn't see nobody.'* They're confusing because the technical meaning is different from their intended meaning. When someone says, *'She didn't do nothing'* they *mean* to emphasize that *'She didn't do anything.'*

To construct a double negative sentence in Italian, you must add a negative word before *and* after the main verb in a sentence. The first word is usually **'non.'**

For example:

Lei non ha niente   *(She doesn't have nothing.)*

noun + **non** + verb + niente

Let's take a look at the following negative and double negative sentences:

La bambina non mangia niente.	*The girl doesn't eat nothing./* *The girl doesn't eat anything.*
Non so niente.	*I know nothing./ I don't know anything.*
Il bambino non capisce niente.	*The boy doesn't understand nothing./* *The boy doesn't understand anything.*
Luigi non compra niente dal fruttivendolo.	*Luigi buys nothing in the fruit store./* *Luigi doesn't buy anything in the fruit store.*
Non abbiamo bisogno di niente.	*We need nothing./ We don't need anything.*

> **Tip**: How do you translate a sentence like **The man doesn't speak Spanish**? Well, in Italian there is no equivalent for the English word *do* or *does* in negative sentences. You simply say **L'uomo** <u>non</u> **parla spagnolo**.

The negative words you use to form **double negative sentences** in Italian are:
1. Adverbs of denial (see below)
2. Indefinite pronouns (*'anything,' 'something,'* etc.)

Adverbs of Denial

no / non	*no - not*
né	*nor - neither*
mai	*never, ever*
neanche / nemmeno	*not even*

To use this in a sentence it would look like:

non + verb + adverb of denial + complement

Examples:
- ⮑ **Non** mi piace **né** il nuoto né il tennis: *I **don't** like swimming **or** tennis*
- ⮑ Maria **non** mangia **né** verdura né frutta: *Maria **doesn't** eat vegetables **or** fruits*
- ⮑ **Non** vado **mai** al ristorante: *I **never** go to a restaurant*
- ⮑ Luigi **non** va **mai** a trovare Elena: *Luigi **never** visits Elena*

Indefinite Pronouns

The other way to create double negative sentences in Italian is with **indefinite pronouns**. They're *'indefinite'* because they're vague about who they are referring to, e.g., *'someone'* or *'anyone.'* They can also be negative like *'no one'* or *'nothing.'*

The order is the same as with adverbs of denial: **non + verb + indefinite pronoun + complement**

These are negative indefinite pronouns:

nessuno	*no one / nobody*
niente	*nothing / anything*
nessuno / nessuna	*anyone / no one*

Examples:

➥ **Non** c'è **niente** da mangiare in casa: *There is **nothing** to eat in the house.*

➥ **Non** capisco **niente** di tedesco: *I **don't** understand **any** German.*

➥ **Non** ha bisogno di **nessuno**: *He/she **doesn't** need **any** of them.*

➥ **Non** c'è **nessuno** in città: *There is **no one** in the city.*

Time to roll up your sleeves and practice!

Practice 11

A. Check this dialogue out and answer the questions below.

Teresa va a cena dalla sua amica Isabella, ma non le importa di mangiare...

(Teresa goes to dinner with her friend Isabella, but it isn't important for her to eat anything.)

Isabella: Vuoi qualcosa da mangiare?
　　　　　(Do you want something to eat?)

Teresa: **No**, grazie. **Non** voglio mangiare **niente**.
　　　　(No, thank you. I won't eat anything.)

Isabella: E qualcosa da bere?
　　　　　(And something to drink?)

Teresa: **Non** voglio **neanche** da bere
　　　　(I won't drink anything either.)

Isabella: Davvero **non** vuoi **niente**?
　　　　　(You really don't want anything?)

Teresa: **Non** mangio **mai** a cena.
　　　　(I never have anything for dinner.)

Isabella: **Non** mangi **mai** la sera?
　　　　　(You never eat anything at night?)

Teresa: **No.** Dormo meglio.
　　　　(No. I sleep better.)

Notice that when the adverbs or pronouns of denial are placed directly **before** the first verb, you don't need the double negative: **Non mangio mai la sera.**

Nessuno / nessuna is an adjective. Therefore, it must agree in number and gender with the noun it modifies: **Non ha nessun**a **camer**a **da letto**.

When **nessuno** is before a masculine singular noun, it shortens to **nessun**.

For feminine nouns, "nessuno" does not shorten; it remains "nessuna" before a consonant and "nessun'" before a vowel: "Nessuna studentessa" (No female student) remains "nessuna studentessa."/"Nessuna amica" (No female friend) becomes "nessun'amica."

Nessuno/a is not used in the plural.

If **nessuno/a** precedes the noun, you don't need a **non: Nessuna persona capisce il latino.**

Remember: the opposite of **nessuno** (*no one*) is **qualcuno** (*someone / some*)

1. Teresa vuole mangiare qualcosa? _____
2. Teresa vuole bere qualcosa? _____
3. Teresa desidera qualcosa? _____
4. Teresa cena mai la sera? _____
5. Teresa dorme meglio senza mangiare? _____

B. Write the opposite of the following words:

1. qualcosa _____
2. qualcuno _____
3. qualcuno _____
4. sempre _____
5. anche _____

6. niente _____
7. nessuno _____
8. nessuno _____
9. mai _____
10. neanche _____

C. Translate the following using **alcun, alcuno, alcuna, qualche, del/della** (*one, a, an, any*), **alcuni, alcune** (*some, any*), and **nessun, nessuno, nessuna** (*none, no one*).

Example: Do you have any idea? → Hai qualche idea?

1. Do you have any sweaters?
2. I don't have any shirts.
3. Did you buy a blouse?
4. No, I didn't buy any blouses.
5. Are there some boys in the pool?
6. No, there aren't any boys in the pool.
7. Do you have any cats at home?
8. No, I don't have any cats at home.
9. Do you have any suitcases in the car?
10. No, I don't have any suitcases in the car.

D. Answer these questions, first affirmatively, and then, negatively.

Example: C'è qualcosa in frigorifero? → <u>Sì, c'è. No, non c'è niente.</u>

1. C'è qualcosa nel forno?

    _____

2. C'è qualcosa nella valigia?

    _____

3. C'è qualcosa sul tavolo?

    _____

4. C'è qualcosa in camera da letto?

    _____

5. C'è qualcosa nel portafoglio? (*wallet*)

    _____

E. Answer these questions, first affirmatively, and then, negatively.

Example: C'è qualcuno in biblioteca? → <u>Sì, c'è qualcuno. No, non c'è nessuno.</u>

1. C'è qualcuno nel giardino? _____

2. C'è qualcuno in casa? _____

3. C'è qualcuno nella pescheria? _____

4. C'è qualcuno nell'ufficio? _____

5. C'è qualcuno per strada? _____

F. Answer these questions, first affirmatively, then, negatively.

Example: Ci sono quadri (paintings) nel museo? → <u>Sì, ce ne sono alcuni. No, non ce ne sono.</u>

Remember: **Nessun, nessuno, and nessuna** do not have a plural form.

1. Ci sono fiori nel giardino? _____

2. Ci sono bambini nel collegio? _____

3. Ci sono libri nella biblioteca? _____

4. Ci sono persone alla festa? _____

5. Ci sono sedie nella classe? _____

G. Express these sentences using double negatives.

Example: C'è qualcosa di interessante al cinema → <u>Non c'è niente di interessante al cinema.</u>

1. C'è qualcosa di buono in cucina: _____

2. Ho qualche fiore nel mio giardino: _____

3. Sofía studia sempre per la lezione: _____

4. Mettono qualcosa nell'auto: _____

5. Ricevono sempre i loro amici a casa: _____

H. Choose among these indefinite pronouns (**niente – nessuno – nessuno – nessuna**) or negative adverbs (**mai – né – neanche – mai**) to complete the sentences.

1. C'è _____ nel frigorifero.
2. Maria e Daniele _____ discutono.
3. Non mi piace _____ la carne _____ il pollo.
4. Non mi piace _____ di quel giovane.
5. _____ sa il suo nome.
6. Non voglio andare al ristorante. _____'io voglio andare.
7. Non c'è _____ hotel in questa città.
8. _____ fiore è bello come questo.
9. Non ho _____ mangiate sushi.
10. Non mi piace _____ vino _____ birra.

I. Answer the following questions with a negative response. Try to use a double negative. Remember: **nessun, nessuno and nessuna** do not have a plural form.

1. Condividete qualcosa?

    No, _____

2. Tommaso riceve qualcosa per il suo compleanno (*for his birthday*)?

    No, _____

3. C'è qualche ristorante in questa (*this*) via?

    No, _____

4. Canti mai?

    No, _____

5. Hanno fatto qualche lavoro per domani (*in the morning*)?

    No, _____

6. Leggete qualche giornale la domenica?

    No, _____

7. C'è qualche fiore in inverno?

    No, _____

8. Vai sempre al supermercato il sabato?

    No, _____

9. I turisti visitano qualche parco?

    No, _____

10. Voi mangiate carne?

    No, _____

J. Turn these sentences into negative ones. In some cases, it will be a double negative. Remember: **Nessun, nessuno and nessuna** do not have a plural form.

Example: Sai qualcosa di francese? <u>No, non so niente di francese.</u>

1. Lei sta sempre giù di morale.

   _____

2. Noi facciamo un po' di sport oggi.

   _____

3. Anche Maria deve comprare dei libri.

   _____

4. Questo supermercato è un po' piccolo.

   _____

5. Qualcuno studia in biblioteca.

   _____

6. Tante bambine ballano al collegio.

   _____

7. Ci sono fruttivendoli qui (here)?

   No, _____

8. Martino beve acqua.

   _____

9. Voi pulite sempre la casa.

   _____

10. Conosco tutti i suoi amici.

    _____

Lo sai che... (Did you know?)

Apparently, homework was invented by Roberto Nevelis, an Italian educator from Venice. Rumor has it that he created it as a punishment for students who didn't work hard during lessons. So, roll up your sleeves, work hard and even though we may dred it, let's thank the Italian Roberto Nevelis with a big GRAZIE for all of the homework we have. Ora, vai a studiare! (*Now, go study!*)

LESSON 12 :

CONJUNCTIONS AND INDEFINITE ADJECTIVES
YOU, AND YOU, AND YOU

12.1 Conjunctions

Don't be intimidated by that big word! Conjunctions are some of the most common components of everyday language. They connect other words, phrases, *and* clauses. For example, in that last sentence, *'and'* was the conjunction, because it unites the rest of the sentence.

Some other examples of conjunctions are *'or'* and *'but.'* They allow us to say things like *'She came by, but she didn't come in.'*

By learning conjunctions in Italian, you'll be able to construct slightly more complex sentences. Although they aren't hard to construct, they help to convey a whole new layer of meaning.

In Italian, there are two types of conjunctions:

- Coordinating conjunctions ('but,' 'and,' 'or')
- Subordinating conjunctions ('because,' 'although')

What's the difference?

Coordinating conjunctions join two parts of a sentence that are equal in importance, e.g., *'Tina loves Instagram and Bob loves Facebook.'* You know they're equal because if you removed the conjunction, you would still understand that Tina loves Instagram and Bob loves Facebook.

Subordinating conjunctions, on the other hand, connect parts of a sentence that don't convey the same message when they're independent. E.g., *'Tina loves Instagram because she's a fan of photography.'* If you removed the conjunction in this sentence, you wouldn't understand that the reason Tina loves Instagram is because she's a fan of photography.

These same differences apply to coordinating and subordinating conjunctions in Italian. Understanding their purpose will help you navigate them.

Here's a table to further illustrate the use of coordinating conjunctions:

Coordinating Conjunctions			
Combine Elements Together (Copulative Conjunctions)	e	*and*	Mangia **e** beve. (*He eats **and** drinks.*)
	né	*nor*	Non mangio **né** pane **né** gallette. (*He doesn't eat bread **nor** crackers.*)
Show an Opposition or Difference (Adversative Conjunctions)	**però/ma**	*but*	È intelligente **però** svogliato. (*He's intelligent **but** lazy.*)
	ma	*but*	Ha un lavoro **ma** non è felice. (*She has a job **but** isn't happy.*)
	tuttavia (usually used after a semi-colon)	*however, nevertheless, but*	Ha molto denaro; **tuttavia**, non lo condivide. (*She has a lot of money; **however** she doesn't share it.*)
	anche se/ sebbene	*even if, though, although*	Il film è bello, **anche se** lungo. (*The movie is good, **even if** it's long.*)
	ma/bensì	*but*	Non mangio carne ma mangio pesce. (*I don't eat meat **but** I eat fish.*)
Show Options (Disjunctive Conjunctions)	o	*or*	Maria ritorna a mezzogiorno **o** alle 13:00. (*María comes back at 12:00 p.m. **or** at 1:00 p.m.*)
	od	*or (used when the word following the disjunctive conjunction "o" begins with the vowel "o" or the silent letter "h" followed by the vowel "o")*	Laura sistema **od** organizza i documenti. (*Laura organizes **or** arranges the papers.*)

Coordinating Conjunctions

	o... o	*either... or*	**O** studi **o** non guardi la TV. (*Either you study, or you don't watch TV.*)
	sia... che	*either... or*	Studiano **sia** al parco, **che** in biblioteca. (*Either they study in the park or in the library.*)
Show Alternation (Distributive Conjunctions)	**tanto... quanto**	*both*	**Tanto** Pietro quanto Maria sono bravi studenti. (**Both** *Pedro and María are good students.*)
	sia... sia	*whether... or*	Il matrimonio è condividere la vita **sia** nelle gioie **sia** nei dolori. (*Marriage is sharing life* **whether** *in happiness or in sorrow.*)

As we all know that practice makes perfect, so let's give it a go!

12.1 Practice

A. Find the right conjunctions: **e – o**. If the sentence is not translated, go ahead, and translate it.

1. There are ten or eleven children: _____

2. Get the key and try to open the door: Prendi la chiave _____ prova ad aprire la porta.

3. He calls and invites us: _____

4. She saw something or heard a noise: Vide qualcosa _____ udì un rumore.

5. She knows how to read and write very well. _____

B. Fill in the blanks with the conjunctions **e, o**, or **ma**

1. Il bambino mangia una banana _____ una mela.

2. Martino lavora _____ studia?

3. Cerco il mio cane _____ non lo trovo.

4. Lo ripeto due _____ tre volte (*times*).

5. Avete cantato _____ ballato tutta la notte.

6. Sono francese _____ vivo in Italia.

7. Vieni alle otto _____ alle nove del mattino.

8. Luisa lavora tanto _____ guadagna (*earns*) poco (*little*).

9. Loro giocano _____ gli altri studiano.

10. Ho visto il Duomo di Milano _____ il Duomo di Firenze.

C. Fill in the blanks with the right conjunction: **però, ma, tuttavia, anche se, bensì.**

1. Mangio poco _____ sono grasso.

2. Non lavora oggi in ufficio _____ domani si.

3. Tommaso sa tante cose _____ è una persona umile (*humble*).

4. Ha l'auto; _____ gli piace camminare.

5. Viaggia tanto, _____ non ha tanto denaro.

D. Circle the correct conjunction in each sentence and write it on the line provided.

1. Cammino tutti i giorni { **perché – tuttavia** } fa bene alla salute.

2. Loro mangiano al ristorante tutti i giorni { **ma – né** } gli altri (*the others*) mangiano casa.

3. Teresa impara il tedesco { **né – anche se** } non ne ha bisogno.

4. { **Anche se – Né** } Elena { **anche se – né** } Cristiano bevono vino.

5. Elena { **e – né** } Ilario sono avvocati.

6. { **Anche se – Tanto** } Pietro { **quanto – né** } Sofia sono francesi.

7. Compriamo { **e – ma** } vendiamo roba usata (*used clothes*).

8. Andiamo al ristorante { **perché – ma** } non c'è da mangiare a casa.

9. Studia tanto; { **anche se – tuttavia** } non impara tanto.

10. Leggiamo il libro { **anche se – quanto** } abbiamo gia letto una volta.

12.2 Subordinating Conjunctions

As we mentioned earlier, subordinating conjunctions connect parts of a sentence that are dependent on each other. Here's a table to further illustrate the use of subordinating conjunctions:

Subordinating Conjunctions			
Showing Cause (Cause Conjunctions)	**perché**	*because*	È stanca **perché** lavora tanto. (*She's tired **because** she works a lot.*)
	poiché/ dato che/ visto che	*since, as, because*	Sto a casa **visto che** piove. (*I'm home **because** it's raining.*)
	siccome	*since, as, because*	**Siccome** è occupato, non ha tempo. (***Since** he's busy, he doesn't have any time.*)

Subordinating Conjunctions			
Elaborating (Relative Conjunctions)	**che**	*that*	Mi ha detto **che** sono il suo migliore amico. (*He told me **that** I was his best friend.*)
Making Comparisons (Comparative Conjunctions)	**così come**	*just as*	José è alto, **così come** sua sorella. (*José is tall, **just as** his sister.*)
	e anche	*so to/and also*	Sa il francese, **e anche** il tedesco. (*He knows French, **and also** German.*)
	tanto quanto	*as...as*	Maria è simpatica **tanto quanto** Clara. (*Maria is **as** nice **as** Clara.*)
To Show an Obstacle Doesn't Prevent Action (Concessive Conjunctions)	**sebbene / anche se**	*although, even though, though*	La biblioteca è chiusa, **anche se** è mezzogiorno. (*The library is closed, **even though** it's 12:00 p.m.*)
	nonostante	*even though, despite the fact that*	È triste, **nonostante** abbia tanti amici. (*He's sad, **despite the fact** that he has lots of friends.*)
To Show Conditions (Conditional Conjunctions)	**se**	*if*	Pago con carta di credito **se** devo. (*I pay with a credit card **if** I need to.*)
	a meno che	*unless*	Corro tutti i giorni **a meno che** non piova. (*I run every day **unless** it rains.*)
To Give a Sense of Time and Order (Time Conjunctions)	**mentre**	*while, meanwhile*	Cammina **mentre** parla al telefono. (*She walks **while** she talks on the phone.*)

Common Mistakes: The conjunction **che** is essential in Italian, even though it is often not translated in English. **Che** is a conjunction which means *that or which*.

Credo che lei sia felice. (*I believe that she is happy*)

Note that in English, you can say, *I believe she is happy* (without "that"). Be careful! You can also say **Credo sia felice** in Italian, omitting **che**. But in some cases, specifically when there is the subject, you need to use **che**.

✓ **Credo che la bambina sia felice.**

Time to roll up your sleeves and practice!

Conjunctions and indefinite adjectives

12.2 Practice

A. Let's practice the relative conjunction **se**. Join these sentences.

Example: Maria | non | sapere | se | Juan | avere bisogno | qualcosa: <u>Maria non sa se Juan ha bisogno di qualcosa.</u>

1. Pietro e Luigi | non | sapere | se | suoi amici | ritornare:

    _____

2. Miriana | domanda (*ask*) | se | c'è | esame | domani:

    _____

3. Giancarlo | decidere | se | salire | sul monte Fitz Roy:

    _____

4. Voi | non | sapere | se | Paula | ha bisogno | qualcosa | per la festa:

    _____

5. Lei | domandare | se | gli impiegati | lavorare | bene:

    _____

B. Let's practice the relative conjunction **che**. Remember? The one you should never omit in Italian. Join these sentences.

Example: Abbiamo una festa. Mi dice. → Mi dice che abbiamo una festa.

1. Abitiamo in via Oro. Lei sa: _____

2. Viaggiamo tutto l'anno. Giorgio pensa: _____

3. Il signor Gardella ripara i forni. Io credo: _____

4. A Giulio piace mangiare. Dice Giovanna: _____

5. È tardi. La professoressa ci dice: _____

C. Join both sentences with a subordinate conjunction.

perché – ma – anche se – che

Example: È un buon professore. Io credo → <u>Io credo che sia un buon professore.</u>

1. Mi piace. I miei figli ordinano da soli.

    _____

2. Lavoro tanto. Guadagno poco.

    _____

3. Fa freddo. C'è il sole.

    _____

4. Sta soffiando troppo vento per correre. Martino crede.

    _____

5. I pomodori sono verdi. Mi spiega il fruttivendolo.

    _____

12.3 Indefinite Adjectives

An indefinite adjective is an adjective used to describe a noun in a non-specific way. It agrees with the noun in quantityand sometimes gender. Many indefinite adjectives in Italian are identical to Italian indefinite pronouns.

Examples of indefinite adjectives are:

C'è **qualche** mela.	(*There are a few apples.*)
C'è **qualche** possibilità di viaggiare.	(*There is a possibility to travel.*)
C'è **tanto** sole.	(*There is a lot of sun.*)
È la **stessa** casa.	(*It's the same house.*)
Mi serve **qualche** vestito.	(*I need some clothes.*)
Il professore insegna **tutti** gli esercizi.	(*The professor teaches all of the exercises.*)

SINGULAR		PLURAL		
masculine	feminine	masculine	feminine	
alcun	alcuna	alcuni	alcune	*some, a few*
nessun	nessuna	-	-	*none, neither*
ogni	ogni	-	-	*each*
certo	certa	certi	certe	*certain*
stesso	stessa	stessi	stesse	*same*
tanto	tanta	tanti	tante	*many, much, a lot*
altro	altra	altri	altre	*other*
poco	poca	pochi	poche	*few, a little*
alcune	-	alcuni	-	*some, any*
tanto	tanta	tanti	tante	*so many, so much*
tutto	tutta	tutti	tutte	*all*
-	-	vari	varie	*several, some*

Common Mistake:

Indefinite adjectives are used in place of an article, **not with one**.

X Don't say: **Ci sono le alcune mele**
✓ Say instead: **Ci sono alcune mele**

Rules, step aside; it's practice time!

Speak Abroad
Academy

12.3 Practice

A. Complete the sentences with the correct indefinite adjective.

Example: Paolo compra solo _____ **mela → Paolo compra solo qualche mela.**

1. _____ persone lavorano solo in casa propria.
2. Ci sono _____ uccelli che Leonardo.
3. Susanna ha una_____ casa sulla spiaggia.
4. _____ persone condividono l'appartamento con gli amici.
5. _____ giorno che passa è peggio (*is worse*).

B. Translate the following sentences using conjunctions and indefinite adjectives:

1. Lei ha tanti cani e gatti.

   _____   _____

2. Marla ha diverse figlie, ma non ha figli.

   _____

3. Sia Luigi che Juan hanno pochi amici.

   _____

4. Non legge né riviste (*magazines)* né quotidiani (*newspapers*).

   _____

5. Conosce altri paesi perché viaggia tanto.

   _____

6. Ha la stessa auto di Laura.

   _____

7. Conosce ogni strada di Parigi, ma non conosce la propria città (*her own city*).

   _____

8. Parla alcune lingue, ma non parla inglese.

   _____

9. È la stessa amicizia, anche se siamo più vecchi.

   _____

10. Tutte le lingue sono utili (*useful*), ma alcune sono più utili (*useful*) di altre.

    _____

C. Elena has a positive outlook on life. Roberto has a negative outlook on life. Change Elena's statements to the opposite to express what Robert thinks.

Example: Ho pochi problemi → <u>Ho tanti problemi</u>.

1. Tutti i giorni sono belli →_____
2. Ho pochi dolori →_____
3. Ci sono tante cose belle nella vita →_____
4. Ho tanti amici →_____
5. Certi giorni sono brutti →_____

Ciao, vorresti sapere qualcosa di interessante? *(Did you know?)*

In Italian, there is only one word to say both 'why?' and 'because'. That word is perché. The difference is in the tone of your voice – naturally when we ask questions we tend to raise our voice at the end and in affirmative statements we keep our tone neutral. Why don't you try, the Italian way!

Perché si mangia la pizza?

Perché è buona!

LESSON 13 :

LIKES AND DISLIKES
I LIKE APPLES

It would be impossible to get to know other people and allow them to get to know you without learning to express likes and dislikes. They convey our opinions and other key parts of our personality. By using **mi piace** (*I like*) and **non mi piace** (*I don't like*), we can finally tell people what we really think!

13.1 Constructions With Mi Piace and Non Mi Piace

Exploring the use of the Italian verb "piacere," is essential for expressing personal preferences in Italian. Unlike the direct English equivalents "like" and "dislike," "piacere" translates more accurately to "to be pleasing to."

Thus, when Italians say "Mi piace leggere," they are literally stating, "Reading is pleasing to me." This structure provides a unique perspective on likes and dislikes, reflecting the subjectivity of preference. We will delve into both positive and negative constructions with "Mi piace" (I like) and "Non mi piace" (I don't like), providing examples and usage tips to help you communicate your preferences effectively in Italian.

The takeaway:

The verb **piacere** is used in Italian to express likes and dislikes:

- ⤷ **Mi piace leggere** (*I like to read*)
- ⤷ **Non mi piace leggere** (*I do not like to read*)
- ⤷ **Mi piacciono i gatti** (*I like cats*)
- ⤷ **Non mi piacciono i gatti** (*I don't like cats*)

But we know that **piacere** does not literally mean *to like*.

Piacere means *to be pleasing (to someone)*. It needs to be used with an indirect object to make complete sense. This indirect object is whatever it is you're expressing your affection or fondness for.

The indirect object can be a pronoun **(mi, ti, gli, le, ci, vi, gli/loro)** or a person/object/animal preceded by a → a + person/name/object+piacere (conjugated).

For example:

A Maria piace il gelato. (*Maria likes ice cream.*)

A me piacciono (mi piacciono) i cavalli. (*I like horses.*)

A Juan e Cristina piace la musica classica. (*Juan and Cristina like classical music.*)

A sentence like, **A Martino piace mangiare** has two indirect objects: **gli** and **a Martino. A Martino** is used to add emphasis or to clarify who or what the indirect object pronoun is (**gli** could be a woman, an animal, or almost anything).

Notice, too, that the verb **piacere** must agree with its subject, i.e., the person or thing that is liked, *not* the person who is being described. In the sentences above, we used both **piace** and **piacciono** to agree with the different nouns.

A Martino piacciono i cavalli → **piacciono** agrees with **cavalli** *(horses)*, not Martín.

A Tommaso piace la pizza → **piace** agrees with **pizza** *(pizza)*, not Tommasso

To say that you *don't* like something, you need to add **non** before the indirect object pronoun or before the verb piacere.

<u>Non</u> mi piacciono i cani. (*I don't like dogs.*)

A loro <u>non</u> piacciono i gatti. (*They don't like cats.*)

<u>Non</u> ci piacciono le moto. (*We don't like motorcycles.*)

Indirect Object Pronouns

mi:	to, for me
ti:	to, for you
gli:	to, for you, him, it
le:	to, for her
ci:	to, for us
vi:	to, for you
gli/ a loro:	to, for you, them

Now check these sentences:

- **A Martino piacciono le mappe**: *Martin likes maps (or Maps are pleasing to Martin).* In this case, since maps is plural, "piacciono" is in the plural form. **Gli** is the indirect object and **A Martino** is used in addition to the indirect object pronoun for clarification or emphasis.

- **A me piace (mi piace) lo sport**: *I like sports (or Sports are pleasing to me).* Again, **sport** agrees with the singular third-person, **piace**. **Mi** is the indirect object pronoun and **A me** is used as emphasis.

↻ **Le piacciono i fiori?:** *Do you like flowers? (Are flowers pleasing to you?)* **I fiori** agrees with the plural, **piacciono**. **Le** is the indirect object. **A Lei (***formal***)** is used for clarification (since **le** can also refer to someone else).

↻ **A loro piace il teatro**: *They like the theater. (The theater is pleasing to them)* **Il teatro** is singular third-person and agrees with **piace.** The indirect object is **gli** and **A loro** is used for emphasis.

Tip: Just as in English, you can combine **piacere + a verb** (*I like running*). In Italian, **piacere** is combined with the **infinitive** of the verb (not the gerund, like in English): **piacere + verbo all'infinito.**

Examples: **Ti piace correre** (*you like running*), **mi piace guardare la TV** (*I like watching TV*), **a loro piace cucinare** (*they like cooking*).

X **Do not say:**   Mi piace correndo.

✓ **Say:**   Mi piace correre.

Vocabulary: Food

Something that we all have strong opinions about is food! It's time to expand your vocabulary and get to know the different Italian words for food. Using what we just learned, can you express which types of food below you like or dislike?

English	Italian	Pronunciation
meat	**carne**	*[kahr-neh]*
chicken	**pollo**	*[poh-yoh]*
fish	**pesce**	*[peh-scheh]*
hamburger	**hamburger**	*[ahm-boor-gehr]*
tomato	**pomodoro**	*[poh-moh-do-roh]*
lettuce	**lattuga**	*[laht-too-gah]*
apple	**mela**	*[meh-lah]*
orange	**arancia**	*[ah-rahn-chee-ah]*
potatoes	**patate**	*[pah-tah-teh]*
banana	**banana**	*[bah-nah-nah]*
onion	**cipolla**	*[chee-pohl-lah]*
bread	**pane**	*[pah-neh]*
milk	**latte**	*[laht-teh]*
water	**acqua**	*[ah-kwah]*

English	Italian	Pronunciation
coffee	**caffè**	*[kahf-feh]*
tea	**tè**	*[teh]*
sugar	**zucchero**	*[tsook-keh-roh]*
candy	**caramelle (plural)**	*[kah-rah-mehl-leh]*
	caramella (singular)	*[kah-rah-mehl-lah]*

Enough scribbling on the language map; let's navigate through the terrain of practice!

13.1 Practice

A. Write the correct indirect object pronoun for each subject pronoun.

1. A noi _____ piace.
2. A voi _____ piace.
3. A Lei _____ piace.
4. A loro _____ piace.
5. A Giulio e Mattia _____ piace.
6. A me _____ piace.
7. A te _____ piace.
8. A Giorgio _____ piace.
9. A Elena _____ piace.
10. A Sofia _____ piace.

B. Translate the sentences.

Example: She likes candy. → <u>A lei piacciono le caramelle.</u>

1. I like the car. _____
2. They like onions. _____
3. We don't like reading. _____
4. You (sing.) like bananas. _____
5. You (plural) like working. _____
6. Marcos likes studying. _____
7. Elsa likes tomatoes. _____
8. My father likes to eat. _____
9. My mother likes fish. _____
10. The boys don't like milk. _____

C. Join the words to make a sentence. Make sure you include two indirect objects (the pronoun + whoever the action is for).

Example: non | piacciono | le | banane | a Mirta: <u>A Mirta non piacciono le banane</u>.

1. correre | a noi | piace: _____
2. non | piacciono | le verdure | ai bambini _____
3. quelle scarpe | piacciono | me _____
4. le feste | a Luigi e Teresa | piacciono _____
5. suonare il piano | a Elena | piace _____

D. Pick one of the items below and say you like it. Pick the other one to say you don't like it. You can switch the items according to what you like. You may use an adversative conjunction (**ma, anche se, tuttavia**) or a copulative conjunction (**e**).

Example: mangiare carne? Mangiare pesce? → <u>Non mi piace mangiare carne, ma mi piace mangiare pesce.</u>

1. Leo Messi? Cristiano Ronaldo?

   _____

2. Mangiare hamburger? Mangiare pasta?

   _____

3. Il caffè? Il tè?

   _____

4. L'attrice Meryl Streep? L'attrice Judy Dench?

   _____

5. Il tennista Medvedev? Il tennista Federer?

   _____

6. Studiare in biblioteca? Studiare in sala da pranzo?

   _____

7. I cani? I gatti?

   _____

8. Viaggiare in treno? Viaggiare in auto?

   _____

9. Giocare a tennis? Giocare a calcio?

   _____

10. Fare la pizza? Fare la lasagna?

   _____

E. Complete the sentences by conjugating **piacere** according to its subject.

Example: A Isabella _____ i bambini → A Isabella piacciono i bambini.

1. A Sebastiano e Nicola _____ lo sport.
2. A voi _____ gli orologi costosi.
3. A te _____ le moto.
4. A noi _____ imparare l'italiano.
5. A me _____ i cioccolatini.

F. Complete these questions making **piacere** agree with the subject and adding the appropriate personal pronoun.

Example: (lui / piacere) _____ il teatro? → A lui piace il teatro?

1. (noi / piacere) _____ le fragole?
2. (Teresa / piacere) _____ la sua università?
3. (loro / piacere) _____ ricevere gente in casa?
4. (te / piacere) _____ fare yoga?
5. (tu / piacere) _____ il pesce?

G. Complete with a + pronoun + pronoun + verb **piacere**.

Example: _____ (io) studiare lingue → A me piace studiare lingue.

1. _____ (noi) lavorare.
2. _____ (voi) vivere da soli.
3. _____ (voi) camminare nel parco il sabato.
4. _____ (Carolina e Luigi) salire sui monti.
5. _____ (tu) invitare amici a casa tua.

H. Rewrite these sentences by correcting the mistakes.

1. A me ci piace le caramelle: _____
2. A te ti piace il pane: _____
3. A voi mi piace il latte: _____
4. A te mi piace il caffè: _____
5. A loro ci piacciono le arance: _____

Vocabulary: Members of the Family

English	Italian	Pronunciation
father	**padre**	*[pah-dreh]*
mother	**madre**	*[mah-dreh]*
daughter	**figlia**	*[fee-lyah]*
son	**figlio**	*[fee-lyoh]*
grandfather	**nonno**	*[nohn-noh]*

Likes and dislikes

Speak Abroad
Academy

English	Italian	Pronunciation
grandmother	**nonna**	*[noh-nah]*
uncle / aunt	**zio/ zia**	*[tsyoh]/ [tsyah]*
cousin	**cugino/a**	*[koo-jee-noh]/ [koo-jee-nah]*
nephew / niece / grandchild	**nipote**	*[nee-poh-teh]*

I. Dove andiamo in vacanza? (*Where do we go on vacation?*)

The Pérez family each have their own idea of a good vacation and where they prefer to go. Turn the suggested separate elements into a sentence. Remember to include the indirect object that clarifies or adds emphasis.

Example: padre / nuotare → Al padre piace nuotare.

1. nonno / cucinare

    _____

2. fratello / fare surf (*to do surf*)

    _____

3. zia / leggere libri

    _____

4. cugini / comprare vestiti (*go shopping for clothes*)

    _____

5. padre / mangiare e bere

    _____

6. figlia / cercare conchiglie sulla riva (*look for seashells on the shore*)

    _____

7. madre / la tranquillità

    _____

8. nipoti / correre sulla spiaggia (*run on the beach*)

    _____

9. Sofia / fare ginnastica (*to do gymnastics*)

    _____

10. nonna / cucire (*sew*)

    _____

13.2 Expressing Wants in a Direct and Polite Way

You've learned how to express your likes and dislikes, but what about your wants? How can you tell someone that you want something?

In Italian, you use the verb **volere** to express **wants**, e.g., **Voglio un caffè** (*I want a coffee*)

How do you say you don't want something? For this, we'll use **non** again.

To say you don't want something, just add a **non** before the verb:
Non voglio un caffè (*I don't want a coffee*)

As with **piacere,** you can also add an infinitive verb after **volere/desiderare** when you *want to do something*, e.g., **Voglio imparare il tedesco** (*I want to learn German*).

Sometimes it's not polite to ask directly for something. For example, if you're asking for a map in a hotel lobby, it's more polite to say, **Vorrei una mappa (***I would like a map)* rather than **Voglio una mappa** (*I want a map*).

When you want to express what you *would like* or *wouldn't like,* in Italian you say, **Vorrei / Non vorrei.**

Of course, **vorrei** is also used when you're wishing or pining for something: **Mi piacerebbe conoscere Luigi** (*I would like to meet Luis*). In other words, it's a way of expressing your wants in a less direct way, which is essential for politeness.

With **vorrei** you can also add an infinitive for something you *would like to do*: **Mi piacerebbe scalare l'Everest.**

Practice makes perfect—let's give it a go!

13.2 Practice

Choose what you would say in each scenario, depending on whether you can be more direct or need to be more polite:

1. You're at a bar and ask the waiter for a glass of water:
   { Voglio – Vorrei } un bicchiere d'acqua.
2. You're expressing your need for sleep to a friend:
   { Voglio – Vorrei } dormire.
3. You're explaining to a professor that you would like to speak Italian well:
   { Voglio – Vorrei } parlare bene l'italiano.
4. You're asking a salesperson at a store to hand you that green dress:
   { Voglio – Vorrei } quel vestito verde.
5. You're telling your friend you want to fix the roof:
   { Voglio – Vorrei } riparare il tetto.

Speak Abroad
Academy

Ciao, voglio dirti qualcosa! *(I want to tell you something...)*

Italians are famous for their beautiful land, fashion, people but most importantly, they are famous for their food! That's right, Italian food is celebrated around the world and is known for being THE BEST! With the best, there are some strict rules to an 'Italian diet'. We already know that pasta and meat are never served together, but did you also know that it's almost considered a crime to order a cappuccino after lunch! Of course, you can still be served a cappuccino at any time of the day but if you want to live like a true Italian, make sure you get your cappuccino fixings bright and early!

PREPOSITIONS I
THE HAT IS ON THE CHAIR

14.1 Introduction to Prepositions

Again, don't be afraid of the big word. We use prepositions all the time and they're not complex. They're words like *'on,' 'over,'* or *'until,'* which are important for describing space and time.

If you're trying to help someone find something, prepositions allow you to describe which part of the room they would find the object in. Is it *under* the bed? *On* the table? *In* the laundry hamper?

They also describe time. If you're trying to organize plans with your friends, prepositions would help you arrange an appropriate time. Can you only hang out *at* 8 PM? *After* work? *Before* your favorite TV show starts playing. Or maybe just *until* you start feeling tired?

The good news is that, unlike most words in Italian, prepositions in Italian don't change! They have no number or gender, and always remain the same. Phew!

Here is the list of simple prepositions:

a	at, to
prima	before
sotto	under
con	with
contro	against
di	of, from
da	after, since, from
durante	during
in	in
su/ sul/ sulla	on
tra/ fra	among, between
verso	toward
fino a	until, up to, as far as
eccetto	except

per	for, in order to	
da	by, for	
tranne	except, save	
secondo	according to	
senza	without	
sopra	on, upon, over, above	
dietro	after, behind	

Most Common Prepositions: in – di – con

Let's start practicing the three most common prepositions in Italian. We will start with these three:

in	*in, on*	States the idea of remaining in a place or time	Juan è **in** camera sua. (*Juan is **in** his bedroom.*)
di	*of, from*	Gives the idea of possession, matter, or origin	La casa è **di** Gabriella. (*The house **belongs to** Gabriela.*) La sedia *di* legno. (*The chair is made **of** wood.*)
con	*with*	Indicates company	Sto **con** i miei amici. (*I'm **with** my friends.*)

Time to roll up your sleeves and practice!

14.1 Practice

A. Complete the following sentences with the prepositions **in, di**, or **con**:

1. Luigi vive _____ una grande città.
2. Maria viaggia sempre _____ sua sorella.
3. La casa è _____ colore giallo.
4. Le scarpe sono _____ pelle (*leather*).
5. Voi state _____ il capo.
6. Ci sono bei parchi _____ questa strada.
7. Il gatto è di _____ Pietro.
8. Mia nipote lavora _____ suo padre.
9. Sto _____ Inghilterra.
10. I bambini stanno _____ la maestra.

B. Again, try to complete these sentences with **in**, **di**, or **con**:
1. Flavia compie gli anni il quattro _____ aprile _____ 2000.
2. Vorrei un caffè _____ latte.
3. Questa cartella è _____ Simone.
4. Torna dall'ufficio _____ bicicletta.
5. Ho un bel rapporto _____ i miei genitori (*my parents*).

C. Try completing the sentences by choosing between **in** and **tra**:
1. I miei nonni viaggiano (*drive*) _____ in auto per la città.
2. Tommaso sta _____ casa sua.
3. Filippo sta seduto (*sitting*) _____ Maria e Paolo.
4. Il signor Polombo ritorna a casa sua _____ le otto e le nove di sera.
5. Regaliamo un cane a Sebastiano _____ gli amici (*among the friends*).

14.2 Prepositions: a – per – senza

a	*to*	Indicates movement towards a goal, whether real or imagined. It is used before an indirect object and a direct object when it's a person.	Vado **a** casa a piedi. (*I walk **to** my house.*) Parlo **a** mia sorella.
per	*for, in order to*	Indicates the aim or purpose of an action	La matita è **per** mia figlia. (*The pencil is **for** my daughter.*)
senza	*without*	Indicates lack of	L'hotel è **senza** turisti. (*The hotel is **without** tourists.*)

What follows a preposition?

⮌ In Italian, prepositions can be followed by verbs in the infinitive form: **Tommaso studia per imparare** (*Tomas studies to learn*) or **Martino parla senza pensare** (*Martin speaks without thinking*).

⮌ Prepositions can be followed by nouns: **Maria compra un fiore per sua madre** (*María buys a flower for her mother*).

⮌ Prepositions can be followed by pronouns: **Il libro è per lei** (*The book is for her*). In Italian, the pronouns that follow prepositions are **subject pronouns**, except for **me** and **te** (instead of **io** and **tu**): **Il caffè è per me** and **Il tè è per te**.

> **Tip:** When you use the preposition **con** together with the **1st and 2nd subject pronoun**, the result is **con me** and **con te**. In fact, **con** is the only preposition that combines with a pronoun.
>
> Example: **Mio marito viaggia sempre con me** (*My husband always travels with me*) or **Parlo con te nel parco** (*I talk with you in the park*).

Eager to dance with phrases? Let's groove through practice!

14.2 Practice

A. Complete the following sentences with the prepositions **a, per**, or **senza**.
1. Il regalo è _____ Marco.
2. MI piace il caffè _____ zucchero.
3. Il padre ritorna _____ casa alle 9:00 di sera.
4. Lei studia _____ imparare.
5. Mia mamma cammina _____ la sala.
6. Elena impara il tedesco _____ professori.
7. Mio zio entra _____ l'ufficio alle 8:00 del mattino.
8. Tommaso viaggia _____ mappe.
9. Sono uscita _____ ombrella oggi mentre pioveva.
10. Abbiamo regalato una borsa _____ suo compleanno.

B. Complete the following sentences adding **a** when it's needed:

Not all sentences require changing!
1. Manfredi domanda _____ Maria quando torna sua mamma.
2. Per favore, descrivi _____ un leone.
3. Teresa cerca _____ i cani per dargli da mangiare.
4. Silvia dà calci _____ la porta.
5. Nell'oceano ci sono _____ pesci.

C. Complete the following sentences choosing **a** or **di**.
1. Gli studenti ritornano _____ casa loro alle otto di sera.
2. Il martedì vado _____ Madrid.
3. Pietro fa esercizio _____ notte, non _____ giorno.
4. Sono le cinque _____ martedì sera.
5. Sofía è _____ Firenze.
6. Suo padre regala _____ sua figlia un cane.
7. Luigi viene _____ parlare con il dottore.
8. Quella bottiglia è _____ plastica.
9. La macchina è fatta _____ metallo.
10. Vado _____ letto perché sono stanco.

D. Complete these sentences choosing between **da** and **di**.
1. Torna _____ la festa alle quattro del mattino.
2. Torna _____ casa a piedi.
3. Mi piacciono i piatti _____ legno.
4. Guardiamo la gente _____ dal balcone.
5. Studia in quel collegio _____ tre anni.

14.3 Prepositions: fino a – da/ per – secondo – per – contro

fino a	until, up to, as far as	Expresses a limit	Cammina **fino alla** cucina. (*He/she walks up to the kitchen.*)
da/ per	by, for	Describes the means or cause for something. Also precedes a quantity of time.	Viaggia **in** barca. (*He/she travels by boat.*) Cammina **da** due ore. (*She walks for two hours.*)
secondo	according to	Used to describe the opinion of others. It's used before names and pronouns.	**Secondo** mia mamma, il film è brutto. (*According to my mom, the film is bad.*)
per	for, in order to	Used for deadlines, and to indicate purpose and destination	Il regalo è **per** la mia amica. (*The present is for my friend.*)
contro	against	Describes opposition	La lotta **contro** il cambiamento climatico. (*The battle against climate change.*)

Excited to play with sentences? Let's do it!

14.3 Practice

A. See if you can complete these sentences with the right preposition from this last group:
fino a – per – da – secondo – contro
1. L'uomo salta _____ finestra.
2. Il regalo è _____ suo figlio.
3. _____ la mia amica, il ristorante non è buono.
4. Camminiamo _____ casa.
5. Lei guarda la TV _____ un'ora.

6. Sono _____ le idee di quel professore.
7. Sta a casa mia _____ martedì.
8. C'è una camera da letto _____ due persone.
9. _____ il dottore, devi mangiare molta verdura e frutta.
10. Devo lavorare _____ tardi stasera.

B. Complete the sentences with the right preposition from this list:

fino a – per – secondo – contro

1. Questo oceano (*ocean*) arriva _____ coste africane (*the African coasts*).
2. _____ mio fratello, oggi le banche sono chiuse.
3. Per la Festa della Mamma, compro un regalo _____ mia mamma.
4. Durante la gara (*race*), nuotano _____ la corrente (*against the current*)
5. Nostro padre lavora _____ le nove di sera.

C. And now that you're more familiar with these prepositions, try to tackle the whole list with these sentences, filling in the blanks. These are the prepositions that you need:

a – tra – sopra – senza – con – per – secondo – fino a – da – su/sul – durante

1. Non corro _____ scarpe da ginnastica.
2. Maria porta la sua borsa _____ lei.
3. Questi regali sono _____ i miei amici.
4. _____ Paolo, il film non è bello.
5. I bambini corrono _____ noi.
6. Il professore parla _____ gli bambini.
7. Luigi corre _____ la maratona.
8. Il libro sta _____ tavolo.
9. L'auto sta _____ i due alberi.
10. Parlo _____ mio padre.

Ciao, vuoi sapere qualcosa di interessante? (*Did you know?*)

When you answer the phone in Italian, never say 'hello – ciao' like we do in English! Italians strictly answer the phone with **'pronto?!'** Yes, that's right, they use the word 'ready?!' to answer phone calls. In any other situation, the word pronto is used to say 'ready' but when answering the phone, **'pronto'** is the only word to use! Try yourself...

ring ring, ring ring

pronto, chi è?

LESSON 15 :

PREPOSITIONS II

THE BOX IS BEHIND THE CHAIR

Did you think we were done with prepositions? There are so many of them, and they're all so important! Let's look at some more of them. These, in particular, are crucial for describing where something is located.

15.1 Prepositions for Talking About Place and Position

Compound prepositions are prepositions that are used to describe a **location** or **position**.

accanto a	*next to*
intorno a	*around*
vicino	*near*
sotto a	*underneath*
sotto	*under (more figurative than **sotto a**)*
davanti a	*before, in front of (physical location)*
di fronte	*before, in front of, in the presence of*
dentro a	*inside of*
dietro a	*behind*
dopo	*after (in a set of expressions)*
in cima a	*on top of*
faccia a faccia, di fronte	*in front of, opposite, facing, across from*
fuori da	*outside of*
vicino a, attaccato a	*close to, right next to*
lontano da	*far from*

Vocabulary: Objects in a Home

A great way to practice these new prepositions you've learned is by using them with common household objects. How is your home arranged? Can you describe it using the prepositions you just learned?

English	Italian	Pronunciation
Bookcase	libreria	[lee-breh-ree-ah]
Desk	scrittoio (scrivania)	[skreet-toh-yoh]
Chair	sedia	[seh-dyah]
Computer	computer	[kohm-pyoo-tehr]
Backpack	zaino	[tsah-een-noh]
Picture	quadro	[kwah-droh]
Clock	orologio	[oh-roh-loh-joh]
Shelf	scaffale	[skahf-fah-leh]
Toys	giocattoli	[joh-kaht-toh-lee]
Ball	palla	[pahl-lah]
Stuffed teddy bear	orso di peluche	[ohr-soh deeh peh-loo-cheh]
Car	automobile	[ahw-toh-moh-bee-leh]
Helicopter	elicottero	[eh-lee-koht-teh-roh]
Pencil/ pencils	matita/matite	[mah-tee-tah]/ [mah-tee-teh]
Pencil holder	portamatite	[pohr-tah-mah-tee-teh]
Plant	pianta	[pyahn-tah]
Box	scatola	[skah-toh-lah]
Rug	tappeto	[tahp-peh-toh]

> **Tip:** In Italian **di + il** contract to form **del: La porta del negozio è aperta** (*The door of the store is open*) and **a + il** contract to form **al/alla: Cammina fino alla sala da pranzo** (*She walks up to the dining room*).

> **Tip:** Notice that when **accanto a** precedes **il,** it becomes **accanto al.** The same happens with other prepositions.

Remember: When talking about location and using prepositions, we normally use the verb **stare** (*to stay-to be*). Sometimes you can also use the verb **essere** (*to be*).

What is the difference?

stare → *to say where someone/something is/to say where something is positioned*

essere → *to say a more permanent state of being, location or quality*

In the examples below, you will be asked to use the verb **stare**, but always keep in mind, in some situations you can also use essere.

La matita sta sulla tavola.

La matita è sulla tavola.

Preposizioni articolate (articulated prepositions) in Italian are formed by combining simple prepositions with definite articles. Here's a table showing the combinations:

Simple Preposition	il	lo	l'	la	i	gli	le
di	del	dello	dell'	della	dei	degli	delle
a	al	allo	all'	alla	ai	agli	alle
da	dal	dallo	dall'	dalla	dai	dagli	dalle
in	nel	nello	nell'	nella	nei	negli	nelle
su	sul	sullo	sull'	sulla	sui	sugli	sulle
con	col*	collo*	coll'*	colla*	coi*	cogli*	colle*
per	pel*	pello*	pell'*	pella*	pei*	pegli*	pelle*

Note: The prepositions "con" and "per" rarely combine with articles in modern Italian; the forms marked with an asterisk (*) are considered archaic or poetic and are not commonly used in contemporary language.

This table includes the most common articulated prepositions, which are used frequently in Italian grammar.

Ready to apply what you know? Let's practice!

15.1 Practice

A. Fill in the blanks with the correct compound preposition.
   1. La palla sta _____ (inside of) la scatola.
   2. La palla sta _____ (outside of) la scatola.
   3. La palla sta _____ (on top of) la scatola.
   4. La palla sta _____ (underneath) la scatola.
   5. La palla sta _____ (right next to) la scatola.

B. Give the opposites of these compound prepositions.
    1. Dentro al → _____
    2. Dietro al → _____
    3. Vicino al → _____
    4. In cima al → _____
    5. Accanto al → _____

C. Fill in the blanks with the correct compound preposition. Remember, that if the compound preposition has a **a** and is followed by the article **il**, you should contract both.

    Example: La bambina sta <u>sotto all'albero</u> (sotto + a + il)
    1. L'auto sta _____ (behind) camion.
    2. Il portafoglio sta _____ (inside of) la borsa.
    3. La sedia sta _____ (in front of) tavolo.
    4. Lo zaino sta _____ (on top of) letto.
    5. Il gatto sta _____ (outside of) casa.

D. In this neighborhood, there is a main square surrounded by a church, the post office and the town hall, one next to the other. Behind the post office is the movie theater. There is a clock on top of the town hall. In the middle of the square there is a large park. On one of the sides of the square, there is a bar. The supermarket is twenty blocks away.

    Choose a word from the first, second, and third column to form sentences. You're also going to need a verb. "Stare" is probably the verb to use. Though you may also use "C'è".

    Example: La chiesa sta davanti alla piazza.

la chiesa	lontano da	il bar
l'ufficio postale	vicino a	la chiesa
il municipio	dietro a	il cinema
il bar	sotto a	l'ufficio postale
il cinema	accanto a	il municipio
la piazza	davanti a	la piazza
il supermercato	sopra a	orologio

1. _____
2. _____
3. _____
4. _____
5. _____

E. Translate the following sentences describing where the objects in a room are located by using the right preposition.

Example: The ball is next to the desk. La palla sta _____ **lo scrittoio. → La palla sta** <u>accanto allo</u> **scrittoio.**

1. The chair is in front of the desk: La sedia sta _____ scrittoio.
2. The computer is on top of the desk: Il computer sta _____ lo scrittoio.
3. The plant is underneath the picture: La pianta sta _____ il quadro.
4. The toys are inside the box: I giocattoli stanno _____ scatola.
5. The stuffed teddy bear is in front of the box: L'orso di peluche sta _____ la scatola.

F. Translate the following sentences describing where the objects in a room are located by using the right preposition.

1. The backpack is far from the bookcase: Lo zaino sta _____ libreria.
2. The painting is near the bookcase: Il Quadro sta _____ biblioteca.
3. The pencils are inside the pencil holder: Le matite stanno _____ il portamatite.
4. The stuffed teddy bear is outside the box: L'orso di peluche sta _____ la scatola.
5. The map is on the wall: La mappa sta _____ parete.

15.2 Expressing origin

In Italian you use the preposition, **da,** to express where you're from: **Sono dal Perú** or **Voi siete dal Belgio**. You can also use the verb **venire** followed by **da** to explain where *you come from*. For example, **io vengo dall'Italia** (*I come from Italy*).

And to ask where you're from, you need to use the preposition **di +** adverb **dove**, as in **Di dove sei tu?** (*Where are you from?*) or we can say **Da dove vieni tu?** (*Where do you come from?*)

Time to roll up your sleeves and practice!

15.2 Practice

Answer these questions according to the clues. Remember that you don't need to use the subject pronoun, as it is already implied in the verb form.

Example: Di dove sei tu? (Francia). <u>Sono dalla Francia.</u>

1. Di dov'è il signor Pérez? (Inghilterra) _____
2. Di dove sono tuoi amici? (Stati Uniti) _____
3. Di dove siete voi? (Italia) voi → noi _____
4. Di dove sono Elena e Julio? (Canada) _____
5. Di dove siete voi? (Spagna) _____
6. Di dov'è Martino? (Germania) _____
7. Di dove sono loro? (Belgio) _____

8. Di dove sei tu? (Brasile) _____

9. Di dov'è Emma? (Italia) _____

10. Di dove sono i tuoi nonni? (Messico) _____

15.3 Giving and following directions

Are you lost? Let us help you! It's useful to know how to speak Italian when asking for directions in an Italian speaking country. Some verbs you'll need to know are:

English	Italian	Pronunciation
To take	**prendere**	[prehn-deh-reh]
To follow	**seguire**	[ech gwee-reh]
To drive forward	**guidare verso**	[gwee-dah-reh vehr-soh]
To turn	**svoltare**	[svohl-tah-reh]
To make a turn	**girare**	[jee-rah-reh]
To explain	**spiegare**	[spee-eh-gah-reh]
To reach/ to arrive	**arrivare**	[ahr-ree-vah-reh]

Adverbs of Time
⮑ dopo (*after*)
⮑ poi (*after, then*)
⮑ allora (*so, then*)
⮑ mentre (*meanwhile/ meantime*)

Vocabulary: The Street

English	Italian	Pronunciation
The block	**l'isolato**	[lee-soh-lah-toh]
The street	**la strada**	[lah strah-dah]
The avenue	**il viale**	[eel vee-ah-leh]
The sidewalk	**il marciapiede**	[eel mahr-chee-ah-pee-eh-deh]
The main square	**la piazza principale**	[lah pyaht-tsah preen-chee-pah-leh]
The traffic light	**il semaforo**	[eel seh-mah-foh-roh]
Straight	**dritto**	[dreet-toh]

English	Italian	Pronunciation
The train tracks	**linea ferroviaria**	*[leeh-neh-ah fehr-roh-vee-ah-ryah]*
To the right	**a destra**	*[ah deh-strah]*
To the left	**a sinistra**	*[ah see-nee-strah]*
The corner	**l'angolo**	*[lahn-goh-loh]*
The bus stop	**la fermata del bus**	*[lah fehr-mah-tah dehl boohs]*
North	**nord**	*[nohrd]*
South	**sud**	*[sood]*
West	**ovest**	*[oh-vehst]*
East	**est**	*[ehst]*
The intersection	**incrocio**	*[een-kroh-tschyoh]*
The traffic circle	**la rotonda**	*[lah roh-tohn-dah]*
The police	**la polizia**	*[lah poh-lee-tsee-ah]*
The officer	**l'agente**	*[lah-jehn-teh]*

Time for words! Let's practice a bit!

15.3 Practice

A.   You're in an Italian-speaking city. How would you ask for these directions?

Example: Excuse me, could you please tell me where there is a public bathroom?
In Italian we'll say: Mi scusi, può dirmi per favore dove c'è un bagno pubblico?

1.   Please, can you tell me where the closest restaurant is?
Per favore, sa dirmi _____?

2.   Excuse me, can you tell me how many blocks there are to the supermarket?
Mi scusi, sa dirmi _____?

3.   Could you please tell me how to get to the main square?
Mi scusi, sa dirmi _____?

4.   Excuse me, can you please tell me where the drugstore is?
Mi scusi, sa dirmi per favore _____?

5.   Could you please tell me where the bus stop is?
Mi scusi, sa dirmi _____?

Speak Abroad
Academy

B. Now see if you can translate the following dialogue

Per strada

TERESA: Buongiorno, sa dove sta la banca?

AGENTE: Sì, le spiego. È a nord. Deve seguire questo viale fino a raggiungere l'incrocio. Poi deve svoltare a destra e procedere fino al semaforo, verso est.

TERESA: Quanti isolati sono fino al semaforo?

AGENTE: Sono cinque isolati fino al semaforo. Al semaforo, deve girare a sinistra, verso nord, e continuare per due isolati. Raggiunta una rotonda, alla rotonda, continui sulla stessa strada per un isolato. Poi deve girare a destra e procedere per altri sette isolati. Dopo svolga di nuovo a sinistra e proceda per un altro isolato. La banca sta all'angolo, sulla destra.

TERESA: Grazie mille, agente. Spero di arrivarci!

C. You're in Italy and you want to help a lost tourist by giving them directions. Translate the following suggestions to Italian.

Example: You should turn left at the light → Deve svoltare a sinistra al semaforo.

1. You should continue on the avenue until you get to the corner:

    _____

2. You should take a right and continue straight:

    _____

3. You should continue straight until you reach the light:

    _____

4. You should make a turn at the light:

    _____

5. You should turn left and continue five blocks until you get to the main square:

    _____

Posso dirti una cosa? *(Can I tell you one thing?)*

Pistacchio is one of the most traditional flavors of gelato. But don't be fooled, make sure you get the real deal! True Italian pistachio gelato is a faded green, almost light brown color – so don't go for the vibrant green pistachio flavor and always remember, no matter how full you may be after all of that pizza, pasta and lasagna there is ALWAYS room for gelato!

SECTION II:
WORDS AND PHRASES

EVERYDAY ESSENTIALS

Conversation essentials

When you learn a new language and interact with people who are native speakers, it is normal that you often don't understand their accents or some of the words they use. For that reason, here are some options to use when the message is not clear.

English	Italian	Pronunciation
Can you repeat that?	Puoi ripeterlo?	[pwoy ree-peh-tehr-lo]
I can't hear you.	Non riesco a sentirti.	[nohn ree-eh-skoh ah sehn-teer-tee]
I don't understand your question.	Non capisco la tua domanda.	[nohn kah-pee-skoh lah twah doh-mahn-dah]
Can you please say that in English?	Puoi dirlo in inglese?	[pwoy'deer-lo in een-gleh-seh]
How do you say ___ in Italian?	Come si dice ___ in italiano?	[koh-meh see dee-cheh ___ in ih-tah-lee-ah-no]

In case you want to sound like a local speaker, to sound more friendly and impress native speakers, you could use these expressions:

English	Italian	Pronunciation
I'm just kidding.	Sto solo scherzando.	[stoh soh-loh skehr-tshn-doh]
That's very impressive.	Questo è davvero notevole.	[kweh-stho eh dahv-veh-roh noh-teh-voh-leh]
Go ahead.	Procedi.	[proh-cheh-dee]
That's very interesting.	Questo è davvero interessante.	[kweh-stho eh dahv-veh-roh een-teh-rehs-sahn-teh]
You have to be kidding me.	Mi stai prendendo in giro.	[mee stah-y prehn-dehn-doh in jih-roh]
You know what I mean.	Sai a cosa mi riferisco.	[sah-y ah koh-sah mee ree-feh-ree-skoh]

In case you need to start a conversation cordially, you should start with the following phrases according to the time of the day:

English	Italian	Pronunciation
Welcome	**Benvenuto**	*[behn-veh-noo-toh]*
Good morning	**Buongiorno**	*[bwon-johr-noh]*
Good afternoon	**Buon pomeriggio**	*[Bwohn poh-meh-ree-joh]*
Good evening	**Buonasera**	*[Bwoh-nah seh-rah]*

If you are visiting a foreign country where Italian is spoken, you have two options: you can ask them if they speak English, or they can ask you if you speak Italian.

Do you speak English?	**Parli inglese?**	*[Pahr-lee een-gleh-seh?]*
Do you speak Spanish?	**Parli spagnolo?**	*[Par-lee spah-nyoh-loh?]*

If this happens, there are two key responses you can identify and two more you can respond to:

English	Italian	Pronunciation
I don't speak English.	**Non parlo inglese.**	*[Nohn pahr-loh een-gleh-seh]*
I speak English.	**Sì, parlo inglese.**	*[See pahr-loh een-gleh-seh]*
I don't speak Italian.	**Non parlo italiano.**	*[Nohn pahr-loh ee-tah-lee-ah-no]*
I speak Italian.	**Sì, parlo italiano.**	*[See pahr-loh ee-tah-lee-ah-no]*

In addition, here are some responses you may hear from locals, and you could use them to sound more friendly.

I speak English a little.	**Parlo un po' di inglese.**	*[Pahr-loh uhn poh dee een-gleh-seh]*
I speak Italian a little.	**Parlo un po' di italiano.**	*[Pahr-loh uhn poh dee ee-tah-lee-ah-no]*

Now let's explore some quick and handy Italian responses! We'll start with a few short answers to help you get the hang of Italian. These snappy phrases will add a touch of Italian charm to your conversations. Ready to dive in? Here are a few to start building your Italian skills:

English	Italian	Pronunciation
Yes	Sí	[See]
No	No	[Noh]
Excuse me	Scusa	[Skoo-zah]
I don't know	Non lo so	[Nohn loh soh]
I don't understand	Non capisco	[Nohn kah-pee-skoh]
I'm sorry	Mi dispiace	[Mee dee-spee-ah-cheh]
Thank you	Grazie	[Grah-tsee-eh]
I hank you very much	Molte grazie	[Mohl-teh grah-tsee-eh]
Please	Per favore	[Pehr fah-voh-reh]
Goodbye [formal]	Arrivederci	[Ahr-ree-veh-dehr-chee]
Goodbye [informal]	Ciao	[Chee-ah-oh]
See you later	Ci vediamo dopo	[Chee veh-dee-ah-moh doh-poh]
Hope to see you again	Spero di rivederti	[Speh-roh dee ree-veh-dehr-tee]
Hope to see you soon	Spero di vederti presto	[Speh-roh dee ree-veh-dehr-tee preh-stoh]

Talking about the weather

It is very important to know how to ask for the weather in the new languages you are looking to learn, because when you travel to an Italian country for tourism, sometimes the weather may vary. Moreover, the weather always makes for a good conversation starter as it breaks the ice pretty fast. For that reason, here are some key questions to ask about the weather:

English	Italian	Pronunciation
What's the weather like today?	Che tempo fa oggi?	[Keh tehm-poh fah?]
What will the weather be like tomorrow?	Come sarà il tempo domani?	[Koh-meh sah-rah eel tehm-poh doh-mah-nee?]
Will it rain tomorrow?	Pioverà domani?	[Pee-oh-veh-rah doh-mah-nee?]
This is a beautiful day.	Oggi è una bella giornata.	[Ohj-jee eh uhnah behl-lah johr-nah-tah]
It will rain most of next week.	Pioverà quasi tutta la prossima settimana.	[Pee-oh-veh-rah kwa-see twt-tah lah prohs-see-mah seht-tee-mah-nah]
The weather is good.	Il tempo è bello.	[eel tehm-poh eh behl-lo]

Moreover, the correct ways of describing the weather can be varied just like in English, so here you will learn how to express yourself correctly, according to the weather of the day.

English	Italian	Pronunciation
Rainy	Piovoso	[Pee-oh-voh-soh]
Sunny	Soleggiato	[Soh-lehj-jah-toh]
Thunder	Tuono	[Twoh-noh]
Windy	Ventoso	[Vehn-toh-soh]
Snowing	Nevoso	[Neh-voh-soh]
Cloudy	Nuvoloso	[Noo-voh-loh-soh]
Fog	Nebbia	[Nehb-beeah]
Storm	Tempesta	[Tehm-peh-stah]
Hail	Grandine	[Grahn-dee-neh]
Hot [weather]	Torrido	[Tohr-ree-doh]
Cold	Freddo	[Frehd-doh]
Warm	Caldo	[Kahl-doh]

Finally, let's chat about the four seasons in Italian: We'll explore the words for each season, making it easy for you to talk about different times of the year in Italian. Get ready to learn about spring, summer, fall, and winter!

Spring	**Primavera**	*[Pree-mah-veh-rah]*
Summer	**Estate**	*[Eh-stah-teh]*
Autumn	**Autunno**	*[Awh-toon-noh]*
Winter	**Inverno**	*[Een-vehr-noh]*

Compliments & Showing Gratitude

Compliments play a crucial role in fostering positive connections and uplifting the human experience. They act as bridges, connecting individuals and fostering a sense of camaraderie. They transcend language barriers, cultural differences, and societal divides, creating moments of shared positivity. This is why it is so important to compliment a place or thing in the native tongue. You can use the following common expressions used by the locals.

Here are some simple sentences to express your compliments:

English	Italian	Pronunciation
You have a beautiful home.	**Hai una casa splendida.**	*[ahy uh-nah kah-sah splehn-dee-dah]*
You've been a great host.	**Sei stato un perfetto padrone di casa.**	*[say stah-toh uhn pehr-feht-toh pah-droh-neh dee kah-sah]*
You've been a wonderful host.	**Sei stato un padrone di casa meraviglioso.**	*[say stah-toh uhn pah-droh-neh dee kah-sah meh-rah-vee-lyoh-soh]*
Thank you for your help.	**Grazie per il tuo aiuto.**	*[Grah-tsee-eh pehr eel twoh ah-yooh- toh]*
Thank you for your assistance.	**Grazie per la tua assistenza.**	*[Grah-tsee-eh pehr eel twoh ah-yooh- toh]*
You've been a great friend.	**Sei stato un ottimo amico.**	*[Say stah-toh uhn oht-tee-moh ah-mee-koh]*
Thank you for your kindness.	**Grazie per la tua gentilezza.**	*[Grah-tsee-eh pehr lah twah jehn-tee-leht-tsah]*
You're very kind.	**Sei molto gentile.**	*[Say mohl-toh jehn-tee-leh]*

Gratitude is the powerful force that transforms ordinary moments into extraordinary experiences. At its core, gratitude is a catalyst for connection. When we express thanks, we strengthen the bonds with those around us, creating a network of appreciation and support. Therefore, being grateful in Italy is essential and the locals appreciate gratitude, so these expressions will help you to adapt to the culture and be more friendly.

English	Italian	Pronunciation
Thank you for cooking this delicious meal.	**Grazie per aver cucinato questa cena deliziosa.**	*[Grah-tsee-eh pehr ah-vehr koo-chee-nah-toh kweh-stah cheh-nah deh-lee-tsyoh-sah]*
Thank you for the hospitality.	**Grazie per l'ospitalità.**	*[Grah-tsee-eh pehr lah twah oh-spee-tah-lee-tah]*
I appreciate your concern.	**Apprezzo la tua preoccupazione.**	*[Ahp-preht-tsoh lah twah preh-ohk-kooh-pah-tseeoh-neh]*
Thank you for organizing this wonderful event.	**Grazie per aver organizzato questo meraviglioso evento.**	*[Grah-tsee-eh pehr ah-vehr ohr-gah-neet-tsah-toh kweh-stoh meh-rah-vee-lyoh-soh eh-vehn-toh]*
Thank you for inviting me.	**Grazie per il tuo invito.**	*[Grah-tsee-eh pehr eel twoh een-vee-toh]*
I own you a great deal.	**Ti devo un favore!**	*[Tee deh-voh uhn fah-voh-reh!]*
You've made my day.	**Mi hai rallegrato la giornata.**	*[Mee ahy rahl-leh-grah-toh lah johr-nah-tah]*
What would I do without you?	**Che farei senza di te?**	*[Keh fah-reh-y sehn-tsah dee teh]*

Italian is the language of romance. This is why there are several types of compliments. Below, you can find some essential sentences to show your appreciation and compliment people:

English	Italian	Pronunciation
You're pretty.	**Sei carina/o.**	*[Say kah-ree-nah]/ [kah-ree-noh]*
You're funny.	**Sei divertente.**	*[Say dee-vehr-tehn-teh]*
You're handsome.	**Sei affascinante.**	*[Say ahf-fah-shee-nahn-teh]*
I love your smile.	**Amo il tuo sorriso.**	*[Ah-moh eel twoh sohr-ree-soh]*
You have beautiful eyes.	**Hai degli occhi belli.**	*[Ahy deh-ly ohk-kee behl-lee]*

Speak Abroad
Academy

English	Italian	Pronunciation
You look good today.	Ti trovo bene oggi.	[Tee troh-voh beh-neh ohj-jee]
You look gorgeous.	Ti trovo bellissimo/a.	[Tee troh-voh behl-lees-see-moh] / [behl-lees-see-mah]
	Ti trovo bello/a.	[Tee troh-voh behl-loh] / [behl-lah]
I like your shirt.	Mi piace la tua maglietta.	[Mee peeah-cheh lah twah mah-lyeht-tah]
I love your attitude.	Amo il tuo modo di essere.	[Ah-moh eel twoh moh-doh dee ehs-seh-reh]
You're the best.	Sei la migliore.	[Say lah mee-lyoh-reh]
	Sei il migliore.	[Say eel mee-lyoh-reh]

BUILDING CONNECTIONS

Italians are maestros in the art of building connections through conversations. Every exchange becomes a bridge between individuals, fostering bonds that extend beyond mere words. In Italy, conversations are more than dialogue; they are a shared experience, a dance of ideas and emotions. Whether sipping espresso at a café or engaging in animated discussions during family dinners, Italians infuse their conversations with warmth and genuine interest. Conversations in Italy are not just a means of communication; they are a celebration of shared moments and a testament to the nation's commitment to building meaningful relationships. This is why it's so important to master the art of basic introductions.

Basic introductions

Let's begin with a simple way to start a conversation when meeting someone for the first time. This way you can introduce yourself to someone new.

Hello, how are you?	**Ciao, come stai?**	*[Cheeah-oh, koh-meh stah-y?]*
Hello, my name is Juan. (In-formal)	**Ciao, mi chiamo Giovanni.**	*[Cheeah-oh, mee kee-ah-moh Joh-vahn-nee]*
Hello, my name is Juan. (formal)	**Salve, il mio nome è Giovanni.**	*[Sahl-veh, eel meeoh noh-meh eh Joh-vahn-nee]*

Here are some other questions you can use to create a conversation with a new person or friend:

English	Italian	Pronunciation
How was your day?	**Com'è andata la tua giornata?**	*[Koh-meh eh ahn-dah-tah lah twah johr-nah-tah?]*
Where are you from?	**Di dove sei?**	*[Dee doh-veh say?]*
What's your name?	**Qual è il tuo nome?**	*[Kwahl ehs eel twoh noh-meh?]*
How old are you?	**Quanti anni hai?**	*[Kwahn-tee ahn-nee ahy?]*
When is your birthday?	**Quando è il tuo compleanno?**	*[Kwahn-doh eh eel twoh kohm-pleh-ahn-noh?]*
Do you have siblings?	**Hai fratelli?**	*[Ahy frah-tehl-lee?]*
Do you have a big family?	**Hai una famiglia grande?**	*[Ahy uhnah fah-mee-lyah grahn-deh?]*

English	Italian	Pronunciation
Do you live alone?	**Vivi da solo?** **Vivi da sola?**	[Vee-vee dah soh-loh?] [Vee-vee dah soh-lah?]
Do you have pets?	**Hai animali domestici?**	[Ahy ah-nee-mah-lee doh-meh-stee-chee?]
Where do you live?	**Dove vivi?**	[Doh-veh vee-vee?]

Some responses you may receive when you start an introductory conversation are as follows:

English	Italian	Pronunciation
Fine, and you?	**Bene, e tu?**	[Beh-neh oh too?]
Nice to meet you.	**Piacere di conoscerti.**	[Peeah-cheh-reh dee koh-noh-shehr-tee]
I'm from Spain.	**Io sono spagnolo/a.**	[Ee-oh soh-noh spah-nyoh-loh]/ [spah-nyoh-lah]
I live in Barcelona.	**Io vivo a Barcellona.**	[Ee-oh vee-voh ah Bahr-chehl-loh-nah]
We live in Barcelona.	**Noi viviamo a Barcellona.**	[Noh-y vee-veeah-moh ah Bahr-chehl-loh-nah]
I have five [5] brothers.	**Ho cinque [5] fratelli.**	[Oh cheen-kweh frah-tehl-lee]
I have five [5] sisters.	**Ho cinque [5] sorelle.**	[Oh cheen-kweh soh-rehl-leh]
I'm an only child.	**Sono figlio unico.** **Sono figlia unica.**	[Soh-noh fee-lyoh oo-nee-koh] [Soh-noh fee-lyah oo-nee-kah]

Now, let's talk about the formal titles that you can use when talking to a person. It is worth noting that for the male term, we have only one variation [Signore]; however, for the female term there are two variations: [Signorina] used to refer to a single person, and [Signora] used to refer to a married person.

Miss	**Signorina**	[See-nyo-ree-nah]
Mrs	**Signora**	[Seeh-nyo-rah]
Mister	**Signore**	[Seeh-nyo-reh]

In addition, here are some small phrases you can use when introducing a person or describing your relationship status:

English	Italian	Pronunciation
This is my friend.	Questo è il mio amico. Questa è la mia amica.	[Kweh-stoh eh eel meeoh ah-mee-koh] [Kweh-stah eh lah meeah ah-mee-kah]
This is my husband.	Questo è mio marito.	[Kweh-sto eh meeoh mah-ree-toh]
This is my wife.	Questa è mia moglie.	[Kweh-stah eh meeah moh-lyeh]
I'm single.	Sono nubile. Sono celibe.	[Soh-noh noo-bee-leh] [Soh-noh cheh-lee-beh]
I'm married.	Sono sposata. Sono sposato.	[Soh-noh spoh-sah-tah] [Soh-noh spoh-sah-tah]
I'm divorced.	Sono divorziata. Sono divorziato.	[Soh-noh dee-vohr-tseeah-tah] [Soh-noh dee-vohr-tseeah-toh]

Work and professions

To find out more about a person, one option is to ask them about their work and what they do. Here you can find some options:

English	Italian	Pronunciation
What do you do for a living?	Cosa fai per vivere?	[Koh-sah fahy pehr vee-veh-reh?]
Where do you work?	Dove lavori?	[Doh-veh lah-voh-ree?]
How often do you work?	Con che frequenza lavori?	[Kohn keh freh-kwehn-tsah lah-voh-ree?]
How much do you earn?	Quanto guadagni?	[Kwahn-toh gwah-dah-nyh?]
How many hours do you work a week?	Quante ore lavori a settimana?	[Kwahn-teh oh-reh lah-voh-ree ah seht-tee-mah-nah?]
What time do you work?	A che ora lavori?	[Ah keh oh-rah lah-voh-ree?]
When is your day off?	Qual è il tuo giorno libero?	[Kwahl eh eel twoh johr-noh lee-beh-roh?]

Speak Abroad
Academy

Below are some answers you can expect to the previous questions asked about a person's job or profession:

English	Italian	Pronunciation
I work from home.	**Lavoro da casa.**	*[Lah-voh-roh dah kah-sah]*
I work freelance.	**Lavoro freelance.**	*[Lah-voh-roh freelance]*
I work a lot.	**Lavoro tanto.**	*[lah-voh-roh tahn-toh]*
I don't work on the weekends.	**Non lavoro il fine settimana.**	*[Nohn lah-voh-roh eel fee-neh seht-tee-mah-nah]*
I'm a ___	**Io sono ___**	*[Eeoh soh-noh ___]*
I work in the hospital.	**Lavoro in ospedale.**	*[Lah-voh-roh een oh-speh-dah-leh]*
My day off is Tuesday.	**Il mio giorno libero è il martedì.**	*[Eel meeoh johr-noh lee-beh-roh eh eel mahr-teh-dee]*
I work from nine [9] in the morning.	**Lavoro dalle nove [9] di mattina.**	*[Lah-voh-roh dahl-leh noh-veh dee maht-tee-nah]*

Here is a brief list of professions in Italian:

English	Italian	Pronunciation
Architect	**Architetto**	*[Ahr-kee-teht-toh]*
Actor	**Attore**	*[Aht-toh-reh]*
Actress	**Attrice**	*[Aht-tree-cheh]*
Dentist	**Dentista**	*[Dehn-tee-stah]*
Doctor	**Dottore**	*[Doht-toh-reh]*
	Dottoressa	*[Doht-toh-rehs-sah]*
Carpenter	**Carpentiere**	*[Kahr-pehn-teeheh-reh]*
Accountant	**Ragioniere**	*[Rah-joh-nyeh-reh]*
	Ragioniera	*[Rah-joh-nyeh-rah]*
Cooker	**Cuoco**	*[Kwoh-koh]*
	Cuoca	*[Kwoh-kah]*
Baker	**Panettiere/a**	*[Pah-neht-tee-eh-reh]*
		[Pah-neht-tee-eh-rah]
Mechanic	**Meccanico**	*[Meh-kah-nee-koh]*
Police Officer	**Poliziotto/a**	*[Poh-lee-tsee-oh-toh] / [Poh-lee-tsee-oh-tah]*

English	Italian	Pronunciation
Psychologist	Psicologo/a	[Psee-koh-loh-goh] [Psee-koh-loh-gah]
Teacher	Professore Professoressa	[Proh-fehs-soh-reh] [Proh-fehs-soh-rehs-sah]
Surgeon	Chirurgo/a	[Kee-roohr-goh] [Kee-rohr-gah]
Pilot	Pilota	[Pee-loh-tah]
Firefighter	Pompiere	[Pohm-pee-eh-reh]
Lawyer	Avvocato Avvocatessa	[Ahv-voh-kah-toh] [Ahv-voh-kah-teh-sah]
Nurse	Infermiera/e	[Een-fehr-mee-eh-rah] [Een-fehr-mee-eh-reh]

Making plans

Once you've made a new friend, the next step is planning some enjoyable activities together. To assist you in coordinating your plans, here are some fundamental questions to consider:

English	Italian	Pronunciation
When are you free to hang out?	Quando sei libero/a per uscire?	[Kwahn-doh say lee-beh-rah pehr oo-shee-reh?]
What time should we meet up?	A che ora ci incontriamo?	[Ah keh oh-rah chee een-kohn-treeah-moh?]
Where should we go?	Dove andiamo?	[Doh-veh ahn-deeah-moh?]
Do you have plans tonight?	Hai programmi per stasera?	[Ahy proh-grahm-mee pehr stah-seh-rah?]
Do you want to go to a party?	Vuoi venire a una festa?	[Woee veh-nee-reh ah uhnah feh-stah?]
Are you free tomorrow?	Sei libero/a domani?	[Say lee-beh-rah doh-mah-nee?]
What are you going to do tonight?	Che fai stasera?	[Keh fahy stah-seh-rah?]
What time will we meet?	A che ora ci incontriamo?	[Ah keh oh-rah chee een-kohn-treeah-moh?]

Speak Abroad
Academy

Certainly, if you're posed with these questions, it's essential to respond appropriately. Here are several different options for your potential answers.

English	Italian	Pronunciation
Let's watch a movie this week.	Andiamo a vedere un film questa settimana.	[Ahn-deeah-moh ah veh-deh-reh uhn feelm kweh-stah seht-tee-mah-nah]
Let's go to the ___ this weekend.	Andiamo al ___ questo fine settimana.	[Ahn-deeah-moh ahl ___ kweh-sto fee-neh seht-tee-mah-nah]
Let's go to a party.	Andiamo a una festa.	[Ahn-deeah-moh ah uhnah feh-stah]
Let's go out tonight.	Usciamo questa sera.	[Ooh ohccah moh kweh-stah seh-rah]
I'm only free in the evening.	Sono libero/a solo la sera.	[Soh-noh lee-beh-roh soh-loh eel fee-neh seht-tee-mah-nah]
I'll meet you at the mall at four [4] in the afternoon.	Ci vediamo al centro commerciale alle quattro [4] del pomeriggio.	[Chee veh-deeah-moh ahl chehn-troh kohm-mehr-cheeah-leh ahl-leh kwaht-troh dehl poh-meh-reej-joh]
I don't have plans tonight.	Non ho programmi per stasera.	[Nohn oh proh-grahm-mee pehr stah-seh-rah]
We should meet in the afternoon.	Incontriamoci nel pomeriggio.	[Een-kohn-treeah-moh-chee nehl poh-meh-reej-joh]

Furthermore, these are some keywords that are likely to help you construct sentences on your own:

English	Italian	Pronunciation
Beach	Spiaggia	[spee-ahj-jah]
Mall	Centro commerciale	[chehn-troh kohm-mehr-cheeah-leh]
Store	Negozio	[neh-goh-tsyoh]
Market	Mercato	[mehr-kah-toh]
House	Casa	[kah-sah]
Living room	Soggiorno	[sohj-johr-noh]
Bedroom	Camera da letto	[kah-meh-rah dah leht-toh]
Bathroom	Bagno	[bah-nyoh]
Cinema	Cinema	[chee-neh-mah]
Restaurant	Ristorante	[reeh-stoh-rahn-teh]

English	Italian	Pronunciation
Super Market	Supermercato	[soo-pehr-mehr-kah-toh]
School	Collegio	[koh-leh-joh]
	Scuola	[skwoh-lah]
University	Università	[ooh-nee-vehr-see-tah]
Library	Biblioteca	[bee-bleeoh-teh-kah]
Pool	Piscina	[pee-she-nah]
Apartment	Appartamento	[ahp-pahr-tah-mehn-toh]
Kitchen	Cucina	[koo-chee-nah]
Dining room	Sala da pranzo	[sah-lah dah prahn-tsoh]

Flirting

Flirting always seems to be the priority when learning a new language and being friendly is the important thing. That's why here are some questions to communicate with someone you want to flirt with and catch their attention.

English	Italian	Pronunciation
Can I buy you a drink?	Posso invitarti a bere qualcosa?	[pohs-soh een-vee-tahr-tee ah beh-reh kwahl-koh-sah?]
Are you single?	Sei single?	[say single?]
Can I join you?	Posso farti compagnia?	[pohs-soh fahr-tee kohm-pah-nyah?]
Can I have your number?	Mi dai il tuo numero?	[mee dahy eel twoh noo-meh-roh?]
Do you have a boyfriend/ girlfriend?	Sei fidanzato/ fidanzata?	[say fee-dahn-tsah-toh/ fee-dahn-tsah-tah?]
Can I give you a kiss?	Posso darti un bacio?	[pohs-soh dahr-tee uhn bah-chyoh?]
Do you like roses?	Ti piacciono le rose?	[tee pee-ah-cheeoh-noh leh roh-seh?]
Do you want to hang out with me?	Ti va di uscire con me?	[tee vah dee ooh-she-reh kohn meh?]
Do you want to be my boyfriend/girlfriend?	Vuoi essere la mia fidanzata/fidanzato?	[woy ehs-seh-reh lah myah fee-dahn-tsah-tah/ fee-dahn-tsah-toh?]

English	Italian	Pronunciation
Are you an angel?	**Sei un angelo?**	*[say uhn ahn-jehl-loh?]*
Do you wanna dance?	**Vuoi ballare?**	*[woy bahl-lah-reh?]*
When can I see you again?	**Quando posso rivederti?**	*[kwahn-doh pohs-soh ree-veh-dehr-tee?]*

In addition to questions, there are also very typical and well-known phrases to flirt with a person in any situation or place. That's why here are some phrases to show your affection towards someone.

English	Italian	Pronunciation
This dress looks amazing on you.	**Questo vestito ti sta benissimo.**	*[kweh-stoh veh-stee-toh tee stah beh-nees-see-moh]*
Your smile is contagious.	**Il tuo sorriso è contagioso.**	*[Tuh sohn-ree-sah ehs kohn-tah-geeoh-sah]*
You're perfect to me.	**Sei perfetta per me.** **Sei perfetto per me.**	*[say pehr-feht-tah pehr meh]* *[say pehr-feht-toh pehr meh]*
I want to be your boyfriend/girlfriend.	**Voglio essere il tuo fidanzato/fidanzata.**	*[voh-lyoh ehs-seh-reh eel twoh fee-dahn-tsah-toh/ fee-dahn-tsah-tah]*
You dance very well.	**Balli molto bene.**	*[bahl-lee mohl-toh beh-neh]*
I'll take you out to eat later.	**Ti invito a mangiare più tardi.**	*[tee een-vee-toh ah mahn-jah-reh pyooh tahr-dee]*
Don't worry. It's on me.	**Non ti preoccupare. Offro io.**	*[nohn tee preh-ohk-koo-pah-reh. Of-roh ee-yoh]*
I like you very much.	**Mi piaci tanto. (couple) / mi vai a genio. (friends)**	*[mee pee-ah-chee tahn-toh/ mee vahee ah jeh-nyoh]*
I like your smile.	**Mi piace il tuo sorriso.**	*[mee pee-ah-cheh eel twoh sohr-ree-soh]*
I like your lips.	**Mi piacciono le tue labbra.**	*[mee pee-ah-tchyoh-noh leh tweh lahb-brah]*
I would like to hang out with you.	**Vorrei uscire con te.**	*[vohr-rehy uh-she-reh kohn teh]*
You look like an angel.	**Ti vedo come un angelo.**	*[teeh veh-doh koh-meh uhn ahn-jeh-loh]*

LEARN ITALIAN
3-IN-1 BUNDLE

Common slang

Now we will talk about some common phrases you may hear in Italian. Below, we will present some phrases with their respective explanations, so that you can understand when to use each.

1. *Fighi/ Fighe*

   The word "Fighi/Fighe" is commonly used by Italians to refer to something that looks or is cool.

These sunglasses are cool.	**Questi occhiali da sole sono fighi.**	[kweh-stee ohk-keeah-lee dah so-leh soh-noh fee-gee]

2. *D'accordo*

   This simple word is the same when an English speaker says "okay".

Okay	**D'accordo**	[dahk-kohr-doh]

3. *Assurdo*

   Italian speakers use it when something happens that they find shocking.

How crazy that you get fired for that situation!	**Assurdo che ti licenziano per quella situazione!**	[ahs-soohr-doh keh tee lee-chehn-tsyah-noh pehr kwehl-lah see-tooah-tseeoh-neh]

4. *Figo*

   Locals use this in a positive way to express how cool objects and places are.

This shopping center is very cool.	**Questo centro commerciale è molto figo.**	[kweh-stoh chehn-troh kohm-mehr-cheeah-leh eh mohl-toh fee-goh]

5. *Che carino*

   Italian speakers use "carini" to describe something as "cute".

How cute are those pants.	**Che carini quei pantaloni.**	[keh kah-ree-nee kwey pahn-tah-loh-nee]

Building connections

6. *A proprio agio*

Use this slang term to describe how comfortable you are. Being "a mio agio" means feeling good in a place or with someone.

I feel comfortable with you.	**Mi sento a mio agio con te.**	*[mee sehn-toh ah meeoh ah-joh kohn teh]*

7. *Zía/Zío*

The literal meaning of "zía" is "aunt" and "zío" means "uncle", but people use it meaning "friend", so when you wanna talk to a friend and sound like a pro, call them "zía" or "zío".

What's up friend?	**Che succede, zia?**	*[keh soo-cheh-deh tsee-ah?]*
	Che succede, zio?	*[keh soo-cheh-deh tsee-oh?]*

8. *Non ci posso credere*

Locals took this slang word from the English verb "to flip" or "flip out," so it's an easy Italian slang word for English speakers to pick up when expressing anger or surprise.

Your mom said that? I can't believe it!	**Tua mamma ha detto così? *Non ci posso credere!***	*[twah mahm-mah ah deht-toh koh-see? Nohn chee pohs-soh kreh-deh-reh]*

Speak Abroad
Academy

SHOPPING AND DINING OUT

Practicalities

Dining in Italy is a sensory celebration of fresh, quality ingredients and rich culinary traditions. From handmade pasta to local wines, each meal tells a story of regional heritage, shared amidst lively conversations and the clinking of glasses. When you want or have to go out to a restaurant with your friends or for an individual dinner; whether you're indulging in a leisurely dinner at a rustic trattoria or savoring a quick espresso at a bustling café; these questions can help you to communicate easily with the waiters.

English	Italian	Pronunciation
Can I book a table for ___ people?	Posso prenotare un tavolo per ___ persone?	[pohs-soh preh-noh-tah-reh uhn tah-voh-loh pehr ___ pehr-soh-neh?]
How long is the wait for a table?	Quanto tempo c'è da aspettare per avere un tavolo?	[kwahn-toh tee-ehm-poh cheh dah ah-speht-tah-reh pehr ah-veh-reh uhn tah-voh-loh?]
Can I reserve a table for tonight?	Posso prenotare un tavolo per stasera?	[pohs-soh preh-noh-tah-reh uhn tah-voh-loh pehr stah-seh-rah?]
A table for two, please?	Un tavolo per due, per favore?	[uhn tah-voh-loh pehr dweh, pehr fah-voh-reh?]
Is this restaurant accessible to wheelchairs?	Questo ristorante è abilitato per le sedie a rotelle?	[kweh-stoh ree-stoh-rahn-teh eh ah-bee-lee-tah-toh pehr leh seh-dyeh ah roh-tehl-leh?]
Are children allowed in this restaurant?	Si ammettono bambini in questo ristorante?	[see ahm-meht-toh-noh bahm-bee-nee een kweh-stoh ree-stoh-rahn-teh?]
Do you serve alcohol?	Servite alcolici?	[sehr-vee-teh ahl-koh-lee-chee?]
Can I have my steak cooked well?	Posso avere il mio filetto ben cotto?	[pohs-soh ah-veh-reh eel meeoh fee-leht-toh behn koht-toh?]
Are you ready to order?	I signori sono pronti per ordinare?	[eeh see-nyoh-ree soh-noh prohn-tee pehr ohr-dee-nah-reh?]
What's on the menu?	Che c'è nel menù?	[keh cheh nehl meh-noo?]

English	Italian	Pronunciation
Is there a vegetarian or vegan menu?	C'è un menù vegetariano o vegano?	[cheh uhn meh-noo veh-jeh-tah-ryah-noh oh veh-gah-noh?]
Do you know sign language?	Conosci il linguaggio dei segni?	[koh-noh-she eel leen-gwaj-joh deyh seh-ny?]
Is there a baby seat?	C'è un seggiolone?	[cheh uhn seh-joh-loh-neh?]

Additionally, sometimes we like to ask for specific things in our order, so here are some sample sentences that might be useful for you:

English	Italian	Pronunciation
I think this is the wrong order.	Credo che sia l'ordine sbagliato.	[kreh-doh keh syah lohr-dee-neh sbah-lyah-toh]
I don't eat meat.	Non mangio carne.	[nohn mahn-joh kahr-neh]
We're ready to order.	Siamo pronti per ordinare.	[see-ah-moh prohn-tee pehr ohr-dee-nah-reh]
I would like a recommendation.	Vorrei un consiglio.	[vohr-rey uhn kohn-see-lyoh]
There is a one-hour wait.	Bisogna aspettare un'ora.	[bee-soh-nyah ah-speht-tah-reh uhn oh-rah]
Yes, tables are available.	Sì, ci sono tavoli disponibili.	[See, chee soh-noh tah-voh-lee dee-spoh-nee-bee-lee]
I would like to try something new.	Vorrei provare qualcosa di nuovo.	[vohr-rey proh-vah-re kwahl-koh-sah dee nwo-voh]
I would like to try local food.	Vorrei provare la cucina locale.	[vohr-rey proh-vah-reh lah koo-chee-nah loh-kah-leh]

Finally, we know that sometimes you like to ask for specific things in your order, so here is a mini glossary about the useful vocabulary you will need:

English	Italian	Pronunciation
Takeaway	A portar via/ Da asporto	[ah pohr-tahr vee-ah]/ [dah ahs-por-toh]
Gluten-free	Senza glutine	[sehn-tsah gloo-tee-neh]
Vegan	Vegano	[veh-gah-noh]
Vegetarian	Vegetariano	[veh-jeh-tah-reeah-noh]
Raw	Crudo	[kroo-doh]
Medium rare	Cottura media	[koht-too-rah meh-dyah]

English	Italian	Pronunciation
Stew	**Stufato**	[stoo-fah-toh]
Sweet	**Dolce**	[dohl-cheh]
Bitter	**Amaro**	[ah-mah-roh]
Sour	**Acido**	[ah-chee-doh]
Fast food	**Fast food**	[fast food]
Dietetic	**Dietetico**	[dee-eh-teh-tee-koh]

Food & drink

Anywhere you go, you will see many kinds of foods and drinks. It is essential to know some of the most common types. So let's start with a mini glossary about foods you must be familiar with.

English	Italian	Pronunciation
Bread	**Pane**	[pah-neh]
Chicken	**Pollo**	[pohl-loh]
Meat	**Carne**	[kahr-neh]
Fish	**Pesce**	[peh-sheh]
Sugar	**Zucchero**	[tzook-keh-roh]
Butter	**Burro**	[boor-roh]
Jelly	**Marmellata**	[mahr-mehl-lah-tah]
Rice	**Riso**	[ree-soh]
Cake	**Torta**	[Tohr-tah]
French fries	**Patatine fritte**	[pah-tah-tee-neh freet-teh]
Noodles	**Noodles**	[noo-duhls]
Soup	**Zuppa**	[tsoohp-pah]
Cookies	**Biscotti**	[bee-skoht-tee]
Cheese	**Formaggio**	[fohr-mah-joh]
Bacon	**Pancetta**	[pahn-cheht-tah]
Pizza	**Pizza**	[pee-tsah]
Hamburger	**Hamburger**	[ahm-buhr-gehr]
Eggs	**Uova**	[woh-vah]
Turkey	**Tacchino**	[tahk-kee-noh]
Pancake	**Pancake**	[pancake]
Ice cream	**Gelato**	[jeh-lah-toh]

Additionally, here you will find a list of the most common beverages that you can order anywhere:

English	Italian	Pronunciation
Soda	**Soda**	*[soh-dah]*
Water	**Acqua**	*[ah-kwah]*
Juice	**Succo**	*[suhk-koh]*
Wine	**Vino**	*[vee-noh]*
Coffee	**Caffè**	*[kahf-feh]*
Lemonade	**Limonata**	*[lee-moh-nah-tah]*
Green tea	**Tè verde**	*[teh vehr-deh]*
Tea	**Tè**	*[teh]*
Apple juice	**Succo di mela**	*[suhk-koh dee meh-lah]*
Infusions	**Infusi**	*[Een-fuh-seeh]*
Orange juice	**Succo di arancia**	*[sook-koh dee ah-rahn-cheeah]*
Champagne	**Champagne**	*[champagne]*
Beer	**Birra**	*[beer-rah]*
Yogurt	**Yogurt**	*[yoh-guhrt]*
Milk	**Latte**	*[laht-teh]*

Now let's look at some words that you might find in a common Italian menu:

English	Italian	Pronunciation
Main course	**Piatto principale**	*[peeaht-toh preen-chee-pah-leh]*
Dessert	**Dolce**	*[dohl-cheh]*
Starter	**Antipasto**	*[ahn-tee-pahs-toh]*
Beverages	**Bibite**	*[bee-bee-teh]*
Salads	**Insalate**	*[een-sah-lah-teh]*
Hot beverages	**Bevande calde**	*[beh-vahn-deh kahl-deh]*
Cold drinks	**Bevande fredde**	*[beh-vahn-deh frehd-deh]*
Appetizers	**Aperitivi**	*[Ah-peh-ree-tee-vee]*
Side dishes	**Contorni**	*[kohn-tohr-nee]*

Dining out phrases

It is essential to express how you feel during an important meal, especially dinner, in a restaurant or similar location. Here you will find important phrases for it:

English	Italian	Pronunciation
This is delicious.	Questo è delizioso.	[kweh-stoh eh deh-lee-tseeoh-soh]
This is my favorite food.	Questo è il mio cibo preferito.	[kweh-stoh eh eel meeoh chee-boh preh-feh-ree-toh]
Are you enjoying your food?	Ti piace il tuo cibo?	[tee peeah-cheh eel twoh chee-boh]
What will you order?	Cosa ordinerai?	[koh-sah ohr-dee-neh-rahy]
Can I try some of ___?	Posso provare un po' di ___?	[pohs-soh proh-vah-reh uhn poh dee ___]
Will you share it with me?	Lo condividi con me?	[loh kohn-dee-vee-dee kohn meh?]
May I have the bill, please?	Mi fa il conto, per favore?	[meeh fahy eel kohn-toh pehr fah-voh-reh]
Enjoy your meal.	Goditi il pasto.	[goh-dee-tee eel pah-stoh]
I'm full	Sono sazio.	[soh-noh sah-tseeoh]
	Sono sazia.	[soh-noh sah-tseeah]
I am thirsty	Sono assetato.	[soh-noh ahs-seh-tah-to]
	Sono assetata.	[soh-noh ahs-seh-tah-ta]
Check, please.	Il conto, per favore.	[eel kohn-toh pehr fah-voh-reh]

Shopping

Continuing with shopping for products necessary for personal hygiene, we have created small glossaries of words that will be useful for you to know.

English	Italian	Pronunciation
Shampoo	Shampoo	[shahm-poh]
Deodorant	Deodorante	[deh-oh-doh-rahn-teh]
Soap	Sapone	[sah-poh-neh]
Toothpaste	Dentifricio	[dehn-tee-free-cheeoh]
Toothbrush	Spazzolino da denti	[spah-tsoh-lee-noh dah dehn-tee]

English	Italian	Pronunciation
Toilet paper	Carta igienica	[kahr-tah ee-jeh-nee-kah]
Hand sanitizer	Disinfettante per le mani	[dee-seen-feht-tahn-teh pehr leh mah-nee]
Towel	Asciugamani	[ah-shee-ooh-gah-mah-nee]
Pads	Salviette igieniche	[sahl-veeht-teh ee-jeh-nee-keh]
Diaper	Pannolini	[pahn-noh-lee-neeh]

In addition to that, while traveling, indulging in a bit of clothes shopping can be a delightful and memorable way to bring back a tangible memento of the journey. Here are some essential words that might come in handy:

English	Italian	Pronunciation
T-shirt	Maglietta	[mah-lyeht-tah]
Pants	Pantalone	[pahn-tah-loh-neh]
Jacket	Giacca	[jahk-kah]
Sneakers	Scarpe da tennis	[skahr-peh dah tehn-nees]
Socks	Calze	[kahl-tseh]
Underwear	Biancheria intima	[beeahn-keh-reeah]
Shirt	Camicia	[kah-mee-cheeah]
Blouse	Camicetta	[kah-mee-che-tah]
Gloves	Guanti	[gwahn-tee]
Glasses	Occhiali	[ohk-keeah-lee]
Dress	Vestito	[veh-stee-toh]
Scarf	Sciarpa	[shee-ahr-pah]
Sandals	Sandali	[sahn-dah-lee]

Finally, there are several items that can be quite important when packing your suitcases, but in case you forget something, you can easily buy it in a supermarket with this vocabulary.

English	Italian	Pronunciation
Charger	Caricatore	[kah-ree-kah-toh-reh]
Headphones	Auricolari	[ahw-ree-koh-lah-ree]
Portable battery	Batteria portatile	[Bah-teh-reeah pohr-tah-tee-leh]
Laptop	Laptop	[Lahp-tohp]

English	Italian	Pronunciation
Cell phone	**Cellulare**	*[chehl-luh-lah-reh]*
Tablet	**Tablet**	*[Tah-bleht]*
Computer	**Computer**	*[Kohm-pyooh-tehr]*

Groceries

In Italy going shopping for fruits and vegetables can be quite cheap and an experience not to be missed! In these local markets you can see many types of fruits and vegetables at very affordable prices. Here is a list of the fruits you can find there:

English	Italian	Pronunciation
Pineapple	**Ananas**	*[ah-nah-nahs]*
Strawberry	**Fragola**	*[frah-goh-lah]*
Watermelon	**Anguria**	*[ahn-goo-reeah]*
Kiwi	**Kiwi**	*[kee-wee]*
Banana	**Banana**	*[bah-nah-nah]*
Apple	**Mela**	*[meh-lah]*
Orange	**Arancia**	*[ah-rahn-cheeah]*
Grapes	**Uva**	*[uh-vah]*
Cherry	**Ciliegia**	*[chee-lyeh-jah]*
Coconut	**Cocco**	*[kohk-koh]*
Pear	**Pera**	*[peh-rah]*
Avocado	**Avocado**	*[ah-voh-kah-doh]*

Next, here you will find a list of the most common vegetables you can find in markets:

English	Italian	Pronunciation
Tomato	**Pomodoro**	*[poh-moh-doh-roh]*
Onion	**Cipolla**	*[chee-pohl-lah]*
Cucumber	**Cetriolo**	*[cheh-tree-oh-loh]*
Garlic	**Aglio**	*[ah-lyoh]*
Ginger	**Zenzero**	*[tsehn-tseh-roh]*
Carrot	**Carota**	*[kah-roh-tah]*
Broccoli	**Broccoli**	*[broh-koh-lee]*

English	Italian	Pronunciation
Potato	**Patata**	[pah-tah-tah]
Sweet potato	**Patata dolce**	[pah-tah-tah dohl-cheh]
Chilli	**Peperoncino**	[peh-peh-rohn-chee-noh]
Pumpkin	**Zucca**	[tsook-kah]
Lettuce	**Lattuga**	[laht-too-gah]
Green peas	**Piselli**	[pee-sehl-lee]
Spinach	**Spinaci**	[spee-nah-chee]

Shopping phrases

When it comes to shopping, you should know all the details about the product you are going to buy. Here are the most common sentences used by Italian speakers:

English	Italian	Pronunciation
I would like to try this.	**Vorrei provare questo.**	[vohr-rey proh-vah-reh kweh-stoh]
I'm looking for ___.	**Sto cercando ___.**	[stoh-chehr-kahn-doh ___]
I need to buy ___.	**Devo comprare ___.**	[deh-voh kohm-prah-reh ___]
I want to buy ___.	**Voglio comprare ___.**	[vo-lyoh kohm-prah-reh ___]
Do you have this in a different color?	**Ce l'hai in un altro colore?**	[cheh lahee een uhn ahl-troh koh-loh-reh]
Can I have some assistance, please?	**Potete aiutarmi per favore?**	[poh-teh-teh ah-yoo-tahr-mee pehr fah-voh-reh]
Can I have a different size?	**Posso avere una taglia diversa?**	[pohs-soh ah-veh-reh uh-nah tah-leeah dee-vehr-sah]
I would like this in size ___.	**Vorrei questo nella taglia ___.**	[vohr-rey kweh-stoh nehl-la tah-lyah ___]
Where are the fitting rooms?	**Dove sono i camerini?**	[doh-veh soh-noh ee kah-meh-ree-nee]
Can I return this?	**Posso restituirlo?**	[pohs-soh reh-stee-too-eer-loh]
How long do I have to return it?	**Quanto tempo ho per restituirlo?**	[kwahn-toh tehm-poh oh pehr reh-stee-too-eer-loh]
What time do you close?	**A che ora chiudete?**	[ah keh oh-rah kyoo-deh-teh]
Is this handmade?	**È fatto a mano?**	[eh faht-toh ah mah-noh]
Can you tell me where I can find ___?	**Sa dirmi dove posso trovare ___?**	[sah deer-mee doh-veh pohs-soh troh-vah-reh ___]

Paying for something

With these phrases you will be able to ask for prices, payment methods, and if there is any kind of discount. In Italian communities it is ok to bargain, so don't miss a chance when you can!

English	Italian	Pronunciation
How much is this?	Quanto costa questo?	[kwahn-toh koh-stah kweh-stoh?]
Is there a discount?	C'è uno sconto?	[cheh uh-noh skohn-toh?]
Do you take credit cards?	Accettate carte di credito?	[ahc-cheht-tah-teh kahr-teh dee kreh-dee-toh?]
Cash only	Solo contanti	[Soh-loh kohn-tahn-tee]
What are the payment methods?	Quali sono i metodi di pagamento?	[kwah-lee soh-noh eeh meh-toh-dee dee pah-gah-mehn-toh?]
It is on sale?	È in offerta?	[eh een ohf-fehr-tah?]
How much less can I get?	Qual è il prezzo minore?	[kwahl eh eel preht-tsoh mee-noh-reh?]
I will pay by credit card.	Pago con carta di credito.	[pah-goh kohn kahr-tah dee kreh-dee-toh]
I will pay in ___ installments.	Pago in ___ rate.	[pah-goh een ___ rah-teh]
I will pay cash, please.	Pago in contante, per favore.	[pah-goh een kohn-tahn-tee pehr fah-voh-reh]
That's on me.	Questo lo pago io.	[kweh-stoh loh pah-goh yoh]

Speak Abroad
Academy

TRAVEL & TRANSPORTATION

Embarking on a journey through the enchanting landscapes of Italy is a voyage into the heart of art, history, and natural beauty. From the iconic architecture of Rome to the romantic canals of Venice, each destination whispers tales of a rich cultural tapestry. The rolling vineyards of Tuscany and the sun-kissed Amalfi Coast offer picturesque scenes that captivate the soul. Exploring the ruins of ancient civilizations, savoring authentic cuisine, and meandering through cobblestone streets, Italy is an immersive experience where every step echoes the whispers of centuries past, creating memories that linger like the aroma of freshly brewed espresso in the air.

However, to enjoy it all you must know some important 'getting around' phrases!

Getting around

If you're trying to find a new place, feel free to ask a Italian speaker. They would be more than happy to help you! Here are some phrases that you can use:

English	Italian	Pronunciation
How do I get to the train station?	Come posso arrivare alla stazione ferroviaria?	[koh-meh posso ahr-ree-vah-reh ahl-lah stah-tsyoh-neh day treh-nee]
What time is the next train to ___?	A che ora c'è il prossimo treno per ___?	[ah keh oh-rah cheh eel prohs-see-oh treh-noh pehr ___]
Where is the bus stop?	Dove sta la fermata del bus?	[doh-veh stah lah fehr-mah-tah dehl buhs]
Where can I buy tickets for ___?	Dove posso comprare i biglietti per ___?	[doh-veh pohs-soh kohm-prah-reh eeh bee-lyeht-tee pehr ___]
Where can I get a bus?	Dove posso prendere un autobus?	[doh-veh pohs-soh prehn-deh-reh eeh bee-lyeht-tee dehl buhs]
Where can I get a taxi?	Dove posso prendere un taxi?	[doh-veh pohs-soh prehn-deh-reh uhn tah-xee]
Is this the right way to ___?	È questa la strada giusta per ___?	[eh kweh-stah lah strah-dah joo-stah pehr ___]
Where is the nearest ___?	Dove sta il ___ più vicino?	[doh-veh stah eel ___ pyoo vee-chee-noh]
It's next to the ___.	È affianco a ___.	[eh ahf-feeahn-koh ah ___]

English	Italian	Pronunciation
It's behind the ___.	È a destra di ___.	[eh ah deh-strah dee ___]
It's around the corner.	Sta dietro l'angolo.	[stah dyeh-troh lahn-goh-loh]
It's to the left/ right.	Sta a sinistra/ destra.	[stah ah see-nee-strah/ deh-strah]
Go straight to ___.	Vai dritto a ___.	[vay dreet-toh ah ___]
Take the first right.	Prendi la prima a destra.	[prehn-dee lah pree-mah ah deh-strah]
Go ahead.	Continua dritto.	[kohn-tee-nwah dreet-toh]
It's between ___.	Sta tra ___.	[stah trah ___]
Go through ___.	Passa per ___.	[pahs-sah pehr ___]
Go back to ___.	Svolta a ___.	[svohl-tah ah ___]

Signs & notices

When you walk through the streets and in shopping malls, you will find different signs, whether they are traffic signs, security or guide signs that will help you during your visit. Always remember to respect these signs.

English	Italian	Pronunciation
Exit	Uscita	[ooh-she-tah]
Entrance	Ingresso	[een-grehs-soh]
Emergency exit	Uscita di emergenza	[ooh-she-tah dee eh-mehr-djehn-tsah]
Restrooms	Bagni	[bah-nyee]
Slow down	Ridurre la velocità	[ree-doohr-reh lah veh-loh-chee-tah]
No smoking	Non fumare	[nohn foo-mah-reh]
Open	Aperto	[ah-pehr-toh]
Out of order	Fuori servizio	[fwoh-ree sehr-vee-tsyoh]
Close	Chiuso	[kyoo-soh]
Stairs	Scale	[skah-leh]
Push	Spingere	[speen-jeh-reh]
Pull	Tirare	[tee-rah-reh]
Stop	Alt	[ahlt]
Caution, wet floor!	Attenzione, pavimento bagnato!	[aht-tehn-tsyoh-neh, pah-vee-mehn-toh bah-nyah-to]

Speak Abroad
Academy

At the airport

If you have any questions about your flight and would like further guidance at the airport, you can always find a customer service representative to help you. Here are some useful phrases:

English	Italian	Pronunciation
Checked baggage	**Bagaglio registrato**	[bah-gah-lyoh reh-jee-strah-toh]
Hand luggage	**Bagaglio a mano**	[bah-gah-lyoh ah mah-noh]
Delay	**Ritardo**	[ree-tahr-doh]
Customs	**Dogana**	[doh-gah-nah]
Passport	**Passaporto**	[pahs-sah-pohr-toh]
What is the departure gate for the flight ___?	**Qual è la porta di uscita per il volo ___?**	[Kwahl ehs lah pohr-tah dee ooh-she-tah pehr eel meeoh voh-loh ___]
I need medical assistance during the flight	**Ho bisogno di assistenza medica durante il volo**	[oh bee-soh-nyoh dee ahs-see-stehn-tsah duh-rahn-teh eel voh-loh]
Direct fly	**Volo diretto**	[voh-loh dee-reht-toh]
I will be traveling alone	**Viaggio da solo/sola**	[vee-ahdj-joh dah soh-lah]
Check-in	**Check-in**	[Check in]
Do you have all your flight tickets?	**Ha tutti i suoi biglietti di aereo?**	[ah tooht-tee ee swoy bee-lyet-tee aeh-reh-eeh]
Are you traveling with a pet?	**Viaggia con animali?**	[vee-adj-jah kohn ah-nee-mah-lee]
I'm late for my flight.	**Sono in ritardo per il mio volo.**	[soh-noh een ree-tahr-doh pehr eel meeoh voh-loh]

Hotel & Accommodation

Wherever you go it is always important to be able to make a hotel reservation. Below you will find phrases to do it according to what you need.

English	Italian	Pronunciation
Receptionist	**Receptionist**	[Reh-sehp-tseeoh-neest]
Room service	**Servizio in camera**	[Sehr-vee-tseeoh een kah-meh- rah]
Maid	**Cameriera**	[kah-meh-ryeh-rah]
Doorman	**Portiere**	[Pohr-tyeh-reh]

English	Italian	Pronunciation
Book a room.	Prenotare una camera.	[preh-noh-tah-reh uh-nah kah-meh-rah]
Gift shop	Negozio di regali	[neh-goh-tsyoh dee reh-gah-lee]
Check in / Check out	Check in / Check out	[Check in / check out]
Reservation	Prenotazioni	[preh-noh-tah-tsyoh-neh]
Swimming pool	Piscina	[Pee-she-nah]
Lobby	Atrio	[ah-tryoh]
Dining area	Zona pranzo	[tsoh-nah prahn-tsoh]
Balcony	Balcone	[Bahl-koh-neh]
Motel	Motel	[Moh-tehl]
Laundry service	Servizio di lavanderia	[Sehr-vee-tseeoh dee lah-vahn-deh-reeah]
Do not disturb	Non disturbare	[Nohn dee-stoor-bah-reh]
Hotel room	Camera di hotel	[kah-meh-rah dee oh-tehl]
Travel guide	Guida di viaggio	[gwee-dah dee vee-ahj-joh]
Buffet	Buffet	[Buh-ffeht]
Do you have any rooms available?	Avete camere disponibili?	[ah-veh-teh kah-meh-reh dee-spoh-nee-bee-lee?]
Does the room come with ___?	La camera include ___?	[lah kah-meh-rah een-kluh-deh ___?]
How much is the room per night?	Quanto costa la camera a notte?	[kwahn-toh koh-stah lah kah-meh-rah ah noht-teh?]
How many nights are you booking?	Quante notti vuole prenotare?	[kwahn-teh noht-tee woh-leh preh-noh-tah-reh?]
I have a reservation.	Ho una prenotazione.	[oh uh-nah preh-noh-tah-tsyoh-neh]
I'd like to stay in a single room.	Vorrei alloggiare in una camera singola.	[vohr-rey ahl-lohj-jah-reh een uh-nah kah-meh-rah seen-goh-lah]
I'd like to stay in a double room.	Vorrei alloggiare in una camera doppia.	[vohr-rey ahl-lohj-jah-reh een uh-nah kah-meh-rah dohp-peeah]
I'd like to make a reservation for ___ people.	Vorrei prenotare per ___ persone.	[vohr-rey preh-noh-tah-reh pehr ___ pehr-soh-neh]

HEALTH NEEDS & EMERGENCIES

Traveling is fun, going to Italy will probably be a life-changing experience. Nevertheless, we're never safe from a health problem or an emergency. In those cases, speaking the local language solves a lot of problems. That's why we are going to provide you with the main phrases and words you need to know if you're facing an emergency in an Italian-speaking country, while hoping you won't need to use it.

General Phrases

Health is important everywhere and everyone has different needs, so here we will teach you phrases that you can use to describe your needs or your health condition.

English	Italian	Pronunciation
I'm pregnant	Sono incinta	[soh-noh een-cheen-tah]
I need a wheelchair	Ho bisogno di una sedia a rotelle	[oh bee-soh-neeoh dee uh-nah seh-dyah ah roh-tehl-leh]
I need to go to the pharmacy/ doctor.	Devo andare in farmacia/ dal dottore	[deh-voh ahn-dah-reh een fahr-mah-cheeah / dahl meh-dee-koh]
Do you take some medication?	Hai preso qualche medicina?	[ahy preh-soh kwahl-keh meh-dee-chee-nah]
I need medication.	Ho bisogno di medicinali	[oh bee-soh-neeoh dee mee-dee-chi-nah-lee]
I need to go to the hospital.	Devo andare in ospedale.	[deh-voh ahn-dah-reh een oh-speh-dah-leh]
I feel sick.	Mi sento male.	[mee sehn-toh mah-leh]
I'm feeling anxious.	Mi sento ansioso/ ansiosa.	[mee sehn-toh ahn-seeoh-soh / ahn-seeoh-sah]
Do you have any type of insurance?	Ha qualche tipo di assicurazione?	[ah kwahl-keh tee-poh dee ahs-see-koo-rah-tsyoh-ne]
Are you allergic to any medication?	Lei è allergico a qualche farmaco?	[lehy eh ahl-lehr-jee-koh ah kwahl-keh fahr-mah-coh?]
Do you have any food allergies?	Sei allergico a qualche alimento?	[say ahl-lehr-jee-koh ah kwahl-keh ah-lee-mehn-toh]

Health Problems

It's important to communicate if you have a condition that requires immediate treatment or assistance. Here you'll find phrases to express it.

English	Italian	Pronunciation
I have a headache.	Mi fa male la testa.	[mee fah mah-leh lah teh-stah]
I'm struggling to breathe.	Fatico a respirare.	[fah-tee-koh ah reh-spee-rah-reh]
I'm going to vomit.	Sto per vomitare.	[stoh pehr voh-mee-tah-reh]
I feel like I might faint.	Sento che sto per svenire.	[sehn-to keh stoh pehr sveh-nee-reh]
My ___ hurts.	Mi fa male ___.	[mee fah mah-leh ___]
Do you feel nauseous?	Senti nausea?	[sehn-tee naw-seh-ah]
Asthma	Asma	[Ahs-mah]
Backache	Dolore alla spalla	[Doh-loh-reh ahl-lah spahl-lah]
Broken leg	Gamba rotta	[gahm-bah roht-tah]
Chest	Petto	[peht-toh]
Cold	Raffreddore	[rahf-frehd-doh-reh]
Cough	Tosse	[tohs-seh]
Eyes	Occhi	[ohk-kee]
Fever	Febbre	[fehb-breh]
Earache	Mal di orecchi	[mahl dee oh-rehk-ky]
Flu	Influenza	[een-floo-ehn-tsah]
Sore throat	Mal di gola	[mahl dee goh-lah]
Stomach ache	Mal di stomaco	[mahl dee stoh-mah-koh]
Sunburn	Insolazione	[een-soh-lah-tsyo-neh]
Toothache	Mal di denti	[mahl dee dehn-tee]
Diabetes	Diabete	[Deeah-beh-teh]
Cancer	Cancro	[Kahn-kroh]

At the pharmacy

If you find yourself at an Italian pharmacy, it's essential to know how to ask about receipts or medications. Interestingly, in certain Italian-speaking regions, pharmacies might surprise you with offerings beyond medicines, featuring items like perfumes and teddy bears or even make-up. Following are some words and phrases you can use:

English	Italian	Pronunciation
May I have your prescription?	**Può darmi la ricetta?**	[pwoh dahr-mee lah ree-cheht-tah]
Pregnancy test	**Test di gravidanza**	[tehst dee grah-vee-dahn-tsah]
Pain relief	**Analgesici**	[ah-nahl-jeh-see-chee]
Cough medicine	**Medicine per la tosse**	[meh-dee-chee-neh pehr lah tohs-seh]
Covid-19 test	**Test di Covid-19**	[tehst dee Covid 19]
I need a thermometer	**Mi serve un termometro**	[mee sehr-veh uhn tehr-moh-meh-troh]
Eye drops	**Collirio**	[kohl-lee-ryoh]
Vitamins	**Vitamine**	[Vee-tah-mee-neh]
Syrup	**Sciroppo**	[she-rohp-poh]
Contraceptive pills	**Pillole contraccettive**	[peel-loh-leh kohn-traht-tchet-tee-veh]
Plan B	**Pillola del giorno dopo**	[peel-loh-lah dehl djohr-noh doh-poh]

Complaints & emergencies

You can always use these phrases in cases of emergency or when you need help. Just look out when you say something like "please leave me alone"; many Italian speakers could take this the wrong way.

English	Italian	Pronunciation
I'm lost	**Mi sono perso/ persa**	[mee soh-noh pehr-so / pehr-sah]
I need to use the toilet	**Devo andare in bagno**	[deh-voh ahn-dah-reh een bah-nyoh]
I can't find my phone	**Non riesco a trovare il mio telefono**	[Noh pweh-doh ehn-kohn-trahr mee teh-leh-foh-noh]
It's too loud	**C'è troppo rumore**	[cheh trohp-poh roo-moh-reh]

English	Italian	Pronunciation
It's too dirty	È troppo sporco	[eh trohp-poh spohr-koh]
Call an ambulance	Chiama un'ambulanza	[Yah-mah ah uh-nah ahm-buh-lahn-see-ah]
Call the police	Chiama la polizia	[kyah-mah lah poh-lee-tsy-ah]
I can't afford this	Non posso permettermelo.	[nohn pohs-soh pehr-meht-tehr-me-loh]
Thief	Ladro	[Lah-droh]
Someone is following me	Qualcuno mi sta seguendo.	[kwahl-koo-noh mee stah seh-gwehn-doh]
There's been an accident	C'è stato un incidente.	[cheh stah-toh uhn een-chee-dehn-teh]
I need help	Ho bisogno di aiuto.	[oh bee-soh-nyoh dee ah-yuh-toh]
Please, leave me alone	Per favore, lasciami in pace.	[pehr fah-voh-reh lah-shyah-mee een pah-cheh]
I don't feel safe	Non mi sento sicuro/sicura.	[nohn mee sehn-toh see-kooh-roh/ see-kooh-rah]
I'm injured	Sono ferito/ ferita	[soh-noh feh-ree-toh / feh-ree-tah]
Go away	Vattene	[vaht-teh-neh]
Help	Aiuto	[Ah-yuh-toh]
Fire	Al fuoco	[ahl fwoh-koh]

Health needs & emergencies

Speak Abroad
Academy

ITALIAN IDIOMS

If your goal is to speak Italian like a native, then at some point you will have to learn how to use a variety of Italian idioms as their meaning is often rooted deep in culture.. In this section we will explain a little more about them. Remember proper use and good understanding mean you are at an advanced level. Some essential everyday sayings are mentioned below:

Everyday sayings

English	Italian	Pronunciation	Meaning
To be a piece of cake	**È una passeggiata.**	*[eh uh-nah pahs-seh-jah-tah]*	It means that something is very easy to do. (*It's bread eaten*)
To be a little crazy	**Stai fuori come un cammello**	*[stah-eeh fwoh-ree koh-meh uhn bahl-koh-neh]*	Use it when somebody is doing something bizarre or a little out of the ordinary. (*To be like a goat*)
To pull someone's leg	**Prendere in giro.**	*[prehn-deh-reh een jee-roh]*	It's used when someone is tricking or making fun of someone else, but in a good-natured way. (*To take the hair*)
To make a mountain out of a molehill	**Perdersi in un bicchier d'acqua.**	*[pehr-dehr-see een uhn beek-kyeh-reh dah-kwah]*	Use it when someone is overreacting about a problem that is easy to solve. (*Drowning in a glass of water*)
To be straightforward	**Non avere peli sulla lingua**	*[nohn ah-veh-reh peh-lee sool-lah leen-gwah]*	Means that someone is a straight shooter and says their mind whenever possible. (*Not to have hairs on the tongue*)
To spare no expense	**Non badare a spese**	*[nohn bah-dah-reh ah speh-seh]*	Means that no expense has been spared or that money is not an object. (*Throw the house through the window*)

English	Italian	Pronunciation	Meaning
To be stunned	Solido come una roccia	[soh-lee-doh koh-meh ooh-nah roh-cheeah]	Normally used when you are extremely surprised and you stay like a stone. (*Stay like a stone*)
To give birth	Dare alla luce	[dah-reh ahl-lah loo-cheh]	Always used to say that someone is giving birth. (*Bring to light*)
Not have a stitch of clothes on	Essere come mamma l'ha fatto	[ehs-seh-reh koh-meh mahm-mah lah faht-toh]	You can use it when you want to say that someone is naked. (*Being in the buff*)
To rain cats and dogs	Piove a catinelle	[peeoh-veh ah kah-tee-nehl-leh]	You can use it when you want to express that it is too rainy out there. (*Pouring rain*)
To have money to burn	Avere soldi da buttare	[ah-veh-reh sohl-dee dah boot-tah-reh]	Means when someone can afford more than expected because they have a lot of money. (*He has more wool than a sheep*)
To be in a bad mood	Essere di cattivo umore	[ehs-seh-reh dee kaht-tee-voh ooh-moh-reh]	When you want to describe someone else's or your own bad mood. (*To have a mood of dogs*)
Give lip-service	Aprire bocca e darle fiato	[ah-pree-reh bohk-kah eh dahr-leh feeah-toh]	Use this when you want to express that a person didn't mean what they said. (*To say from the mouth outward*)
To be extremely angry	Essere molto arrabbiato	[ehs-seh-reh mohl-toh ahr-rahb-beeah-toh]	Use this when you want to say that a person is very angry (*Being a chili*)
Strike the right note	Colpire il bersaglio	[kohl-pee-reh eel behr-sah-lyoh]	When you want to say that someone is right about something (*Hit the target*)

Speak Abroad
Academy

English	Italian	Pronunciation	Meaning
Be the black sheep of the family	**Essere la pecora nera della famiglia**	*[ehs-seh-reh lah peh-koh-rah neh-rah dehl-lah fah-mee-lyah]*	When you want to express that someone is different than the rest in a group
You snooze, you lose	**Chi dorme non piglia pesci**	*[kee dohr-meh nohn pee-lyah peh-shee]*	Originally refers to the negative consequences of laziness. (*Shrimp that falls asleep, it's taken away by the current*)
Look at something through rose-tinted glasses	**Vedere tutto rosa**	*[veh-deh-reh tuht-toh roh-sah]*	This can be used when referring to someone who thinks that everything in life is well intentioned. (*Look everything color pink*)
Cat got your tongue?	**Il gatto ti ha mangiato la lingua?**	*[eel gaht-toh tee hah mahn-jah-toh lah leen-gwah]*	You can say this when a person is quieter than usual. (*A cat ate your tongue*)
Curiosity killed the cat	**La curiosità uccise il gatto**	*[lah kuh-reeoh-see-tah uch-chee-she eel gaht-toh]*	It is used to warn that someone is inquiring into dangerous matters or matters that are none of their business.
Be everywhere	**Essere come il prezzemolo**	*[ehs-seh-reh koh-meh eel preht-tseh-moh-loh]*	When there is some topic or person that is being talked about all day long at all times. (*To be even in the soup*)
You lost the plot!	**Ti manca una rotella**	*[tee mahn-kah uh-nah roh-tehl-lah]*	You say it when you want to express that someone is a little bit crazy. (*You are missing a screw*)
Browse	**Gettare un occhio**	*[jeht-tah-reh uhn ohk-keeoh]*	When you want to ask someone to look at something. (*Throw an eye*)
Put one's foot in it	**Rovinare tutto.**	*[roh-vee-nah-reh tuht-toh]*	When you want to say someone has ruined something or has made a mistake.

English	Italian	Pronunciation	Meaning
Speak of the devil	**Parli del diavolo**	*[pahr-lee dehl deeah-voh-loh]*	You can say it when someone appears exactly when you are talking about them. (*Talking about the king of Rome*)
Close enough to use the same toothpick	**Sono pappa e ciccia**	*[soh-noh pahp-pah eh cheech-cheeah]*	When you want to express that two people are too close and do everything together. (*To be like nail and dirt*)
Add fuel to the flames	**Gettare benzina sul fuoco**	*[jeht-tah-reh behn-zee-nah suhl fuoh-koh]*	Use it when someone raises a controversial or problematic topic. (*Add wood to the fire*)
Be between a rock and a hard place	**Stare tra l'incudine e il martello**	*[stah-reh trah lihn-kuh-dee-neh eh eel mahr-tehl-lo-]*	When you want to express that someone has to choose between two bad options. (*Be between the sword and the wall*)
There's always enough for one more	**Dove si mangia in due, si mangia in tre**	*[doh-veh see mahn-jah ihn duh-eh, see mahn-jah ihn treh]*	When you want to say there's always enough food to share with someone else. (*Where two eat, three eat*)
Turn the tables	**Girare la frittata**	*[jee-rah-reh lah freeht-tah-tah]*	It means to make a situation look different or to change it completely. (*Turning the tortilla*)

SECTION III:
SHORT STORIES

In this section, we'll try to introduce new words and expressions in a fun way, through different short stories. We believe that learning a new language should be an entertaining experience, and the Italian language is way easier when it's introduced in this way. We'll gradually increase the level of the vocabulary and the tenses used while keeping it adequate for beginners. We encourage you to read the stories as often as needed to get comfortable with the language. The vocabulary words are explained at the end of each story. This will clear up any confusion you may have had and provide you with the tools to progress. You can use these stories to practice reading or writing in Italian.

Now that it's all clear, let's continue our journey!

STORY #1 : La pausa pranzo di martedì

(Tuesday Lunch Break)

Mi chiamo Gianni e oggi è **martedì**. Il **martedì** esco di casa **presto** per **lavorare**. Il mio **luogo di lavoro** non è **lontano** da casa, per questo sto **camminando**. Mi piace **camminare** la **mattina** perché alleno le **gambe**. Mi piace **allenarmi** al **mattino**, per questo mi piace **camminare**.

Quando raggiungo il **luogo di lavoro**, saluto i miei **colleghi**. Il **martedì** mattina al lavoro è tutto normale. Mi siedo alla **scrivania** per **iniziare** il lavoro. Oggi devo completare molti documenti prima della fine della giornata. All'ora di **pranzo** faccio una pausa per mangiare. Mangio un piatto di pasta alla carbonara. Mi piace la pasta alla carbonara. A Roma, sono famosi per la pasta alla carbonara.

Dopo pranzo continuo a lavorare. **Lavoro** fino alle cinque di pomeriggio. Il mio **lavoro** termina nel pomeriggio. Prima che finisca il mio **orario di lavoro**, la mia collega Sara mi domanda se desidero andare a casa sua perché i **colleghi** di **lavoro** terranno una riunione lì. "Perché mi invitano all'ultimo momento?", penso. Credo che non pensano che io vada e mi sento molto **triste** e **dispiaciuto**. Dico a Sara che ho degli impegni dopo il mio **orario di lavoro**. "Scusa, Sara. Non posso venire." Sara si allontana **dopo** e la vedo **bisbigliare** con gli altri. Concludo i miei rapporti di lavoro prima della fine dell'orario di lavoro, quindi prendo le mie cose e me ne vado dal **luogo di lavoro**. Vedo Sara e i miei **colleghi** di lavoro **ridere** mentre vado via. Non mi importa.

Di **martedì**, dopo il lavoro, mi piace andare al mio ristorante preferito. Si chiama "L'Osteria Antica"". Ordino sempre la carbonara perché é la mia preferita. Inizio a **camminare** verso il mio ristorante preferito, mentre la **luna** comincia a sorgere. Oggi, come tutti i **martedì**, sto nel mio ristorante preferito per mangiare la pasta alla carbonara. Quando sono **seduto** al bar, una **sconosciuta** si siede accanto a me. Ordino le mie amate patatine fritte, mentre la **sconosciuta** ordina la stessa cosa. Penso di parlare con la **sconosciuta**, però mi **vergogno**.

Quando arriva il mio ordine di pasta alla carbonara, mi sento **meglio**. La pasta rende **migliore** la mia giornata. Sto **pensando** a quello che farò domani, **dopo** l'**orario di lavoro**. Io vivo da solo. Non c'è niente da fare a casa. Mangio la mia pasta. La **sconosciuta** inizia a mangiare la mia pasta! Penso di essermi **sbagliato**, però la **sconosciuta** non smette di mangiare la mia pasta alla carbonara. Guardo da un'altra parte perché sono **arrabbiato**. Non voglio **litigare** con una **sconosciuta**. "Che devo fare?", penso. Devo parlarle, questo devo fare.

Mi domando perché la **sconosciuta** mangia la mia pasta alla carbonara, perché la **sconosciuta** non **mangia** la sua pasta. **Ho sentito** quando la **sconosciuta** ha ordinato la sua pasta alla carbonara. Perché mangia la mia pasta? Mi **voltò** a guardare la **sconosciuta**. Sta mangiando la pasta e le dico: "Perché mangi la mia pasta e non le tue?" La **sconosciuta** è sorpresa, ma io lo sono di più. "Scusa, ma queste non sono la tua pasta alla carbonara." Che sta dicendo la **sconosciuta**? Questa è la mia pasta alla carbonara. "Tu stai **sbagliando**, queste sono la mia

pasta alla carbonara." Quando finisco di parlare, vedo la **cameriera** che lascia il piatto di pasta accanto a me. Mi rendo conto che la pasta alla carbonara che sto mangiando era la pasta della **sconosciuta**. "Per favore, scusami. Credevo che fosse la mia pasta alla carbonara." La **sconosciuta** inizia a **ridere** di me e io sono così imbarazzato. Mi scuso molte volte finché la **sconosciuta** mi dice: "Non preoccuparti, eri molto **distratto** per sapere che queste non era la tua pasta alla carbonara ma la mia pasta alla carbonara." La **sconosciuta** mi sorride e anch'io le sorrido.

Mi presento alla **sconosciuta**. "Ciao, mi chiamo Gianni. E tu come ti chiami?", le domando, imbarazzato. "Ciao, mi chiamo Maria. Piacere di conoscerti, Gianni." Che sorpresa! Andiamo molto d'accordo. Parlo con Maria tutta la notte nel mio ristorante preferito. Mangiamo **insieme** la pasta alla carbonara e ridiamo molto.

Alle dieci di sera vado a casa molto felice. Mi **lavo** i **denti** e mi cambio i vestiti. **Penso** a Maria per tutto il tempo. Credo che mi piace perché è una persona molto cordiale. Penso di **chiamarla**. **Ricordo** che non ho il suo numero di telefono. "Che **stupido**, non ho il suo numero di telefono!", penso. Molto triste mi **stendo** nel **letto**. **Penso** di avere un rapporto perfetto con Maria. **Lentamente** mi addormento e sogno Maria.

La mattina **seguente** inizio la giornata con un **sorriso**. Sento se posso incontrare Maria nel mio ristorante preferito, "L'Osteria Antica". Vado al mio **luogo di lavoro**. Quando arrivo, vedo Maria che entra nell'**ufficio** del mio **capo**. Per caso Maria **inizierà** a **lavorare** nel mio **luogo di lavoro**? Sono più felice e, quando Maria esce dall'**ufficio** del mio **capo**, la affianco e le dico: "Ciao, mi chiamo Gianni. È un piacere conoscerti." Lei sorride e mi stringe la mano.

GLOSSARY		GLOSSARY	
Martedì	Tuesday	**Pensare**	Think
Presto	Early	**Triste**	Sad
Lavoro	Work	**Dispiaciuto**	Disappointed
Luogo di lavoro	Workplace	**Bisbigliare**	Mumbling
Mattine	Mornings	**Ridere**	Laugh
Esercizio	Exercise	**Dopo**	After
Gambe	Legs	**Luna**	Moon
Camminare	Walk	**Seduto**	Sitting
Colleghi	Co-workers / Colleagues	**Sconosciuta**	Unknown person
Scrivania	Desk	**Vergogna**	Embarrassment
Pranzo	Lunch	**Migliore**	Better
Orario di lavoro	Shift	**Sbagliando**	Mistaken

3-IN-1 BUNDLE

GLOSSARY		GLOSSARY	
Solo(a)	Alone	Lavare	Wash
Cominciare/Iniziare	Start	Denti	Teeth
Discutere	Discuss	Chiamare	Call
Arrabbiato	Angry	Stendersi	Lay down
Ascoltare/Sentire	Listen/Hear	Letto	Bed
Comprare	Buy	Stupido	Dumb
Girarsi	Turn around	Ricordare	Remember
Cameriera	Waitress	Lentamente	Slowly
Distratto	Distracted	Seguente	Next
Sorriso	Smile	Ufficio	Office
Insieme	Together	Capo	Boss

After diving into the story and hopefully having a good time with it, let's see how well you caught on! Answer the following questions to test your understanding:

1. Che giorno é oggi nella storia?

   _____

2. Cosa mangia Gianni a pranzo?

   _____

3. Cosa domanda Sara a Gianni prima che finisca il suo orario di lavoro?

   _____

4. Come si chiama la sconosciuta?

   _____

5. Come si chiama il ristorante preferito di Gianni?

   _____

Italian idioms

STORY #2 : Una vacanza a Positano

(A Vacation in Positano)

L'anno scorso ho fatto un viaggio con la mia migliore amica, Mayra, che conosco fin dal collegio. Siamo stati in Italia durante il mese di febbraio, perché avevamo le ferie e volevamo trascorrere il tempo insieme. Volevamo **festeggiare** il compleanno di Mayra. **Decidemmo** di andare a Positano perché sapevamo che era un luogo che aveva delle bellissime spiagge, hotel puliti e splendidi paesaggi.

Maria e io stiamo in un hotel chiamato "L'hotel Cinque Stelle". L'hotel è vicino alla mia spiaggia preferita di Positano, che è il Gabbiano Blu. In quei luoghi, la gente è **straniera** e desidera conoscere il posto. I **lavoratori** sono Italiani. Sono stati molto **cordiali** con noi durante tutta la nostra **permanenza** in Italia. L'hotel era molto grande, **spazioso** e **rustico**. Lo avevamo prenotato un mese prima del viaggio. **Scegliemmo** una camera doppia per stare **comode**. Il nostro pacchetto in hotel comprendeva la colazione. Il clima era soleggiato e le spiagge erano sempre piene di gente, ma il luogo era bello lo stesso.

Un giorno andiamo in gita guidata all'Isola di Capri, un luogo che Maria ed io desideravamo conoscere da molto tempo. Era un'attività di gruppo di **circa** venti persone. Maria ed io eravamo felici ed emozionate di visitare un'isola tanto conosciuta e splendida. A noi è sempre piaciuto stare in spiaggia e **abbronzarci**.

Il viaggio per l'isola fu parecchio **stressante**. C'era un bambino chiamato Ethan che voleva sempre giocare. Tentavamo di ascoltare quello che ci diceva la nostra **guida turistica**, ma Ethan faceva troppo **chiasso**. Il viaggio in **motoscafo** durò venti minuti e alla fine conoscemmo quel luogo tanto bello, dove le acque sono cristalline e tranquille. Amiamo quel luogo e posso dire che ha superato le nostre **aspettative**. Più tardi, quello stesso giorno, continuiamo il giro e stavolta riuscimmo a vedere i pesci e a nuotare con loro. Per un attimo, Maria ed io ci fermammo a guardare Fabbio, il bambino **giocherellone**, che si divertiva tanto a nuotare con i variegati pesci del luogo. Dopo aver nuotato e passeggiato, ci venne fame, così **assaggiamo** un **pasto tipico** dell'isola di Capri, a base di pesce.. La cena era deliziosa. Al momento di tornare, Maria ed io notammo che Fabbio dormiva. La gita era stata molto divertente ed era durata tutto il giorno. Fabbio non aveva resistito ed era crollato.

Dopo questo, arrivò il giorno più atteso per noi: il compleanno di Maria. **Decidemmo** di cenare in un bel posto chiamato "La Conchiglia". Era vicino al nostro hotel. Ordinammo i nostri piatti italiani preferiti. Questa volta, **scegliemmo** un antipasto, frittura di mare, il preferito di Maria, insieme a un'abbondante **varietà** di cibo italiano. Per Maria, acqua gassata, e per me, acqua naturale. Maria ed io condividiamo un'**esperienza** molto **gradevole**. Il cameriere incaricato, di nome Cesare, ci mostrò come si prepara il tiramisù. Il posto era **spazioso** e offrivano un eccellente servizio. Quella sera era davvero speciale. Maria ed io parlavamo dei nostri piani futuri e ci divertimmo molto. Cesare e i suoi compagni cantarono "That's Amore" per Maria. Le regalarono il tiramisù per soffiare le candeline. Al termine della cena, Maria ed io andammo a spasso e comprammo dei **ricordini** da portare a casa. **Dall'altra parte**, io scelsi di comprare un piatto fatto di ceramica che sono **fatte a mano** e sono molto **pittoresche.** In quel luogo conoscemmo Luca.

Lui è diventato nostro amico ed è stato con noi nei nostri ultimi giorni in Italia. Luca ci invitava ad una **discoteca** perché gli dicemmo che era il compleanno di Maria. Tale **discoteca** si chiama "La Farfalla Bianca". Luca era molto **gentile** e ci divertimmo tanto. Ci presentò a un gruppo di amici suoi. Alcuni di questi erano **stranieri**. I **ballerini** della Farfalla Bianca erano bravissimi. L'ambiente era il meglio. Maria ed io ci stanchiamo tanto, ballando e divertendoci. Sicuramente torneremo in **discoteca**. Il giorno seguente, tutti e tre andammo in spiaggia ad **abbronzarci** e a riposare. L'attività preferita di Maria **mentre** è in spiaggia. La mia è nuotare. Amo nuotare. Luca **preferisce abbronzarsi**. La **sbronza** della notte precedente era stata **forte**. Dopo aver riposato qualche ora in spiaggia, ci dedicammo alla nostra ultima attività: le immersioni. È una **esperienza** meravigliosa. Ci immergemmo **a fondo**. Avevamo una **guida** incredibile, che ci insegnò tante cose sulla vita marina. Ci spiegò quali sono gli **animali marini** a rischio di estinzione. Scattammo foto pazzesche. Vedemmo tanti **animali marini** ed è stato il miglior post-compleanno di Maria.

Ricordo che Maria ed io eravamo molto **nostalgiche**. Non volevamo che quei nostri giorni a Positano e in quelle splendide spiagge finissero, però giunse il momento di tornare al nostro paese. Abbiamo stretto grandi amicizie, abbiamo vissuto momenti meravigliosi, ci siamo godute paesaggi **paradisiaci**, abbiamo fatto **esperienze** incredibili. Senza dubbio, è stato un viaggio fantastico che rifarei volentieri.

GLOSSARY		GLOSSARY	
Straniero (a)	Foreigner	**Giacché**	Since
Lavoratore (trice)	Worker	**Chiasso**	Noise
Stressante	Stressful	**Aspettativa**	Expectation
Mentre	While	**Motoscafo / Barca**	Boat
Amabile	Kind	**Gradevole**	Pleasant
Rustico	Rustic	**Provare**	Try
Paradisiaco	Paradisiacal	**Sabbia**	Sand
Abbronzatura	Tan	**Discoteca**	Nightclub
Sbronza	Hangover	**Fatto a mano**	Handmade
Nostalgico (a)	Nostalgic	**Costoso**	Expensive
Guida turistica	Tourist guide	**Pittoresco**	Full of color / Picturesque
Quadro	Picture	**Ricordino**	Souvenir
Giocherellone	Playful	**Ballerino (a)**	Dancer
Pasto tipico	Typical food	**Forte**	Strong
Soggiorno	Stay	**Animale marino**	Sea animal
Variegato (a)	Varied	**Esperienza**	Experience
Comodo (a)	Comfortable	**Preferire**	Prefer
Spazioso	Spacious	**Resistere**	Resist

GLOSSARY	
Scegliere	Choose
Profondo	Deep
Celebrare	Celebrate
Dall'altra parte	On the other hand

GLOSSARY	
Circa	About / Around
In anticipo	In advance
Decidere	Decide

Now that you've finished the story, let's see how much you caught on! Answer the following questions to test your understanding:

1. Che mese sono stati in Italia, a Positano per le ferie?

   _____

2. Come si chiama l'hotel dove stanno Maria e la sua amica?

   _____

3. Quante persone sono andate in gita?

   _____

4. Come si chiama la discoteca?

   _____

5. Chi tipi di animali hanno visto durante l'ultima attività: le immersioni?

   _____

STORY #3 : Buon appetito!

(Enjoy!)

Carolina è una youtuber. Crea **contenuti** sulle **reti social**. Carolina viene dall'Italia In Italia si parla italiano. Carolina fa **contenuti** di cucina sulle **reti social**. Oggi Carolina preparerà la pappa al pomodoro, un **piatto stellare toscano**. Prima di iniziare a **cucinare**, Carolina **cerca** la telecamera. Nel frattempo, suo **marito** torna a casa con tutti gli **ingredienti**.

"Sono tornato!", dice il **marito** di Carolina. *"Sono in camera da letto!"* grida Carolina. Suo **marito** va verso la stanza e vede Carolina che cerca la telecamera. *"Non ricordo dove ho messo la telecamera"*, dice Carolina a suo **marito, infastidita**. *"Tranquilla, l'hai messa nell'armadio."* Il **marito** di Carolina va verso l'**armadio** e tira fuori la telecamera da un **cassetto**. *"Wow, non lo ricordavo, scusa."* Il **marito** di Carolina le dà la telecamera e insieme vanno in **cucina**. *"Inizi a registrare?"* domanda il **marito** di Carolina. *"Sì, inizio a **registrare**."* Carolina controlla tutti gli **ingredienti** che suo **marito** ha portato dal supermercato. Tutti gli **ingredienti** sono nella **busta**. Carolina mette la telecamera di fronte a sé e organizza tutti gli **ingredienti** sul tavolo della **cucina**. Prima di **registrare**, Carolina **fa un respiro** e dice **a se stessa**, *"Puoi farcela, tranquilla e azione"*. Poi accende la telecamera e inizia a **registrare**.

"Il mio nome è Carolina. Benvenuti a un nuovo video!", dice Carolina mentre **saluta** la telecamera. *"Oggi **cucineremo** un piatto **tipico Italiano**, dalla toscana chiamato Pappa al Pomodoro. Avete mai sentito parlare di questo piatto?"* A Carolina piace registrarsi mentre cucina o parla delle sue esperienze. È pronta per cucinare questo piatto stellare del Perù. *"Gli **ingredienti** che andremo ad utilizzare sono: una (1) **cipolla**, cinque (5) **pomodori**, tre (3) pezzi di **aglio**, **un po'** di **basillico**, tre cento grammi **(300 grams)** di pane vecchia, quello croccante **pepe**, **sale** e **olio di oliva**."* Il **marito** di Carolina è molto emozionato perché lui ama la pappa al pomodoro Carolina continua a spiegare quello che fa nel video, mentre suo marito va al bagno a fare una doccia. Dopo la **breve** introduzione del **piatto stellare italiano**, Carolina inizia a triturare la **cipolla** e il **pomodoro**.

L'inizio del **piatto stellare** è **facile**: triturare il **pomodoro** e la **cipolla**. Triturare la cipolla fa piangere Carolina. Tritare il pomodoro è più **facile** per lei. Per Carolina parlare alla telecamera è **facile**. Dopo aver tritato le verdure, si **aggiunge l'olio, la cipolla** in una **ciotola**. Dopodiché *"si **aggiunge il pomodoro** nella **ciotola** e si aggiunge il basilico ed un po 'di acqua ambiente"*, dice Carolina mentre guarda la telecamera. Carolina non è una bravissima **cuoca**, però le piace tanto **diffondere** la sua **cultura** ai suoi **sostenitori**. Carolina ne approfitta per tagliare la carne a strisce. *"Non dovete **dimenticare di aggiungere il sale e il pepe** sempre!,"* Carolina **spiega** questa cosa con molta enfasi perché è necessario seguire **passo dopo passo**, per **ottenere il sapore italiano**.

Carolina sta quasi per terminare di **cucinare** il **piatto stellare italiano. La pappa al pomodoro** è famosa in tutta la Toscana, soprattutto durante l'estate che può essere servita anche fredda! Mischia tutti gli ingredienti finché il pane vecchio diventa morbido. Dopo aver **aggiunto** uno **spicchio d'aglio** , è pronto per essere servito. " Dopo aver terminato di registrare il video e

di fare degli scatti in più, Carolina serve due piatti per lei e suo **marito**. *"**Amore**, ho appena terminato di **registrare** e di **cucinare**, vuoi un po' di pappa al pomodoro?"* Carolina finisce di **parlare** e suo **marito grida** dalla **camera da letto**, *"Sì, voglio **un po'** di pappa al pomodoro."*

Quando Carolina si siede a tavola con suo marito, iniziano a parlare dei **successivi** video tutorial sul cibo italiano che lei vuole fare. *"Devi cucinare cotoletta alla milanese,"* le dice suo **marito** pensando a un altro **piatto italiano** che Carolina sa **cucinare**. *"Tu vuoi **cucinare** solo cibo italiano*, vero?" Carolina **ride** e suo **marito** continua a mangiare il **piatto stellare italiano**.

GLOSSARY		GLOSSARY	
Contenuto	Content	**Canale di YouTube**	Youtube channel
Reti social	Social media	**Fare una doccia**	Take a shower
Cibo	Food	**Un po'**	A little
Piatto stellare	Star dish	**Mezzo chilo**	Half a kilo
Peruviano	Peruvian	**Cucina**	Kitchen
Cucinare	Cook	**Piccola**	Small
Fidanzato	Boyfriend	**Triturare/ tagliare**	Chop
Ingredienti	Ingredients	**Facile**	Easy
Cercare	Look	**Prendere**	Turn on
Infastidita	Annoyed	**Riscaldare**	Heat
Armadio	Closet	**Fornello**	Stove
Cassetto	Drawer	**Piangere**	Cry
Borsa	Bag	**Olio**	Oil
Fare un respiro	Take a breath	**Diffondere**	Spread
A se stessa	To herself	**Cultura**	Culture
Salutare	Greet	**Sostenitori**	Subscribers
Cipolla	Onion	**Chef / cuoca**	Chef / Cook
Pomodoro	Tomato	**Aggiungere**	Add
Aglio	Garlic	**Strisce**	Strips
Ciotola	Bowl	**Dimenticare**	Forget
Carne	Meat	**Raggiungere**	Achieve/ Reach
Salsa di soia	Soy Sauce	**Passo dopo passo**	Step by step
Pepe	Pepper	**Sapore**	Taste
Sale	Salt	**Pronto**	Ready
Menzionare	Mention	**Servito**	Served
Riso	Rice	**Oggi**	Today
Carismatica	Charismatic	**Scatti aggiuntivi**	Additional shots

GLOSSARY	
Registrare	Record
Amore	Love
Parlare	Talk

GLOSSARY	
Gridare	Shout / Scream / Yell
Ridere	Laugh

Having wrapped up the story, it's quiz time! Test your comprehension by answering the following questions:

1. Di dove Carolina?

   _____

2. Che tipo di contenuti fa Carolina?

   _____

3. Cosa fa Carolina prima di registrare?

   _____

4. Cosa cucina Carolina?

   _____

5. Carolina dice, *'non dovete dimenticare...'* cosa?

   _____

Speak Abroad
Academy

STORY #4 : Giovedì Mattina

(Thursday Morning)

Il mio nome è Ernesto e una volta mi è successa una cosa molto **particolare**. Io vivo a Milano, Italia. Vicino a dove vivo, c'è una stazione ferroviaria chiamata Milano Stazione Centrale. **Solitamente** prendo un treno per andare al lavoro e sono sempre **puntuale**.

Quel giovedì non arrivai in tempo per prendere il treno. Il mercoledì era stato il compleanno di mia madre. Faccio sempre il possibile per prendere il treno giusto. In realtà, stavo per prendere quello **sbagliato**, perché avevo dormito poco il giorno precedente. Ad ogni modo, non potevo mancare il compleanno di mamma, che ha compiuto cinquant'anni. Quella mattina **correvo** più veloce che potevo per non perdere il treno delle sette e trenta. C'erano così tanta gente, che dovevo dire continuamente *"Mi dispiace tanto"*. In realtà, la gente è molto distratta.

Dopo aver aspettato **circa** venticinque minuti, quando normalmente il treno passa ogni dodici minuti, usciva un **avviso** alla stazione, che diceva: *"Ci dispiace molto informare i **cittadini** che, a causa di un **incidente**, il servizio di trasporti delle prossime tre ore sarà bloccato. Ricordate che potete chiedere assistenza all'Ufficio dei servizi alternativi di trasporto. Vi chiediamo **pazienza**, dato che stiamo lavorando per **risolvere** questo **problema** nel modo più rapido possibile."* Sentendo questo, pensai che non poteva esserci niente di **peggio**. Per giunta, la mia **titolare**, che era di malumore, già mi chiamava per chiedere dove stavo. Le mie parole **esatte** furono: *"Mi dispiace tanto di essere **in ritardo** oggi, ma il treno ha avuto un **imprevisto**, che **sarà risolto** entro tre (3) ore. Devo capire come posso fare per arrivare il prima possibile"*.

D'un tratto, si **avvicinò** Maria, che in quel momento era una totale **sconosciuta**, e mi domandava: *"Salve. Sa dove posso **trovare** l'**Ufficio** dei servizi alternativi? È che ho perso il treno e ho un tour turistico tra un'ora"*. Appena la vedo, sono rimasto colpito. Devo **ammettere** che Maria è una donna bellissima. Le rispondevo in modo **cortese** che sì, lo sapevo e che l'avrei **accompagnata** molto volentieri. Nel tragitto verso questo ufficio, la conversazione tra noi **fluì** con naturalezza. Ho dimenticato per un momento quanto stava andando male quel giovedì mattina. Innanzitutto, le domandavo: *"Dove si tiene il giro turistico che deve fare?"*. Mi diceva che era per Torino e che non aveva avuto l'**opportunità** di venire prima, ma non le rimaneva tanto tempo. Questo non le **avrebbe permesso** di visitare il centro storico della città. Mi sono sentito molto a mio agio a parlare con Maria. Arrivati all'**ufficio** di assistenza, che non era tanto lontano, Maria mi diceva: *"Ti dispiace aspettare un momento? Non mi trattengo troppo."* Dopo tutto, pensai che non avevo tanta fretta, perché erano passati solo venti minuti dall'**annuncio**, così risposi *"Sì, non preoccuparti. Se ti danno qualche soluzione, avvisami. Starò qua fuori."* C'era molta gente fuori dall'**ufficio**, ma Maria era una delle prime ad essere **servita**. Io non mi preoccupavo molto, perché avevo già avvertito al lavoro che non sarei arrivato in tempo per **circostanze** del servizio **inefficiente**.

Una soluzione rapida era che la mia titolare mi permetteva di lavorare da casa, almeno quel giorno. Pensavo di dirglielo, ma non mi sono sentito di farlo. Fortunatamente, non mi aspettavo molto lavoro, essendo quasi il fine settimana. Maria usciva dopo poco e non sembrava molto **contenta**. Le domandavo cosa le avevano detto e mi rispondeva che,

fintanto che non si **risolve** i problemi tecnici, non c'era un percorso **alternativo**, a meno che non prendeva un autobus.

Mancavano ancora due ore per poter contare di nuovo sul servizio; allora le **proposi**: "*Ti va di andare a prendere un caffè?*", al che lei mi disse: "*D'accordo. Andiamo.*"

Durante il tragitto per la caffetteria, mi venne da chiederle se poteva parlare con la gente del tour turistico. Mi diceva che ormai lo davano per perso. Non mi sembrava **giusto**, dato che non era **colpa** sua. Allora le dicevo di provare a parlare con loro. L'opzione migliore era di **riprogrammare** il tour per un'altra volta. Maria mi ringraziò tanto per averla **tirata su**. Al contempo, mi arrivò un messaggio della mia titolare, che diceva di non preoccuparmi, perché potevo lavorare da casa.

Dopo tutto, quella mattina di giovedì non andava così tanto male, perché ho potuto conoscere Maria. Da quel giorno, siamo diventati grandi amici. E in più, la mia titolare mi ha dato il permesso di lavorare da casa. Non avrei mai pensato di sentirmi tanto grato per un guasto alla stazione ferroviaria.

GLOSSARY		GLOSSARY	
Puntuale	Punctual	**Risolvere/ sistemare**	Fix /Solve
Solito	Usual	**Avvicinare**	Approach
Particolare	Peculiar	**Sconosciuto (a)**	Unknown
Sbagliato	Wrong	**Trovare**	Find
Correre	Running	**Ufficio**	Office
Scontrarsi	Stumble	**Colpire**	Shock
Girarsi	Turn over	**Ammettere**	Admit
Fermare	Stop	**Cortese**	Polite
Ritmo	Pace	**Accompagnare**	Go with / Join
Circa	Around	**Fluire**	Flow
Incidente	Incidence	**Entrambi**	Both
Cittadino	Citizen	**Pazienza**	Patience
Risolvere	Solve	**Permettere**	Allow
Problema/ questione	Matter	**Circostanze**	Circumstances
Peggiore	Worst / Worse	**Inefficiente**	Inefficient
Avviso	Alert	**Servire**	Attend to
Titolare	Boss	**Annunciare**	Announce
Esatto	Exact	**Alternativo**	Alternative
Ritardo	Delay	**Contenta**	Happy

.

Speak Abroad
Academy

GLOSSARY	
Imprevisto	Unforeseen
Mentre/ fintanto che	While
Proporre	Propose
Accettare	Like

GLOSSARY	
Tirare su/ incoraggiare	Encourage
Colpa	Fault
Giusto	Correct
Riprogrammare	Reschedule

You've reached the end of the story—great job! To gauge your understanding, answer the following questions:

1. Come si chiama la stazione ferroviaria vicino a dove vive Ernesto?

   _____

2. A che ora era il treno?

   _____

3. Perché il treno era in ritardo?

   _____

4. Come si chiama la ragazza ha conosciuto Ernesto?

   _____

5. Ernesto ha lavorato da casa?

   _____

STORY #5 : L'esame Finale

(The Final Exam)

Elena è una **studentessa** del **liceo** che ha un **esame finale** oggi. Per superare l'**anno scolastico**, Elena deve superare l'**esame finale**. Elena sta **studiando** in camera sua per l'**esame finale** che si tiene oggi, tra quattro ore. Elena pensa di **studiare** fino a due ore prima dell'**esame finale** e poi di prepararsi per andare a **scuola**.

Elena è seduta alla sua **scrivania** con un **libro** di **matematica** sul **tavolo**. Elena sta **studiando** per il suo **esame finale** di matematica. Mentre Elena continua a **studiare**, sua mamma passa in camera di Elena e la vede tanto **concentrata**, che le chiede se ha bisogno di **aiuto**. Elena le **risponde** che va tutto bene, ma la mamma non è **convinta**, quindi decide di portarle un **tè** e degli **spuntini**.

Elena sta seduta alla **scrivania** della sua camera a **leggere** il **libro** di **matematica**. Sulla sua **scrivania** ci sono alcuni **materiali scolastici** per l'**esame finale**. A iniziare dal **libro** di **matematica** e il **quaderno di matematica**, una **matita** per compilare l'**esame finale**, **colori** per **disegnare grafici**, una **gomma** per cancellare qualche errore sull'**esame finale**, **appuntamatite**, se la punta della **matita** si rompe, una **riga** per **disegnare grafici** e, per finire, **forbici** e **colla**.

Mentre Elena risolve alcuni **esercizi di matematica** per finire di **studiare**, sua mamma entra in camera con un piatto di **biscotti** con **gocce di cioccolata**, un po' di **latte fresco** e un fiore. *"Spero che ti vada tutto bene al tuo **esame finale**, tesoro. Non pretendere troppo da te stessa."* Sua mamma le dà un **bacio** sulla **fronte** ed Elena **sorride**. *"Grazie, mami. Farò il meglio che posso."* Nel frattempo, Elena finisce di **leggere** un paio di formule per risolvere le **equazioni**.

Un'ora dopo, Elena si sente più **fiduciosa** per affrontare l'**esame finale**, ma continua a **leggere** altre formule per essere più preparata per l'**esame finale**. Elena decide di **riposare** venti minuti, per **liberare** la **mente** e continuare a studiare l'**ultima parte** dell'**esame finale**. Elena si alza dalla **scrivania** e **si stiracchia**. Ormai si sente pronta per l'**esame finale**. L'**esame finale** di **matematica** non sembra **difficile** adesso.

Elena inizia a preparare il suo **zaino** per andare al **liceo** a presentare il suo **esame finale** di **matematica**. Elena **mette** nel suo **zaino** tutti i **materiali scolastici** che le servono. Quando finisce, si **volta** verso la sua **scrivania** e nota i **biscotti** e il **latte fresco** che sua mamma le aveva lasciato. Quasi se n'era **dimenticata**. Elena si siede di nuovo alla **scrivania**, stavolta un po' più **rilassata**, per mangiare gli **spuntini** che sua mamma le aveva portato in camera.

D'un tratto, sua mamma si affaccia alla **porta**, **sorridente**, e le domanda. *"Ti sono piaciuti gli spuntini?"*. Elena alza lo sguardo e trova sua mamma seduta sul suo **letto**. *"Sono deliziosi, mi piacciono i **biscotti** con **gocce di cioccolato**."* La mamma di Elena sa che le piacciono i **biscotti** con **gocce di cioccolato**. Dopo aver **chiacchierato** per altri cinque minuti, la mamma di Elena esce dalla camera, mentre Elena torna alla sua **scrivania** a **studiare** per l'ultima volta. .

Speak Abroad
Academy

Quando Elena termina di **studiare matematica**, si alza dalla sua **scrivania**, felice e pronta per affrontare l'**esame finale**. Si **stiracchia** un po' e lascia cadere il suo **corpo** sul **letto**, per poi **mandare un messaggio** alla sua **migliore amica**, Rachele: *"Ho finito di **studiare**, sto andando a **scuola**."* Elena è **orgogliosa** di se stessa, perché è riuscita a capire tutte le formule. Mancano ancora due ore all'**esame finale**, per cui Elena decide di **riposare** un paio di minuti sul **letto**, e **chiude** gli **occhi**. Senza pensare, Elena si **addormenta** per un'ora e mezza e si sveglia al suono del suo **telefono**. *"Pronto?"* risponde Elena con **voce roca** e assonnata. *"Elena, dove sei? L'**esame finale** inizia fra **mezz'ora** e tu non sei ancora qui!"* Era Rachele al **telefono**. Elena **salta** giù dal **letto** ed esce **di corsa** da **casa** sua senza pensare. *"Arrivo tra venti minuti. Di al **professore** di non **chiudere la porta**, per favore!"*. Dopo aver detto questo, Elena riattacca il **telefono** per entrare nella sua **auto** e **guidare** fino a **scuola**.

GLOSSARY		GLOSSARY	
Studentessa	Student	Gomma per cancellare	Eraser
Liceo	High school	Appuntamatite	Sharpener
Esame finale	Final exam	Riga	Ruler
Anno scolastico	School year	Disegnare	Draw
Studiare	Study	Forbici	Scissors
Scrivania	Desk	Colla	Glue
Scuola	School	Zaino	Bag
Libro	Book	Su	On
Matematica	Math	Letto	Bed
Tavolo	Table	Cuscino	Pillow
Concentrata	Focused	Lenzuolo	Bedsheet
Aiuto	Help	Esercizi di matematica	Math exercises
Rispondere	Answer	Biscotti	Cookies
Tè	Tea	Gocce di cioccolato	Chocolate chips
Spuntini	Snacks	Latte fresco	Fresh milk
Leggere	Read	Profumo	Smell
Materiali scolastici	School supplies	Bacio	Kiss
Quaderno di matematica	Math notebook	Fronte	Forehead
Matita	Pencil	Sorridere	Smile
Colori	Colors	Equazioni	Equations
Colorare	Paint	Fiduciosa	Confident
Grafico	Graphic	Riposo / pausa	Break / Rest

GLOSSARY		GLOSSARY	
Pulire	Clean	Confusa	Unclear / Confused
Mente	Mind	Riposare	Rest
Ultima parte	Last part	Chiudere	Close
Stiracchiare	Stretch	Occhi	Eyes
Corpo	Body	Dormire	Sleep
Difficile	Hard	Telefono	Phone
Mettere	Put	Voce roca	Gritty voice
Girarsi	Turn around	Mezzora	Half an hour
Dimenticare	Forget	Saltare	Jump
Rilassata	Relaxed	Correre	Run
Porta	Door	Professore	Teacher
Mandare un messaggio	Send a message	Riattaccare	Hang up
Migliore amica	Best friend	Auto	Car
Orgogliosa	Proud	Guidare	Drive

The story's done, but the challenge isn't over! Test your grasp by answering the following questions:

1. Cosa deve fare Elena per superare l'anno scolastico?

   _____

2. Quale libro sta sulla scrivania?

   _____

3. Cosa ha mangiato Elena?

   _____

4. Come si chiama la migliore amica di Elena?

   _____

5. Elena va a scuola in macchina o in bicicletta?

   _____

STORY #6 : Viva Gli Sposi

(Long Live the Newlyweds)

Il mese **prossimo** mi sposo con l'amore della mia vita. Da poco abbiamo fatto una cena **meravigliosa** e molto divertente. Il mio fidanzato ed io ci conosciamo da dieci anni e siamo fidanzati da tre. Il nostro anniversario è il venti dicembre. Il mio fidanzato ed io siamo molto emozionati, perché si avvicina il giorno delle nostre **nozze**. Abbiamo deciso di sposarci in un locale. Il mio fidanzato è **socio** di questo locale da quando era bambino. La nostra organizzatrice di **nozze** si chiama Elisa. Elisa è nostra amica da tanti anni. **Confidiamo** ciecamente che ci offra il miglior servizio e che **realizzi** i nostri desideri. Io **parlo di** Elisa come della sorella che non ho mai avuto. È molto **simpatica** ed **estroversa**. Ha un buon senso dell'umorismo, è **appassionata** del suo lavoro, **empatica** e molto **organizzata**. Non ci sbagliamo a sceglierla come nostra organizzatrice di **nozze**.

Il giorno della cena, il mio fidanzato ed io siamo arrivati tardi, perché, a causa delle feste natalizie, il nostro lavoro **aumenta**. **Tuttavia, penso** che la **sorte** sia sempre al nostro fianco, visto che arrivammo prima di Elisa. Il **motivo principale** della **riunione** era **ordinare** i tavoli secondo la risposta degli **invitati**. Io ho invitato un centinaio di persone e il mio **fidanzato** altre centocinquanta.

Il tavolo principale sarà il nostro. A quel tavolo, ci sarà mio padre, che è un eccellente **oratore** e sono sicura che farà il **discorso** migliore per noi; mia madre, che è molto **emotiva** e si **emoziona** fino alle **lacrime** quando sente le parole di ogni **discorso**. Ci saranno anche i genitori di Giacomo, il mio fidanzato. Mia **suocera**, di nome Fiorella, è molto **diretta, amabile** e **loquace**. Al contrario, mio **suocero**, di nome Roberto, è una persona **riservata, paziente** e **puntuale**. Ci farà bene tenerli vicini, perché ci daranno la **calma** che ci servirà in quel giorno tanto **movimentato**.

Anche i nostri fratelli e i **testimoni** di **nozze** si siederanno accanto a noi; senza dubbio, gli invitati che più amiamo dopo i nostri genitori. Io ho tre fratelli. Mio fratello Mario, che è il **centro dell'attenzione** la maggior parte del tempo, è molto **divertente** ed è alto. Mia sorella Gemma, che è la maggiore tra noi, è la più **intelligente** e **originale** e sono **sicura** che ci **proporrà** idee per rendere il mio **matrimonio** più **memorabile**. In ultimo, mio fratello minore, di quindici anni, di nome Mauro, continua ad essere un ragazzino molto **giocherellone**, ma senza smettere di essere **obbediente**. È molto **educato** e **mangione**. D'altra parte, Giacomo ha un solo fratello minore, di nome Alessandro, che è molto **simile** a suo padre. Tra loro fanno **molte battute**, cosa che mi **sembra** assai **tenera**.

I nostri **testimoni** di **nozze** sono i nostri **migliori amici**. La mia **migliore amica** si chiama Giuliana e ha la stessa età nostra. Ci conosciamo dalle **elementari**. Quando le chiesi di farmi da testimone, si **emozionò** tanto. **Penso** che sia molto **affidabile, intelligente, decisa** e **paziente**. Poi c'è il nostro **testimone**, che è il **migliore amico** di Giacomo da quando erano molto piccoli. Si chiama Marco ed è molto **estroverso** e **leale**, è un **ballerino** e un po' **ribelle**.

Speak Abroad
Academy

La cosa migliore per Giacomo e per me è che Marco e Giuliana vanno molto d'accordo. Noi diremmo che si piacciono. Non vogliamo **intrometterci**, ma **pensiamo** che formino una bella **coppia**. Chissà cosa può succedere il giorno delle **nozze**. **Anche** Elisa la pensa come noi. Durante la conversazione, Elisa disse: "Mi *sembra* che tra Marco e Giuliana ci sia un'attrazione *reciproca*." Noi ci guardammo un po' sorpresi, perché pensavamo di essere gli unici ad averlo notato, per cui scoppiammo a ridere. Era un momento piacevole durante la cena.

La nostra cena non poteva andare meglio. Javier, Elisa ed io siamo riusciti a confermare i tavoli degli invitati e a controllare anche gli ultimi dettagli. Javier si incaricò di procurare i fiori per i centrotavola. Trova rose bianche con nastri bianchi intorno. Io ho scelto il sapore della torta: millefoglie con una crema mascarpone con frutta di bosco, una torta tradizionale per matrimoni qui in Italia..

Il giorno delle **nozze**, tutto è andato meravigliosamente. Non ce l'avremmo fatta senza il sostegno del mio attuale marito e di Elisa. Finimmo con sorpresa, perché al momento di lanciare il bouquet, Giuliana lo afferrò e Marco fu incoraggiato a chiederle di uscire, confermando la teoria di cui avevamo parlato con Elisa, Giacomo ed io durante la cena. Alla fine, non ci eravamo sbagliati così tanto

GLOSSARY	
Prossimo	Next
Sembra	Seem
Anche	Even
Bouquet	Bouquet
Leale	Loyal
Intromettersi	Intrude
Coppia	Couple
Padrini	Godparents
Ballerino (a)	Dancer
Ribelle	Rebel
Fiduciosa	Reliable
Intelligente	Smart
Deciso (a)	Assertive
Piuttosto/ abbastanza	Plenty
Elementari	Primary
Miglior amico (a)	Best friend
Emozionare	Excite
Lacrime	Tears

GLOSSARY	
Battutine	Inside jokes
Obbediente	Obedient
Innovativo (a)/ originale	Innovative
Divertente	Funny
Memorabile	Memorable
Tenero	Tender
Condividere	Share
Centro dell'attenzione	Center of attention
Meraviglioso (a)	Wonderful
Nozze	Wedding
Socio (a)	Member
Confidare	Trust
Esaudire	Fulfill
Parlare di	Describe
Gradevole	Nice
Estroverso (a)	Extrovert
Appassionato (a)	Passionate
Empatico (a)	Empathetic

Speak Abroad
Academy

GLOSSARY	
Organizzato (a)	Organized
Tuttavia	However
Considerare	Consider
Sorte / Fortuna	Luck
Aumentare	Increase
Riunione	Meeting
Ordinare	Order
Motivo principale	Main reason
Invitato (a)	Guest
Emotivo (a)	Emotional
Sicuro (a)	Sure
Diretto (a)	Straightforward

GLOSSARY	
Amabile	Kind
Suocera	Mother-in-law
Suocero	Father-in-law
Loquace	Talkative
Oratore	Speaker
Discorso	Speech
Riservato (a)	Private/ Reserved
Paziente	Patient
Calma	Calm
Movimentato	Eventful
Sposo	Groom

That concludes the story session. Ready to flex your comprehension muscles? Answer the following questions:

1. Per quanti anni si conoscono e per quanti anni sono fidanzati?

   _____

2. Come si chiama la organizzatrice di nozze?

   _____

3. Descrivi Roberto.

   _____

4. Chi sono i testimoni dello matrimonio?

   _____

5. Tra chi c'è un'attrazione reciproca?

   _____

STORY #7 : Mangiamo Insieme

(Let's Eat Together)

Il mio nome è Liliana, ho due figli. Mia figlia maggiore si chiama Francesca e ha 12 anni. Quando **nacque**, tutto **cambiò** per me. Lei è il mio **angelo** e uno dei miei **tesori** più **preziosi**. Dopo 7 anni, nacque mio figlio, di nome Giulio. È un bambino molto bello e parte della mia grande **ispirazione**; **tuttavia**, ultimamente sto avendo **problemi** per farlo mangiare, cosa che non mi è mai successa con Francesca.

Il **problema** è che a Giulio non piace né la frutta né la verdura di nessun tipo. Mio marito Tommaso mi dice di non **preoccuparmi**, che a nostro figlio piaceranno frutta e verdura con il tempo. In più sono una buona **cuoca**; ho fatto dei corsi vicino a casa mia per poter preparare altre **ricette**. Mio marito ama la mia cucina: il suo piatto preferito è la bistecca fiorentina, accompagnata con patate al forno e verdure grigliate.. Quello di mia figlia è il risotto e il mio è la lasagna con un bel bicchiere di vino rosso accanto.

Giulio non ha ancora un cibo preferito e, dato che è in età di **crescita, provo** a dargli ogni tipo di frutta, come cocco, ananas, fragola, anguria, banana, **pesca** e **frutto della passione**, ma non gliene piace **nessuna**, e di verdure come **peperone**, cetriolo, carota, broccoli, lattuga, **sedano, verza, mais** e **zucchina**.

Qualche tempo fa, andavamo in famiglia a un ristorante dove serve cibo delizioso, non tanto lontano da casa. Io chiesi un purè di patate con carne. Mio marito ordinò il piatto del giorno, che era pesce fritto con insalata. Francesca ordinava baccalà con insalata e non sapevamo cosa chiedere per Giulio, dato che nelle ultime settimane, se non erano patate fritte, non **mangiava** niente. **Tentammo** di dargli un po' di zuppa che **decidemmo** di ordinare, ma non **funzionò**. Alla prima **cucchiaiata** di zuppa, Giulio si mise a piangere. Il ristorante era **pieno** e gli **altri commensali** si stavano già **infastidendo**. Passarono 10 minuti e Giulio si **calmò**. Era una **lotta costante** alimentare mio figlio.

Ricordo ancora quando faceva i primi **capricci** perché non voleva mangiare la verdura. La mia verdura preferita è il cetriolo, così **decisi** di dargli insalata di cetrioli tagliati a **fette** per qualche mese. All'inizio, tutto andò bene. La **prima** fetta la mangiava, ma dopo un po' faceva una smorfia di **disgusto** e iniziava a **gridare**. Fu quasi sul punto di **lanciare** il **piatto**. Lo stesso accadde quando gli davo la banana. Ugualmente la tagliò a **fette** e ne mangiò un paio, ma dopo si **arrabbiò** e non ne volle più.

Non sapevo con chi **parlare** per farmi aiutare a trovare un modo **efficace**, perché Giulio **cominciasse** a mangiare poco a poco frutta e verdura, così, parlando con Tommaso, **decidemmo** di andare da uno **specialista** in **nutrizione**. Abbiamo richiamato una **clinica**, vicino a dove viviamo, e lì ci accolse la dottoressa Olivia Luca, **specializzata** in **nutrizione** pediatrica.

Arrivati allo studio della dottoressa, le riferiremo qual era il nostro **problema** con Giulio e quanto ci stava costando che mangiasse frutta e verdura. La **dottoressa** Luca ci spiegò con molta pazienza che per l'età è **possibile** che Giulio mostrasse un rifiuto verso frutta e

verdura. E poi, che l'ideale era che il cibo **sano diventasse** un'**abitudine**, e non solo di tanto in tanto. Di **tentare** con **pappe, purè, succo** o insalate. Ci disse che dovevamo essere pazienti e non **obbligarlo** a mangiare, se proprio non voleva. E anche di dare l'esempio e non fargli mangiare frutta e verdura **insieme**. Mio marito ed io uscivamo tranquilli dallo studio medico. La **dottoressa** ci aveva dato le informazioni che ci servivano. Dovevamo applicare quello che ci aveva insegnato durante la visita medica. Anche Giulio era felice, perché la **dottoressa** gli ha dato una lecca-lecca all'uscita dalla visita medica. Il **lecca-lecca** è il dolce preferito di mio figlio.

Il giorno seguente, sono andata al supermercato a comprare frutta e verdura **fresche**. Ho comprato arance, uva, banana, spinaci, formaggio, pomodori, patate, uova e pasta. Per colazione, preparavo la macedonia (insalata di frutta). Per pranzo, cucinavo una frittata di patate con spinaci, accompagnata da succo di arancia, e per cena, pasta al forno. Giulio ha fatto un grande **progresso** da quel giorno in poi. **Ha mangiato** tutta la sua macedonia senza **arrabbiarsi**, ha mangiato gran parte della frittata che gli ho servito a pranzo e ha bevuto tutto il succo. Per ultimo, a cena, **ha mangiato** tutto la pasta al forno. Tommaso, Francesca ed io siamo rimasti molto soddisfatti quel giorno, perché abbiamo condiviso un bel momento in famiglia e, da allora, tutto è cambiato.

GLOSSARY		GLOSSARY	
Nascere	To be born	**Efficace**	Effective
Parlare	Talk	**Arrabbiarsi**	Angry
Fresche	Fresh	**Cominciare**	Start
Progresso	Progress	**Cambiare**	Change
Specialista	Specialist	**Angelo**	Angel
Lecca-lecca	Lollipop	**Prezioso**	Precious
Pappe	Baby food	**Tesoro**	Treasure
Purè	Puree	**Ispirazione**	Inspiration
Succo	Juice	**Tuttavia**	However
Obbligare	Force	**Preoccuparsi**	Concern
Insieme	Together	**Problema**	Problem
Possibile	Possible	**Cuoco (a)**	Chef / Cook
Diventare	Become	**Preparare**	Prepare
Abitudine	Habit	**Ricette**	Recipes
Clinica	Clinic	**Corsi**	Courses
Sano	Healthy	**Crescita**	Growth
Dottore (essa)	Doctor	**Anona**	Custard apple
Nutrizione	Nutrition	**Frutto della passione**	Passion fruit

GLOSSARY	
Pesca	Peach
Nessuno (a)	None/ No one
Provare	Try
Ricordare	Remember
Mangiare	Eat
Decidere	Decide
Calmare	Calm
Pieno	Full
Funzionare	Work
Infastidirsi	Discomfort
Cucchiaiata	Scoop
Altri	Other
Commensali	Diners

GLOSSARY	
Lotta	Struggle
Costante	Constant
Fette	Slices
Peperone	Bell pepper
Sedano	Celery
Zucchina	Squash
Mais	Corn
Verza	Cabbage
Capriccio	Tantrum
Disgusto	Displeasure
Lanciare	Throw away
Piatto	Plate
Gridare	Scream / Yell

Now that you've savored the story, let's check your understanding. Answer the following questions to test your comprehension:

1. Quanti figli ha Lilliana? Come si chiamano?

   _____

2. Cos'è il piatto preferito di Tommaso, il marito di Lilliana?

   _____

3. Come si chiama la specialista di nutrizione?

   _____

4. Che cos'è il dolce preferito di Giulio, il figlio di Lilliana?

   _____

5. Cosa ha preparato Lilliana per cena?

   _____

Speak Abroad
Academy

STORY #8 : Amici Pelosi

(Furry Friends)

Dopo 8 anni da **sposati**, due **viaggi** per diversi **paesi** all'**anno** e zero **figli** all'orizzonte, mio marito Alberto e io (Carmella) decidiamo alla fine di prenderci una responsabilità oltre a noi stessi **o al matrimonio**. Siamo una normale **coppia sposata**. Alberto ed io ci conoscevamo da quando andavamo all'università, lui studiava legge e io studiavo per diventare disegnatrice di moda. Il nostro amore **nacque** quando meno ce lo aspettavamo.

Alberto era il fidanzato della **mia migliore amica** e io avevo un fidanzato del liceo. Ero al mio **secondo anno** di università, quando abbiamo iniziato di **uscire**. Certo, lui **come prima cosa,** chiuse il rapporto che aveva con la allora mia **migliore amica**, la quale, stranamente, ora è **sposata** con mio fratello, ma questa è un'altra storia.

Alberto ed io abbiamo cominciato una **relazione** il giorno in cui i miei **genitori** hanno deciso di **trasferirsi** dalla città. Quel giorno i miei **genitori** mi hanno detto che non potevamo **trasferirci** per diverse ragioni, che francamente ora non ricordo più. Ma Alberto pensava che me ne sarei andata via, per cui, si presentò nel mio giardino cantando una **canzone romantica** con un **cartello** scritta: "*Vuoi sposarmi?*"

Prima di poter spiegare quello che succedeva davvero, Alberto mi diceva che prima che me ne andassi dalla **città**, lui voleva confessare i suoi **sentimenti** per me. Io mi sono messa a ridere, ma lui quasi iniziò a piangere. Gli dissi che sì, volevo essere sua moglie e che non me ne sarei andata dalla **città**. Il suo **viso** divenne **rosso** come un pomodoro! Fu così che iniziò la nostra storia d'amore vera e propria.

Dieci **anni** dopo quel giorno, **oggi** siamo qui nella sala di casa nostra, a decidere che tipo di **animale** ci piacerebbe adottare. Per avere una responsabilità, oltre a quella delle nostre vite. La verità è che questo si sta rivelando un po' difficile, perché lui ama i **cani** e io amo i **gatti**. Cosa possiamo fare di fronte a questa tremenda differenza? Tuttavia, entrambi siamo sufficientemente **maturi** per capire che questa decisione deve essere presa da tutti e due.

"*Magari possiamo adottare un **cagnolino***", dice Alberto. "*Non mi piacciono i **cani**. Perché invece non adottiamo un **gatto**, che è **indipendente** e **pulito**?*" Nella mia mente, questa cosa ha senso. "*I **gatti graffiano** tutto in casa, le loro **feci** sono maleodoranti e fuggono quando vogliono*". Sento dire da Alberto. "*Invece i **cani** sono **chiassosi, puzzolenti** e attaccano chiunque.*" Dopo aver detto questo, Alberto rimane **zitto** per un momento, per poi riprendere a parlare. *Ok, facciamo così, allora: andiamo al negozio di **animali** per vederne qualcuno. Quello con cui ci troveremo meglio, lo adotteremo.*" È stata la cosa più **razionale** che ho sentito dire da Alberto in questa discussione.

Dopo avergli dato ragione, ci siamo diretti a un **negozio di animali**, per poter conoscere Il nostro futuro animaletto. Quando arrivammo, un'amabile commessa del posto, ci mostrò il negozio di animali e, dopo aver ascoltato il nostro piano di adozione, iniziò a spiegarci. "*In questo momento abbiamo due opzioni di **animali** da adottare, un **cane** e un **gatto**. Vi*

piacerebbe conoscerli?" Quando la ragazza ci portò a vedere gli animali, il primo che abbiamo notato fu un grazioso **gatto bianco; aveva** occhi grandi e azzurri ed era molto **peloso**. Il suo **pelo** era **morbido** e **setoso**. *"Che **gattino** stupendo e tenero. Credo che dovremmo adottare"*, dico con voce innamorata, ma mio marito subito risponde. *"No, dov'è l'altro **animale**?"* La commessa ci dirige verso l'altro **animale** e mio marito inizia a parlare. *"Questo cagnolino è perfetto, **occhi assonnati, piccolino**, con **le rughe, color caffè**. Mi piace!"* Così come mi aveva detto lui quando io stavo guardando lo splendido gattino, dissi: *"No, non c'è un'altra opzione da vedere?"*

La commessa ci guardò con un'espressione di **tristezza** e ci confermò di non avere altre opzioni da adottare. Ci incamminammo verso l'uscita principale del negozio, quando la commessa si mise davanti a noi e ci disse: *"In realtà mi sono appena ricordata che c'è un'altra opzione, vi interessa conoscerlo?"* I nostri volti si **illuminarono** come a **Natale**. Mio marito ed io dissimodi sì all'**unisono**. La commessa iniziò a camminare dalla parte opposta e ci fece entrare in una stanza. *"Aspettate qui, mettetevi comodi, potete sedervi sul **pavimento**, per conoscerlo meglio, è molto **piccolo**."* Anche se non avevamo idea di quello che ci avrebbe portato, mio marito ed io facevamo quello che ci diceva e ci siamo messi a sedere sul **pavimento**, senza scarpe. Dopo **un paio** di minuti, lei ritornò con qualcosa tra le mani.

"Vi presento il porcellino d'India, che ci è arrivato da poco ed è in cerca di una famiglia." Mio marito ed io restammo **attoniti**: era un **minuscolo porcellino d'India** color **caffè**, grandi **occhi marroni**, super **peloso**, e stava giocando con i nostri piedi! È molto **carino** e non riuscimmo a resistergli. Inaspettatamente, mio marito stava giocando sul **pavimento** con lui e io stavo per piangere. *"Credo che sia quello giusto. Ne sono sicurissima."* Guardai mio marito, che aveva ancora il **porcellino d'India** tra le mani. *"Sì, sono totalmente d'accordo."*

Dopo aver fatto tutti i **documenti**, potremmo portarci a casa il **porcellino d'India**, ma restava ancora una cosa importante da fare. Quando arrivammo a casa, lasciammo che il nostro nuovo **porcellino d'India** esplorasse un po' il luogo. Ovviamente ci assicuriamo che non si perdesse. Mentre il **porcellino d'India** continuò a camminare e ad esplorare, chiesi a mio marito: *"Hai già pensato a un nome?"*. Mio marito subito mi disse di sì, e allora decidemmo di dirlo nello stesso momento. Uno...due...tre... Io dissi "Camillo" e lui disse "Merced". Sul serio?! *"Non si chiamerà Merced." "Nemmeno Camillo."* Ed **ecco che ci risiamo**...

GLOSSARY		GLOSSARY	
Dopo	After	**Migliore amica**	Best friend
Sposati	Married	**Secondo**	Second
Viaggio	Trip	**Anno**	Year
Paese	Country	**Uscire**	Date
Figli	Children	**Come prima cosa**	First
Matrimonio	Marriage	**Relazione**	Relationship
Coppia	Couple	**Stranamente**	Curiously
Nascere	To be born	**Genitori**	Parents

Speak Abroad
Academy

GLOSSARY

Trasferirsi	Move
Città	City
Giardino	Yard
Canzone romantica	Romantic song
Cartello	Poster
Sentimenti	Feelings
Viso	Face
Rosso	Red
Oggi	Today
Animaletto	Pet
Gatto	Cat
Cane	Dog
Entrambi	Both
Maturo	Mature
Piccolo	Small
Indipendente	Independent
Pulito	Clean
Graffiare	Scratch
Feci	Stools
Chiassoso	Loud
Puzzolente	Smelly / Stinky
Zitto	Quiet
Ragionevole	Reasonable
Negozio di animali	Pet shop
Amabile	Kind
Bianco	White

GLOSSARY

Occhi	Eyes
Grande	Big
Azzurro	Blue
Peloso	Furry
Pelo	Hair
Morbido/ soffice	Soft
Setoso	Fluffy
Bellissimo	Pretty
Tenero	Cute
Assonnati	Sleepy
Piccolo	Small/ little
Rughe	Wrinkles
Caffè	Brown
Tristezza	Sadness
Illuminarsi	Shine/ Illuminate
Natale	Christmas
A suo agio	Comfortable
Pavimento	Floor
Un paio	A couple
Porcellino d'India	Guinea pig
Attoniti	Stunned
Marroni	Brown
Piedi	Feet
Documenti	Paperwork/ documents
Ecco che ci risiamo	Here we go again

You've reached the end of the story journey! To see how much you absorbed, answer the following questions and let the comprehension challenge begin:

1. Come si chiamano gli sposi?

   _____

2. Cosa studiavano all'università?

   _____

3. Quale animale piace ad Alberto – Quale animale piace a Carmella?

   _____

4. Descrivi il primo gatto che hanno visto.

   _____

5. Quale animale hanno deciso di adottare?

   _____

CONCLUSION

Congratulations! You've embarked on an exciting journey to learn Italian, and you've successfully reached the end of this book. Whether you've been exploring the intricate dance of grammar, memorizing essential words and phrases, or immersing yourself in our short stories, you've taken significant strides toward fluency. This book has been designed to provide you with a comprehensive foundation in the Italian language, and by completing it, you've equipped yourself with valuable tools for communication and cultural understanding.

Learning a new language is much like exploring a new world; it's filled with surprises, challenges, and the incredible joy of discovery. Each lesson you've tackled, every word you've mastered, and every story you've read has brought you one step closer to speaking Italian with confidence and ease. Reflect on your progress: from mastering subject pronouns and the verb essere, to navigating the nuances of prepositions and idiomatic expressions. Each section of this book was crafted to build your skills systematically, ensuring that you develop a strong grasp of both the technical and practical aspects of the language.

As you close this book, keep in mind that the adventure doesn't end here. Practice, patience, and perseverance are your best companions. Language learning is a dynamic and ongoing process, and the key to true mastery lies in continuous engagement. Engage with native speakers whenever possible; conversation is one of the most effective ways to improve your fluency. Don't be afraid to make mistakes; they are an essential part of the learning process. Each error is an opportunity to learn and grow.

Immerse yourself in Italian media. Watch Italian films, listen to Italian music, and read Italian books and newspapers. These activities will not only enhance your language skills but also deepen your understanding of Italian culture and society. Try to think in Italian as much as possible, and use the language in your daily life. Whether it's labeling objects around your house with their Italian names or writing a journal in Italian, these small practices can make a big difference in your fluency over time.

Whether you're dreaming of sipping espresso in a quaint Roman café, strolling through the picturesque streets of Florence, or simply enjoying Italian culture from your own home, you now have the tools to make those dreams a reality. The practical phrases and vocabulary you've learned in this book will serve you well in a variety of everyday situations, from shopping and dining out to handling travel and emergency scenarios.

The short stories you've read are not just exercises in comprehension; they are windows into Italian life and culture. Each narrative has provided you with context and nuance, helping you to see how the language is used in real-life situations such as leisure time, vacation, lunch breaks and exams. These stories also offer cultural insights that enrich your understanding of Italy and its people so that you can immerse yourself more wildly into the fabric of Italian culture.

As you continue your journey, consider joining Italian language groups or online forums. Connecting with fellow learners can provide mutual support and motivation. Additionally, you might explore advanced courses or even consider a language immersion program in Italy to further hone your skills.

In closing, we hope this book has inspired a lifelong passion for the Italian language and culture. Continue to explore, practice, and enjoy the beautiful journey of learning Italian. The world of Italian speakers is now more open to you than ever before. Buona fortuna, and may your path to fluency be as enjoyable and rewarding as the language itself! Arrivederci!

ANSWER KEY

LESSON 1

PRACTICE 1.1

A	1. noi	2. io	3. loro/ esse	4. loro essi	5. voi	6. tu	7. voi	8. noi	9. noi	10. loro
B	1. io	2. noi	3. voi	4. voi	5. loro/ essi					
C	1. lui e lei/ loro	2. loro	3. voi	4. voi	5. noi	6 lui/ egli	7. lei/ ella	0. loro/ esse	9. lui	10. lei

PRACTICE 1.2

A	1. tu	2. tu	3. lei	4. lei	5. tu	6. lei	7. lei	8. tu	9. tu	10. lei
B	1. voi	2. voi	3. voi	4. voi	5. tu					

PRACTICE 1.3

A	1.c	2. d	3. e	4. g	5. f	6. a	7. b	8. k	9. h	10. i
B	1. Buon pomeriggio	2. Buongiorno		3. Buonanotte		4. Buonanotte		5. Buongiorno		
C	1. Scusate/ Scusa	2. Permesso		3. Non è niente / Non fa niente		4. Permesso/ Scusate		5. Scusate/ Scusa		
D	1. e. Di niente	2. c. Bene, E tu?		3. d. Molto bene, grazie		4. a. A dopo		5. b. Non fa niente		
E	1. Come va?	2. E tu?		3. bene		4. A domani		5. Arrivederci / Ciao, a domani!		

LESSON 2

PRACTICE 2.1

1. la	2. il	3. la	4. la	5. l'	6. la	7. la	8. il	9. la	10. il
11. la	12. l'	13. la	14. la	15. il	16. la	17. il	18. il	19. la	20. il

PRACTICE 2.2

A	1. gli uomini	2. le amiche	3. le conversazioni	4. gli animali	5. i sistemi
	6. i bambini	7. le case	8. i treni	9. le città	10. i dottori
B	1. la verità	2. il televisore	3. la mano	4. la forchetta	5. la matita
	6. la bambina	7. la radio	8. la cena	9. la sedia	10. la gamba

PRACTICE 2.3

A	1. alcuni nonni	2. alcune conversazioni	3. alcuni cani	4. alcune donne	5. alcuni studenti
	6. alcuni dottori	7. alcuni hotel	8. alcuni treni	9. alcune matite	10. alcune città
B	1. gli studenti	2. i pianeti	3. una dottoressa	4. alcune foto	5. la lingua
	6. i turisti	7. alcuni amici	8. un pomodoro	9. la conversazione	10. alcune verità

C	1. la	2. una	3. la / un	4. una	5. alcune	6. il	7. una	8. le	9. la	10. un

D	1. the book- il libro	2. the house- la casa	3. the flowers- i fiori	4. the young man- il ragazzo	5. the brothers- i fratelli
	6. the coffee- il caffè	7. the train- il treno	8. the planets- i pianeti	9. a cat- un gatto	10. some dogs- alcuni cani
	11. the telephone-il telefono	12. the hands- le mani	13. a program- una programma	14. some systems- alcuni sistemi	15. the books- i libri

E	1. la	2. alcuni	3. un	4. il	5. una	6. i	7. il	8. un	9. le	10. la
F	1. una	2. la	3. un	4. la	5. il	6. una	7. le	8. un	9. un	10. gli

LESSON 3

PRACTICE 3.1

A	1. alta	2. povero	3. fedele	4. bella	5. difficile
	6. buono/bravo	7. felice	8. interessante	9. forte	10. debole
B	1. bassa	2. eccellente	3. piccola	4. simpatico/ amichevole	5. vecchio
	6. cattivo	7. intelligente	8. fedele	9. laborioso	10. grassa
C	1.la tema difficile	2. Il bambino alto	3. Il ristorante vuoto	4. La bambina simpatica	5. Il cane grande
D	1. i pomodori grandi	2. gli uomini alti	3. i cani intelligenti	4. le bambine forti	5. le persone laboriose
	6. le città piccole	7. i gatti magri	8. le donne allegre	9. i libri difficili	10. i cibi eccellenti
E	1. eccellenti	2. laboriosa	3. bella	4. piccoli	5. bella
	6. buone	7. grassi	8. simpatici	9. nuova	10. comode

PRACTICE 3.2

1. americana	2. francese	3. inglese	4. italiana	5. spagnola
6. tedesca	7. italiano	8. americana	9. francese	10. portoghese

PRACTICE 3.3

A	1. intelligente - bella	2. allegro - interessante	3. grande - interessante	4. buono - simpatico	5. cattivi - bianchi
B	1. buono, interessante, simpatico	2. interessante, laboriosa	3. grasso, interessante, simpatico, bello, buono, grande	4. grande, simpatico, grasso, buono, bello	5. grande, simpatico, grasso, buono, bello
C	1. francese	2. italiano	3. tedesco	4. spagnola	5. portoghese
D	1. italiano	2. spagnolo	3. inglese	4. italiano	5. spagnolo

LESSON 4

PRACTICE 4.1

A	1. fedele, intelligente, vecchia	2. nuovo, marrone	3. intelligente, laboriosa, interessante, felice, fedele	4. veloce, nuovo, marrone	5. interessante, moro, veloce, felice, intelligente, fedele, alto, ricco
	6. cara, vecchia, nuova, economica, marrone	8. trabajadora, interesante, feliz, inteligente, vieja, fiel, anciana	9. cara, vieja, nueva, barata	10. trabajadora, interesante, feliz, inteligente, vieja, fiel, anciana	11. interesante, difícil, nuevo, fácil
	7. nuovo, ricco, delizioso, marrone	8. laborioso, interessante, felice, intelligente, vecchia, fedele, anziana	9. cara, vecchia, nuova, economica	10. laboriosa, interessante, felice, intelligente, vecchia, fedele, anziana	17. interessante, difícil, fácil
	11. interessante, difficile, nuovo, facile	12. laboriosa, interessante, felice, intelligente	13. interessante, difficile, veloce, nuovo, facile	14. interessante, moro, veloce, felice, intelligente, fedele, alto, ricco	15. cara, interessante, vecchia, nuova
	16. cara, vecchia, nuova, economica, marrone	17. interessante, difficile, facile	18. nuovo, ricco, delizioso	19. buono, grasso, intelligente	20. grasso, veloce, marrone
B	1. gialla	2. blu	3. arancione	4. bianca	5. nera
	6. grigio	7. verde	8. rosato / rosa	9. marrone	10. rosso
C	1. Anche lui è gentile.	2. Anche questa è facile.	3. Anche loro sono laboriosi.	4. Anche loro sono grassi.	5. Anche lei è buona.
D	1. alta, laboriosa, bionda, felice e ricca.	2. grande, brutta, vecchia, e cara.	3. povero, stupido, moro, basso, pigro e giovane.	4. alto, vecchio, biondo e magro.	5. veloce, corto e felice.

PRACTICE 4.2

A	1. Questa camicia è bella	2. Queste scarpe sono care.	3. Questo maglione è di lana.	4. Questi vestiti sono di seta.	5. Questi pantaloni sono economici.
B	1. Quella camicia è bianca	2. Quella maglietta è rossa	3. Quelle gonne sono corte	4. Quella giacca è molto economica	5. Quelle scarpe sportive sono belle

C	1. Chi è quel dottore? Questo dottore è un cardiologo.	2. Questa pianeta è molto grande.	3. Quella casa è bella.	4. Quel treno è lungo.	5. Questa moto è nuova.
D	1. È felice questa bambina? No, è triste.	2. Sono ricchi questi ragazzi? No, sono poveri.	3. È brutto quel cane? No, è bello.	4. Sono vecchi questi edifici? No, sono nuovi.	5. È anziana questa donna? No, è giovane.
	6. Sono forti queste ragazze? No, sono debole.	7. È grande questa casa? No, è piccola.	8. È alto questo bambino? No, è basso.	9. Sono debole queste ragazze? No, sono forti.	10. È felice questa bambina? No, è triste.

PRACTICE 4.3

A	1. Quella casa è molto grande.	2. Quell'edificio è l'ufficio postale e quell'albero è molto vecchio.	3. Quella strada è nuova e quei cani sono cattivi.	4. Quel viale è ampio.	5. Quell'aeroporto è grande.
B	1. Questo sistema è eccellente.	2. Queste pescherie sono care.	3. Questa città è bella.	4. Questo teatro è piccolo.	5. Quegli uffici sono nuovi.

LESSON 5

PRACTICE 5

A	1. Luigi è degli Stati Uniti.	2. Tomás è francese.	3. Stanno a Madrid.	4. Sono turisti.	5. La signora è di Madrid.
B	1. Luciano Pavarotti è dell'Italia. È italiano.	2. Frida Kahlo è del Messico. È messicana.	3. Johnny Depp è degli Stati Uniti. È americano.	4. Albert Einstein è della Germania. È tedesco.	5. Coco Chanel è della Francia. È francese.
	6. Rafael Nadal è della Spagna. È spagnolo.	7. Cristiano Ronaldo è del Portogallo. È portoghese.	8. Paul McCartney è dell'Inghilterra. È inglese.	9. Donald Trump è del Stati Uniti. È Americano.	10. Carlos Santana è del Messico. È messicano.
C	1. Mick Jagger è inglese (identification).	2. Le sedie sono di plastica (materiale).	3. Noi siamo della Colombia (origin).	4. I tavoli sono di legno (material).	5. Il cibo è per la bambina (possession).
	6. È lunedì (day of the week).	7. Marco e Luigi sono avvocati (profession).	8. La festa è nel club (location).	9. Il cane è di Maria (possession).	10. Il libro è giallo (description).
D	1. È di plastica o di vetro	2. È di legno o di plastica	3. È di mattoni	4. Sono di pelle	5. Sono di vetro
	6. È di legno	7. È di metallo	8. È di carta	9. È di legno.	10. È di plastica o di gomma (rubber).
E	1. è	2. sono	3. è	4. sono	5. sono
F	1. Loro sono della Germania	2. Tu e Alejandra/Voi siete dell'Argentina	3. Voi siete della Colombia	4. Noi siamo del Messico	5. Io sono della Francia.
G	1. siete	2. sono	3. siamo	4. è	5. sono
	6. sei	7. siete	8. è	9. siete	10. sono
H	1. sono le tre del pomeriggio	2. è il primo di maggio	3. è il 3 di novembre	4. è mercoledì	5. sono le dieci del mattino

I	1. Sì, lei è simpatica	2. Sì, siamo studenti	3. No, non è piccola la casa di Marianna (or Sì, è piccola la casa di Marianna)	4. Elena è dell'Inghilterra	5. È importante studiare
J	1. I cani sono del bambino	2. Il libro è del collegio	3. Quella casa è del signore ricco	4. La moto è del giovane	5. Il cibo è del ristorante

LESSON 6

PRACTICE 6.1

A	1. Parigi e Lione stanno in Francia (location).	2. La bambina sta male (health).	3. Sta giù di morale (changing mood).	4. Gianmarco sta a pezzi (changing condition).	5. Noi stiamo qui (location).
	6. Questo vestito ti sta bene (personal opinion).	7. Voi state calmi (changing mood).	8. Tu stai dormendo (changing condition)	9. Lei sta lavorando (location)	10. Loro stanno alla partita (location).
B	1. Il tavolo e le sedie sono sporchi.	2. Lui è un avvocato.	3. Noi siamo stanchi	4. È importante studiare.	5. Voi siete all'università.
	6. Martino e Luigi sono intelligenti.	7. Il caffè è per la donna.	8. La città è bella.	9. Tu sei una turista.	10. Io sono di Milano.
	11. La lezione è facile.	12. Il bambino sta nel collegio.	13. Voi state bene.	14. Noi siamo italiani.	15. Sara è triste.
C	1. Tim è spagnolo.	2. Il ristorante è chiuso.	3. Le figlie di Pietro sono bionde e intelligenti.	4. Il problema è molto facile.	5. Il libro è interessante.
	6. Tu sei furioso.	7. La banana è gialla.	8. Noi siamo felice.	9. La foto sta sulla sedia.	10. La macchina è rossa.

D	1. è	2. è	3. è	4. stanno	5. è	6. è	7. è	8. è	9. sta	10. sono
E	1. X	2. ✓	3.✓	4. ✓	5. X	6. X	7. ✓	8. X	9. X	10. ✓

F	1. Teresa e Miguel stanno nel cinema	2. ✓		3. ✓	4. ✓		5. Tu sei una brava avvocatessa
	6. Io sono del Perú	7. ✓		8. Le sedie sono di plastica	9. Susanna è intelligente		10. ✓

PRACTICE 6.2

1. abbiamo	2. hanno	3. avete/ avete	4. ha	5. ho
6. ha	7. ha	8. abbiamo	9. hai	10. ha

PRACTICE 6.3

A	1. hanno		2. ho	3. hai		4. abbiamo		5. avete	
	6. ha		7. ha	8. ha		9. ha		10. abbiamo	
B	1. X	2. X	3. ✓	4. ✓	5. X	6. X	7. X	8. X	9. ✓	10. ✓

C	1. Noi abbiamo sessant'anni.	2. Voi avete quarant'anni.	3. ✓	4. ✓	5. Tu hai quindici anni.
	6. Maria ha sei anni.	7. Tu e Michele avete settant'anni.	8. Josefina ha ventitré anni.	9. ✓	10. ✓
D	1. ho	2. abbiamo	3. ha	4. hai	5. avete
	6. ha	7. hanno	8. avete	9. ha	10. ha

LESSON 7

PRACTICE 7.1

1. un	2. una	3. un	4. uno	5. un	6. un	7. una	8. un	9. un	10. una

PRACTICE 7.2

A	1. X C'è un tappeto in casa.	2. X Ci sono tigri allo zoo.	3. ✓	4. ✓	5. X Ci sono uffici nell'edificio.
	6. ✓	7. X Ci sono turisti in città.	8. X Ci sono persone nel cinema.	9. X C'è una pizza sul tavolo.	10. ✓
B	1. Are there flowers in your garden?	2. Are there chairs in your office?	3. Are there cats on the street?	4. Are there hotels in the city?	5. Is there a television in the house?
	6. Are there doctors at the hospital?	7. Is there a dog in the court?	8. Is there a radio in the automobile?	9. Are there two women in the fish store?	10. Are there tables in the restaurant?
C	1. Non ci sono animali nello zoo.	2. Non ci sono tanti bambini al parco.	3. Non c'è tanta gente nel ristorante.	4. Non c'è un buon hotel in città.	5. Non ci sono tanti pianeti in cielo.
D	1. sta	2. C'è	3. sta	4. sta	5. ci sono
	6. ci sono	7. C'è	8. C'è	9. sta	10. C'è

PRACTICE 7.3

A	1. fa caldo	2. fa freddo	3. c'è vento/sta soffiando il vento	4. c'è il sole	5. sta piovendo/c'è pioggia/piove
	6. c'è neve/sta nevicando/nevica	7. si sta annuvolando/ci sono nuvole	8. sta piovendo/c'è pioggia/piove	9. fa freddo/c'è neve/sta nevicando	10. fa caldo/ c'è sole
B	1. facciamo	2. fanno	3. faccio	4. fanno	5. fa
	6. fa.	7. fai	8. fate	9. fa	10. fa

PRACTICE 7.4

A	1. quanti	2. quanto	3. quanti	4. quante	5. quanto
B	1. Ci sono sette giorni in una settimana.	2. Ci sono quattro settimane in un mese.	3. Ci sono 12 mesi in un anno.	4. Ci sono due giorni in un fine settimana.	5. Ci sono ventotto giorni nel mese di febbraio.
	6. Ci sono cinque dita nella mia mano.	7. Ci sono due (number varies) ospedali nella mia città.	8. Ci sono diversi (number varies) televisori in casa mia.	9. Ci sono tre (number varies) alberi nel mio giardino.	10. Ci sono venti (number varies) sedie nella mia casa.
C	1. Ci sono due università in città.	2. Ci sono venti mele nel cestino.	3. Ci sono dodici mesi in un anno.	4. C'è una Statua della Libertà a New York.	5. Ci sono due occhi sul viso.

LESSON 8

PRACTICE 8.1

1. sappiamo	2. sai	3. sapete	4. sa	5. so	6. sa	7. sanno	8. sa	9. sanno	10. sa

PRACTICE 8.2

A	1. conoscono	2. conosce	3. conoscete	4. conosciamo	5. conosco
	6. conosce	7. conosci	8. conosce	9. conosco	10. conoscono
B	1. conosce	2. sapete	3. sanno	4. sa	5. conosce
	6. conosci	7. so	8. conoscete	9. sappiamo	10. conosce
C	1. conosco	2. sappiamo	3. conoscete	4. conosce	5. sai
	6. sanno	7. conosco	8. conosce	9. sanno	10. conosce

PRACTICE 8.3

A	1. Novak Djokovic sa giocare a tennis.	2. LeBron James sa giocare a pallacanestro/basket.	3. Tiger Woods sa giocare a golf.	4. J. K. Rowling sa scrivere molto bene..	5. Lionel Messi e Cristiano Ronaldo sanno giocare a calcio.
	6. Taylor Swift sa cantare.	7. Michael Phelps sa nuotare.	8. Shakira sa ballare e cantare.	9. Meryl Streep sa recitare.	10. Simone Biles sa fare ginnastica artistica.
B	1. Sherlock Holmes conosce Watson.	2. Ashton Kutcher conosce Mila Kunis.	3. Rhett Butler conosce Scarlett O'Hara.	4. Chris Martin conosce Dakota Johnson.	5. Adamo conosce Eva.
C	1. Io conosco il professor De Luca.	2. Mia sorella ed io conosciamo la madre di Gianmarco.	3. Maria e Luigi conoscono Sergio.	4. Voi conoscete il direttore dell'area commerciale.	5. Tu conosci la zia Teresa.
D	1. Io so la verità	2. Lei conosce Maria	3. Loro sanno nuotare	4. Pietro e Elena conoscono New York	5. Sappiamo la risposta
	6. Conosciamo lo studente.	7. Tu sai il mio nome .	8. Lui conosce/ sa la verità.	9. Il cane conosce Lorenzo.	10. So suonare il pianoforte.
E	1. sa	2. conosco	3. conosci	4. sanno	5. conosce

LESSON 9

PRACTICE 9.1

A	At the Grocer's				
	LUISA:	Good morning, do you have bananas?			
	GROCER:	Good morning. Yes, I do have bananas.			
	LUISA:	Oh, how much are they?			
	GROCER:	They are 20 pesos for a kilogram.			
	LUISA:	Very well. I need to buy two kilograms.			
	GROCER:	Ok. Here you are.			
	LUISA:	Thank you very much. Goodbye.			

B	1. io	2. noi	3. loro	4. Lei/ lui/ lei	5. io
	6. tu	7. Lei/ lui/ lei	8. voi	9. loro	10. tu

C	1. falso	2. falso	3. vero	4. falso	5. falso

D	1. lavora	2. guardano	3. cercate	4. insegna	5. compro
	6. viaggiano	7. spieghiamo	8. ripara	9. cucina	10. gioca

E

Infinito	parlare	insegnare	lavorare	guardare
io	parlo	insegno	lavoro	guardo
tu	parli	insegni	lavori	guardi
egli/ ella/ lui/ lei	parla	insegna	lavora	guarda
noi	parliamo	insegniamo	lavoriamo	guardiamo
voi	parlate	insegnante	lavorate	guardate
esse/ essi/ loro	parlano	insegnano	lavorano	guardano

PRACTICE 9.2

A	1. No, siamo quindici persone al tavolo.	2. Sì, lavoriamo tutti nello stesso ufficio.	3. Sì, abbiamo pollo e pesce.	4. No, abbiamo un tavolo grande.	5. No, ho una bambina mora.
B	1. comprende	2. prendono	3. corre	4. vendiamo	5. mangiate
	6. scriviamo	7. leggo	8. apprendi	9. vedono	10. lavora

C

Infinito	mangiare	vendere	credere	apprendere
io	mangio	vendo	credo	apprendo
tu	mangi	vendi	credi	apprendi
egli/ ella/ lui/ lei	mangia	vende	crede	apprende
noi	mangiamo	vendiamo	crediamo	apprendiamo
voi	mangiate	vendete	credete	apprendete
esse/ essi/ loro	mangiano	vendono	credono	apprendono

PRACTICE 9.3

A	1. condividono	2. salgono	3. vive... vive	4. apro	5. ricevi
	6. divertite	7. discutiamo	8. decidi	9. finisce	10. sento

B

Infinitive	partire	spedire	aprire	offrire
io	parto	spedisco	apro	offro
tu	parti	spedisci	apri	offri
egli/ella/lui/lei	parte	spedisce	apre	offre
noi	partiamo	spediamo	apriamo	offriamo
voi	partite	spedite	aprite	offrite
esse/essi/loro	partono	spediscono	aprono	offrono

LESSON 10

PRACTICE 10.1

A	1. Sono le nove e dieci	2. Sono le sei e cinque	3. Sono le sette e venticinque	4. Sono le dodici e un quarto	
B	1. Sono le quattro meno un quarto	2. Sono le undici in punto	3. È l'una e mezza	4. Sono le sette meno un quarto.	5. Sono le otto e un quarto
	6. Sono le nove e venti	7. Sono le otto meno un quarto.	8. È mezzogiorno/ Sono le dodici in punto.	9. È mezzanotte/ Sono le dodici in punto.	10. Sono le cinque e mezza.
C	1. Sono le otto. È ora di lavorare.	2. Sono le dieci. È ora di passeggiare.	3. È l'una e un quarto. È ora di pranzare.	4. Sono le quattro e mezza. È ora di ritornare a casa.	5. Sono le sei. È ora di andare a prendere i miei figli.
D	1. A che ora partiamo per Parigi? Alle dodici in punto.	2. A che ora partiamo per Madrid? All'una in punto.	3. A che ora partiamo per Praga? Alle cinque e mezza.	4. A che ora partiamo per Lima? Alle nove e un quarto.	5. A che ora partiamo per Washington? Alle sei meno un quarto.

PRACTICE 10.2

A	1. A mezzogiorno.	2. Alle quattro del pomeriggio.	3. Alle otto del mattino.	4. Alle undici di mattina.	5. A mezzanotte.
B	1. Sono le undici in punto.	2. Sono le otto e mezza.	3. Sono le otto del mattino.	4. Sono più o meno le tre del pomeriggio.	5. Sono le dieci e mezza.
	6. Sono le cinque e mezza.	7. Sono le sette e venti.	8. È l'una meno venti.	9. Sono le due meno cinque.	10. Sono le due meno venticinque.

PRACTICE 10.3

A	1. Vanno a messa o al bar per colazione.	2. La nonna cucina il pranzo.	3. Si guarda la partita a casa.	4. Si scende in piazza per un aperitivo.	5. I bambini preparano lo zaino per la scuola domani.
B	1. Alle quattro e un quarto.	2. Alle nove e un quarto.	3. Alle dieci e mezza.	4. Dal lunedì al venerdì.	5. I sabato

PRACTICE 10.4

A	1. Il mio compleanno è il (answer varies) .	2. L'indipendenza degli Stati Uniti si celebra il 4 luglio.	3. L'estate inizia il 21 giugno in Europa.	4. Natale è il 25 dicembre.	5. Capodanno è il 1° di gennaio.
B	1. Fiori → primavera. In primavera ci sono i fiori.	2. Sole → estate. In estate c'è il sole.	3. Foglie secche → autunno. In autunno ci sono le foglie secche.	4. Caldo → estate. In estate fa caldo.	5. vento → autunno. In autunno c'è vento.

LESSON 11

PRACTICE 11

A	1. No, Teresa non vuole mangiare niente.	2. No, Teresa non vuole bere niente.	3. No, Teresa non vuole niente.	4. No, Teresa non mangia mai la sera.	5. Sì, Teresa dorme meglio senza mangiare.
B	1. niente	2. nessuno	3. nessuno	4. mai	5. neanche
	6. qualche	7. qualcuno	8. alcuno	9. sempre	10. anche
C	1. Hai un maglione?	2. Non ho nessuna maglia.	3. Hai comprato una camicia?	4. No, non ho comprato nessuna camicia.	5. Ci sono bambini in piscina?
	6. No, non c'è nessun bambino in piscina.	7. Hai dei gatti in casa?	8. No, non ho nessun gatto in casa.	9. Hai qualche valigia nell'auto?	10. No, non ho nessuna valigia nell'auto.
D	1. Sì, Ho qualcosa. No, non c'è niente.	2. Sì, c'è qualcosa. Non c'è niente.	3. Sì, c'è qualcosa. No, non c'è niente.	4. Sì, c'è qualcosa. No, non c'è niente.	5. Sì, c'è qualcosa. No, non c'è niente.
E	1. Sì, c'è qualcuno. No, non c'è nessuno.	2. Sì, c'è qualcuno. No, non c'è nessuno.	3. Sì, c'è qualcuno. No, non c'è nessuno.	4. Sì, c'è qualcuno. No, non c'è nessuno.	5. Sì, c'è qualcuno. No, non c'è nessuno.
F	1. Sì, ci sono alcune. No, non ce n'è nessuna.	2. Sì, ci sono alcuni. No, non ce n'è nessuno.	3. Sì, ci sono alcuni. No, non ce n'è nessuno.	4. Sì, ci sono alcune. No, non ce n'è nessuna.	5. Sì, ci sono alcune. No, non ce n'è nessuna.
G	1. Non c'è niente di buono in cucina.	2. Non ho nessun fiore nel mio giardino.	3. Sofia non studia mai la lezione.	4.Non mettono niente nell'auto.	5. Non ricevono mai i loro amici a casa.
H	1. niente	2. mai	3. né... né	4. niente	5. nessuno
	6. Neanche'	7. nessun	8. nessuna	9. mai	10. né... né

I	1. No, non condividiamo niente.	2. No, Tommaso non riceve niente per il suo compleanno.	3. No, non c'è nessun ristorante in questa via.	4. No, non canto mai.	5. No, non hanno fatto nessun lavoro per domani.
	6. No, non leggono nessun giornale la domenica.	7. No, non c'è nessun fiore in inverno.	8. No, non vado mai al supermercato il sabato.	9. No, i turisti non visitano mai nessun parco.	10. No, voi non mangiate carne.
J	1. Lei non sta giù di morale.	2. Noi non facciamo nessuno sport oggi.	3. Neanche Maria deve comprare dei libri.	4. Questo supermercato non è affatto piccolo.	5. Nessuno studia in biblioteca.
	6. Nessuna bambina balla al collegio.	7. No, non c'è nessun fruttivendolo qui.	8. No, Martino non beve niente.	9. Voi non pulite mai la casa (or - Voi non pulite mai niente).	10. Non conosco nessuno dei suoi amici (or - Non conosco nessun amico di lui).

LESSON 12

PRACTICE 12.1

A	1. Ci sono dieci o undici bambini.	2. Prendi la chiave e cerca di aprire la porta.	3. Lui ci chiama e ci invita.	4. Ho visto qualcosa e ho sentito un rumore.	5. Sa leggere e scrivere molto bene.

B	1. e	2. o	3. ma	4. o	5. e	6. ma	7. o	8. ma	9. ma	10. e

C	1. ma		2. bensì **		3. ma		4. tuttavia		5. anche se	

D	1. perché		2. ma		3. anche se		4. Né... né		5. e	
	6. Tanto... quanto		7. e		8. perché		9. tuttavia		10. anche se	

PRACTICE 12.2

A	1. Pietro e Luigi non sanno se i loro amici ritornano.	2. Miriana domanda se c'è un esame domani.	3. Giancarlo decide se salire sul monte Fitz Roy.	4. Voi non sapete se Paola ha bisogno di qualcosa per la festa.	5. Lei domanda se gli impiegati lavorano bene.
B	1. Lei sa che abitiamo in via Oro.	2. Giorgio pensa che viaggiamo tutto l'anno.	3. Io credo che il signor Gardella ripari forni.	4. Giovanna dice che a Giulio piace mangiare.	5. La professoressa ci dice che è tardi.
C	1. Mi piace che i miei figli ordinino da soli.	2. Lavoro molto ma guadagno poco.	3. Anche se fa freddo, c'è il sole	4. Martino crede che stia soffiando troppo vento per correre.	5. Il fruttivendolo mi spiega che i pomodori sono verdi.

Speak Abroad
Academy

PRACTICE 12.3

A	1. tante	2. molti	3. stesso	4. altra	5. alcune
B	1. She has many dogs and cats.	2. Maria has several daughters, but she has no sons.	3. Both Luigi and Juan have few friends.	4. She/he doesn't read magazines or newspapers.	5. She/he knows other countries since she/he travels a lot.
	6. She/he has the same car as Laura.	7. She/he knows every street in Paris, but she/he doesn't know her/his own city.	8. She/he speaks some languages, but she/he doesn't speak English.	9. It's the same friendship, though we're older.	10. All languages are useful, even if some are more useful than others.
C	1. Nessun giorno è bello	2. Ho tanti dolori	3. Ci sono così poche cose belle nella vita	4. Ho pochi amici	5. Tutti i giorni sono brutti.

LESSON 13

PRACTICE 13.1

A	1. ci	2. vi	3. gli	4. gli	5. a loro	6. mi	7. ti	8. le	9. le	10. le
B	1. Mi piace l'auto.		2. A loro piacciono le cipolle.		3. Non Ci piace leggere.		4. Ti piacciono le banane		5. A voi piace lavorare.	
	6. A Marcos piace studiare.		7. A Elsa piacciono i pomodori.		8. A mio padre piace mangiare.		9. A mia madre piace il pesce.		10. Ai bambini non piace il latte.	

C	1. Ci piace correre.	2. Ai bambini non piacciono le verdure.	3. Mi piacciono quelle scarpe.	4. A Luigi e Teresa piacciono le feste.	5. A Elena piace suonare il piano.
D	(Answers may vary) 1. Non mi piace Cristiano Ronaldo, ma mi piace Leo Messi.	2. Non mi piace mangiare la pasta, ma mi piace mangiare l'hamburger.	3. Non mi piace il caffè; tuttavia, mi piace il tè.	4. No me gusta la actriz (actress) Judy Dench, pero me gusta la actriz Meryl Streep.	5. No me gusta el tenista Medvedev, aunque me gusta el tenista Federer.
	6. Non mi piace studiare in sala da pranzo, ma mi piace studiare in biblioteca.	7. Non mi piacciono i gatti, però mi piacciono i cani.	8. Non mi piace viaggiare in treno; tuttavia, mi piace viaggiare in auto.	9. Non mi piace giocare a tennis, ma mi piace giocare a calcio.	10. Non mi piace fare la pizza, ma mi piace fare la lasagna.
E	1. a loro piacciono	2. vi piacciono	3. ti piacciono	4. ci piace	5. mi piacciono
F	1. Ci piacciono le fragole?	2. A Teresa piace la sua università?	3. A loro piace ricevere gente in casa?	4. Ti piace fare yoga?	5. Ti piace il pesce?
G	1. Ci piace lavorare.	2. Vi piace vivere da soli.	3. Vi piace camminare nel parco il sabato.	4. A Carolina e Luigi piace salire sui monti.	5. Ti piace invitare amici in casa tua.
H	1. Mi piacciono le caramelle.	2. Ti piace il pane.	3. Vi piace il latte.	4. Ti piace il caffè.	5. A loro piacciono le arance.
I	1. Al nonno piace cucinare.	2. Al fratello piace fare surf.	3. Alla zia piace leggere libri.	4. Ai cugini piace comprare vestiti.	5. Al padre piace mangiare e bere.
	6. Alla figlia piace cercare conchiglie sulla riva.	7. Alla madre piace la tranquillità.	8. Ai nipoti piace correre sulla spiaggia.	9. A Sofia piace fare ginnastica.	10. Alla nonna piace cucinare

PRACTICE 13.2

1. Vorrei un bicchiere d'acqua.	2. Voglio dormire.	3. Vorrei parlare bene lo spagnolo.	4. Vorrei quel vestito verde.	5. Voglio riparare il tetto.

LESSON 14

PRACTICE 14.1

A	1. in	2. con	3. di	4. di	5. con	6. in	7. di	8. con	9. in	10. con
B	1. di... di		2. con		3. di		4. in		5. con	
C	1. in		2. in		3. tra		4. tra		5. tra	

PRACTICE 14.2

A	1. per		2. senza		3. a		4. per		5. a	
	6. senza		7. a		8. senza		9. senza		10. per	
B	1. a		2. X		3. a		4. X		5. X	
C	1. a	2. a	3. di... di	4. di	5. di	6. a	7. a	8. di	9. di	10. a
D	1. da		2. da		3. di		4. da		5. da	

PRACTICE 14.3

A	1. da		2. per		3. secondo		4. fino a		5. da	
	6. contro		7. fino a		8. per		9. secondo		10. fino a	
B	1. fino a		2. secondo		3. per		4. contro		5. fino a	
C	1. senza	2. con	3. per	4. secondo	5. fino a	6. sopra	7. durante	8. su	9. tra	10. a

LESSON 15

PRACTICE 15.1

A	1. dentro	2. fuori da	3. sopra	4. sotto	5. accanto a
B	1. fuori da	2. davanti a	3. lontano da	4. sotto a	5. lontano da
C	1. L'auto sta dietro al camion.	2. Il portafoglio sta dentro la borsa.	3. La sedia sta davanti al tavolo.	4. Lo zaino sta sul letto.	5. Il gatto sta fuori dalla casa.
D	1. L'ufficio postale sta accanto al municipio.	2. Il cinema sta dietro all'ufficio postale.	3. Il supermercato sta lontano dalla piazza.	4. Il bar sta davanti alla piazza.	5. Sopra al municipio c'è un orologio.
E	1. La sedia sta di fronte allo scrittoio	2. Il computer sta sopra allo scrittoio	3. La pianta sta sotto al quadro	4. I giocattoli stanno dentro la scatola	5. L'orso di peluche sta davanti alla scatola.
F	1. Lo zaino sta lontano dalla libreria.	2. Il quadro sta vicino alla biblioteca.	3. Le matite stanno dentro al portamatite.	4. L'orso di peluche sta fuori dalla scatola.	5. La mappa sta sulla parete.

PRACTICE 15.2

1. Viene dall'Inghilterra.	2. Vieni dagli Stati Uniti.	3. Veniamo dall'Italia.	4. Vengono dal Canada.	5. Venite dalla Spagna.
6. Viene dalla Germania	7. Vengono dal Belgio.	8. Vengo dal Brasile.	9. Viene dagli Stati Uniti.	10. Viene dal Messico.

PRACTICE 15.3

A	1. Per favore, sa dirmi dove sta il ristorante più vicino?	2. Mi scusi, sa dirmi quanti isolati ci sono fino al supermercato?	3. Per favore, sa dirmi come arrivare alla piazza principale?	4. Mi scusi, sa dirmi per favore dove sta la farmacia?	5. Per favore, sa dirmi dove sta la fermata del bus?

B	TERESA:	Good morning. Do you know where the bank is?
	AGENTE:	Yes, let me explain. It's towards the north. You need to follow this avenue until you reach the intersection. Then, turn right and keep on going until you reach the light, towards the east.
	TERESA:	How many blocks are there until the streetlight?
	AGENTE:	It's five blocks until the streetlight. At the light, you should turn left, towards north, and continue two blocks. You'll reach a traffic circle. Drive around it and continue on the same road for a block. Then turn right and keep going straight for seven blocks. Then turn left again and go one more block. The bank will be on the corner to the right.
	TERESA:	Thank you very much, officer. I hope I get there!

C	1. Deve seguire il viale fino all'angolo.	2. Deve prendere a destra e proseguire dritto.	3. Debe seguir derecho hasta llegar al semáforo.	4. Debe girar en el semáforo.	5. Debe doblar a la izquierda y seguir cinco cuadras hasta llegar a la plaza principal.

SHORT STORIES

#1	1. Oggi è martedì.	2. Gianni mangia la pasta alla carbonara	3. Sara domanda se Gianni decide di andare a casa sua.	4. Si chiama Maria.	5. Il ristorante preferito di Gianni si chiama 'L'Osteria Antica'
#2	1. Sono stati in Messico durante il mese di febbraio.	2. Stanno in un hotel chiamato Cinque Stelle	3. Circa venti persone.	4. La discoteca si chiama La Farfalla Bianca	5. L'hanno visto animali marini.
#3	1. Carolina è del Perù.	2. Carolina fa contenuti di cucina.	3. Carolina fa un respiro e dice a se stessa, 'puoi farcela, tranquilla e azione.'	4. Carolina cucina un piatto italiano chiamato pappa al pomodoro.	5. Di aggiungere il sale e il pepe.
#4	1. Si chiama Milano Stazione Centrale	2. Alle sette e trenta.	3. Perché c'era un incidente.	4. Si chiama Maria.	5. Sì, Emilio ha lavorato da casa.
#5	1. Elena deve superare l'esame finale.	2. Un libro di matematica.	3. Biscotti e latte fresco.	4. Si chiama Rachele.	5. Elena va in Macchina.
#6	1. Si conoscono da dieci anni e sono fidanzati per tre anni.	2. Si chiama Elisa.	3. Roberto è riservata, paziente e puntuale.	4. Giuliana e Marco.	5. Tra Marco e Giliana
#7	1. Lilliana ha due figli. Si chiamano Francesca e Giulio.	2. Il piatto preferito di Tommaso è la lombata saltata.	3. Si chiama Olivia Luca.	4. Il dolce preferito di Giulio è la lecca-lecca.	5. Lilliana ha preparata patate dolci fritte e latte.
#8	1. Si chiamano Alberto e Carmella.	2. Alberto studiava legge e Carmella studiava disegnatrice di moda.	3. Alberto piacciono i cani e Carmella piacciono i gatti.	4. Era un grazioso gatto bianco e aveva occhi grandi e azzurri ed era molto peloso.	5. Hanno scelto un porcellino d'India.